TARGET STOPPED

OSPREY
PUBLISHING

DEDICATION

For Mia, Otto, and Cece. Thank you.

Sam Cranny-Evans

TARGET STOPPED

THE HISTORY OF THE MODERN TANK

OSPREY PUBLISHING
Bloomsbury Publishing Plc
Kemp House, Chawley Park, Cumnor Hill, Oxford OX2 9PH, UK
Bloomsbury Publishing Ireland Limited,
29 Earlsfort Terrace, Dublin 2, D02 AY28, Ireland
Bloomsbury Publishing Inc.
1359 Broadway, 12th Floor, New York, NY 10018, USA
E-mail: info@ospreypublishing.com
www.ospreypublishing.com

OSPREY is a trademark of Osprey Publishing Ltd

First published in Great Britain in 2026

A catalogue record for this book is available from the British Library.

ISBN: HB 9781472873712; eBook 9781472873736; ePDF 9781472873682; XML 9781472873699; Audio 9781472873705

26 27 28 29 30 10 9 8 7 6 5 4 3 2 1

Plate section image credits and captions are given in full in the List of Illustrations and Maps (pp. 7–11).

Maps by www.bounford.com
Index by Alan Rutter
Typeset by Lumina Datamatics Ltd
Printed and bound in Great Britain by Clays Ltd, Elcograf S.p.A.

Editor's note

For ease of comparison please refer to the following conversion table:

1km = 0.621 miles
1m = 1.094yd / 3.28ft
1cm = 0.394in
1mm = 0.039in
1 tonne = 0.984 tons (UK long) / 1.102 tons (US)
1kg = 2.204lb
1g = 0.035oz
1kW = 1.341hp
1kPa = 0.145psi
1 MPa = 145.038psi
1 Nm = 0.738 ft-lb

MIX
Paper | Supporting responsible forestry
FSC® C018072

Osprey Publishing supports the Woodland Trust, the UK's leading woodland conservation charity.

To find out more about our authors and books visit www.ospreypublishing.com. Here you will find extracts, author interviews, details of forthcoming events and the option to sign up for our newsletter.

For product safety related questions contact productsafety@bloomsbury.com

Contents

List of Illustrations and Maps

PLATE SECTION ILLUSTRATIONS

Soldiers rest on a painted M46. The heavy armour of the tank was more than a match for the T-34s fielded by the North Korean forces. But mines and the terrain were a challenge, as much as they are now for its successor, the M1 Abrams. (Photo12/ Universal Images Group via Getty Images)

A soldier prepares to fire a bazooka during the Korean War. Shoulder-fired weapons have always been a threat to the tank, driving many changes in situational awareness and protection. (Harold M. Lambert/Lambert/Getty Images)

Second Era: 1954–65

A Soviet T-55 fires on a target during the Hungarian Uprising. The modern Russian tank has evolved through several similar deployments. (Bettmann Archive/Getty Images)

A Centurion provides fire support to British commandos during the 1956 Suez Crisis. Any hopes of a peaceful era following World War II had largely faded by this point, and the developments that would lead to the modern tank were underway. (Manchester Mirror/Daily Mirror/Mirrorpix via Getty Images)

Tanks become more exposed in a city or town as everything is closer, allowing people to throw Molotov cocktails onto engine decks or lay explosives under turrets. This was as true for this T-34-85, destroyed on the streets of Budapest during the 1956 Hungarian uprising, as it was for Merkava Mk 4s deployed to Gaza in 2023. (Universal History Archive/Universal Images Group via Getty Images)

Troops from the US 11th Airborne Division watch a nuclear explosion at close range in 1951. These exercises were quite common, and the modern tank evolved around the expectation that it would be used after nuclear weapons had been deployed. (Bettmann Archive/Getty Images)

Two fighters stand guard over their Russian T-34-85 tank in Yemen in 1964. Despite newer designs being released and widely accepted into service, the T-34-85 has found a role in conflicts around the world. (Central Press/Getty Images)

Third Era: 1965–73

Fourth Era: 1973–91

A front view of the XM1 Abrams, which carried the L7 rifled gun that would later be replaced by the M256. The M1 presented a significant departure in US tank design, with its welded turret (as opposed to cast) setting the mould for the modern Abrams we know today. (HUM Images/Universal Images Group via Getty Images)

One of the original Leopard 2s in 1981. The Leopard 2 has become the predominant tank in European NATO but the modern version is almost unrecognisable from this image. (Sahm Doherty/Getty Images)

The hole surrounded by rust on this image was caused by some form of anti-armour round. Possibly one of the depleted uranium or tungsten APFSDS deployed by US and British forces during the Gulf War. (Scott Peterson/Liaison)

An Iraqi Type 59 or T-55 lies abandoned in March 1991, after the fighting had come to an end. The T-54, which the Type 59 is based upon, had upset a lot of the West's planners when it first emerged. By 1991, however, it was hopelessly outmatched by tanks like Challenger 1 and the M1 Abrams. (Jacques Langevin/Sygma/Sygma via Getty Images)

Soviet troops prepare their T-72s to leave East Germany in 1989. NATO had caught rare glimpses of Soviet vehicles and done its best to build an understanding of them, but the fall of the Berlin Wall allowed for unprecedented access. (Leif Skoogfors via Getty Images)

A 120mm barrel for an M256 is heated to nearly 2,000 degrees just prior to moving to the rotary forge at the Watervliet Arsenal. When this image was taken, the Arsenal was using the same Austrian forge it had acquired in the 1980s, which was the same forge used by the Soviets. (John Snyder/US DoW. The appearance of US Department of Defense (DoW) visual information does not imply or constitute DoW endorsement.)

Fifth Era: 1992–2025

A Russian T-72 driving through a Chechen village in 1996. The heavy losses suffered by the Russians reflected poor doctrine and training, and threw some of the design flaws of Soviet armour into sharp relief. (Eric BOUVET/Gamma-Rapho via Getty Images)

MAPS

Introduction

It's a warm morning in November 2023 as an Israeli officer peers out from the hatch of his Merkava Mk 4 and adjusts the GoPro he fixed to the turret roof. His tank and two others have been making their way through Gaza for the past week following the 7 October Hamas attack. The fighting has been heavy and many of the buildings around the tanks have collapsed into piles of rubble, hiding the tunnels that enable Hamas to move around the area undetected. From the officer's left, a Hamas fighter and his cameraman emerge from one of those tunnels; on the fighter's shoulder is an Al-Yassin 105, a shoulder-fired anti-armour weapon carrying a high-explosive anti-tank (HEAT) warhead that has been manufactured in a small workshop beneath Gaza City. He aims at the tank; he can see the officer adjusting his GoPro. Perfect.

The fighter fires his rocket, and in that moment decades of engineering and thinking around the design of armoured vehicles come into play. The rocket travels fast, 300 metres per second (m/s); it will take less than half a second to reach the officer and his tank. At 50m from the tank, a radar that forms part of the Trophy active protection system emits a series of electromagnetic pulses fractions of a millisecond apart. Those pulses bounce off the rocket and back to the radar; its processor uses that information to conclude that this rocket is heading for the vehicle, and fast. The rocket is 4 milliseconds from the tank and the exposed commander. The computer that the radar is connected to has realized this, and 1 millisecond later rotates a launcher loaded with explosively formed projectiles. Using complex algorithms and the input from the radar, the computer has told the launcher when to detonate its projectile. With 2 milliseconds to go, the launcher detonates, sending a cluster of explosively formed projectiles into the rocket's path. The rocket is now one millisecond from the vehicle and commander when the spray of projectiles smashes into the warhead causing it to detonate metres from the vehicle, leaving the officer unharmed. All the officer was able to process in that length of time was the sound of the rocket being launched, and the sound of the interceptor detonating the rocket – to him, both happened at almost the same time.

Below the officer, in the cramped turret of the tank, the gunner's computer is flashing and offering him a prompt. He presses a button and the turret begins to rotate; the officer climbs down from the roof and takes his place. The turret comes to a stop, and the officer gives the order to fire, having confirmed that he can see the Hamas fighters through his thermal imager. A 120mm high-explosive round hurtles towards the fighters and collapses the room they are sheltering in. The entire engagement has lasted less than a minute. Decades of technological evolution mean that the odds were always against the Hamas fighters. Even without Trophy intercepting the Al-Yassin 105, the Merkava Mk 4 is protected by layers of advanced composite armour designed to minimize the lethality of the rocket.

The Merkava is not alone; it is one of dozens of armoured vehicles and tanks around the world protected in this way. Externally, the Merkava would be recognizable as a tank to any soldier from 1939. Internally, and in the technology that protected the Israeli officer and his crew, it is dramatically different. Over 80 years the tank has evolved to become a marvel of modern engineering. The Merkava Mk 4 and others like it have grown out of focused and dedicated research: research that continues even when the vehicles prove hard to destroy. This is the story of the modern tank.

PART I

1945–53: South Korea and the makings of the main battle tank

Our story begins with Lieutenant Francis Nordstrom, an officer serving in the US 89th Medium Tank Battalion in North Korea, October 1950. The weather was beginning to turn cold as Lt Nordstrom and his battalion of M4A3E8 Shermans were attached to the 27th Commonwealth Brigade – a collection of infantry regiments from the British Commonwealth. The US, British, and South Korean forces had recently advanced to take PyongYang, and were now charged with racing to the Yalu River. On 29 October, a significant North Korean presence had been detected in a valley ahead of the 27th Brigade, and Nordstrom had been selected to command the lead tank of the formation that would break through the Chongju Valley and continue the advance. Nordstrom embraced the challenge of leading and controlling an action. He moved forward with his tank and four others.

Two other tank platoons were supporting the action, around 450m to his rear; they were charged with seizing the hills either side of the road in support of infantry assaults. Nordstrom may have felt nervous as his tank advanced down the road. Like most tank commanders, he had his hatch open with his head and shoulders exposed. The murky glass in his periscopes would give a very limited understanding of the world around him – otherwise known as situational awareness. Even if he decided to duck down inside the turret of his 'Easy Eight', he was quite exposed. To his front was around 6.35cm of cast steel armour set at a maximum angle of 56 degrees; this increased the line-of-sight thickness to around 7.7cm.[1] The 85mm ZiS-S-53 tank gun that armed North Korean T-34-85 tanks could penetrate at least 11cm of armour at a range of 500m.[2] As Nordstrom's tank advanced into the valley he was unable to see the four enemy tanks ahead of him, which were camouflaged, but he did notice the North Korean infantry as they moved into position. Nordstrom's machine gunner opened fire, and his gunner soon joined the fray, firing a high-explosive round against a machine-gun team. The blast from the shell displaced the camouflage on a nearby T-34, which immediately fired on Nordstrom's tank. The shell passed between Nordstrom's head and the hatch to his rear – remarkably leaving him unscathed. Instinctively he called for armour-piercing shells and his gunner engaged the target with three rounds, leading to the destruction of the enemy tank.

The scene at this point would have been overwhelming. Thick black smoke was pouring from the T-34 less than 100m from Nordstrom's tank and obscuring the hills around him. Tank fire, which can be momentarily deafening, would have been joined by the rattle of machine guns and rifles as the infantry began their assaults to take the high ground either side of the road. Soon, another North Korean tank was identified and destroyed by Nordstrom's gunner; the rate of fire from the US tanks increased as they attempted to locate possible enemy tanks and support their attacking infantry. Then – disaster – faulty ammunition jammed the 76mm guns in both Nordstrom's tank and the tank behind him. In what must have been a panicked few minutes, he ordered a third tank to provide fire support while the blockages were cleared. Back in the fight, Nordstrom continued engaging likely enemy positions using only his 'mark one eyeball' and his assessment of the situation. An 85mm round hurtled over his turret once more and slammed into one of the tanks supporting the infantry advance to Nordstrom's left. The round would have been heavy and overwhelmed the armour of the Sherman before detonating inside. The commander of the platoon that had suffered the casualty, Lt Cook, inserted a pencil into the hole left by the North Korean shell to figure out where the round had come from; he radioed the approximate location to Nordstrom, who promptly ordered three tanks to engage the position.

The fighting continued until the infantry assaulting the hills on either side of the road had secured their objective. Nordstrom and his tanks, now running low on ammunition, formed a defensive position and prepared for the night. As darkness fell, North Korean infantrymen went onto the offensive with the goal of destroying the tanks.

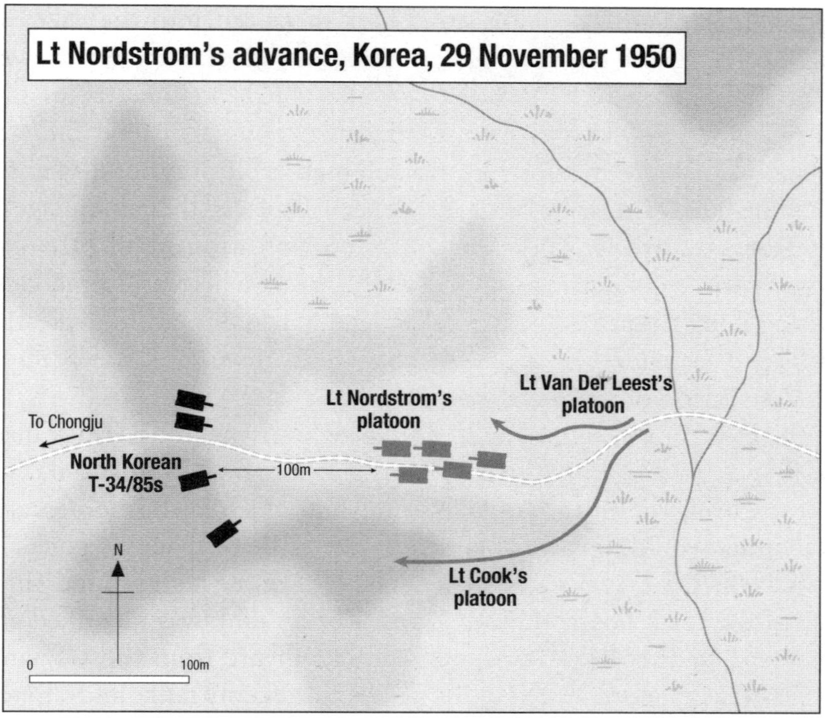

Nordstrom and his crews switched on their headlights and engaged the attacking infantry with small arms and their pistols. By morning, the action was over.[3] Nordstrom would continue fighting in the Korean War and earn a Silver Star with a Bronze Oak Leaf cluster for his actions. His experience of combat was raw – it relied on his own ability to see and understand the situation. Luck was key: he was protected, yes. But if either of the shells that passed above his tank had found their mark, it is unlikely he would have survived. The M4A3E8 was better than the Shermans that had defeated Nazi Germany, but it was a far cry from the South Korean K2 Black Panther that defends the south of the peninsula today. So, what was Nordstrom's tank made of? How did it work?

Chapter 1

Tanks are all about the guns

The history of tanks, or at least the technology used in them, can be traced back to the late 1800s. They were principally designed to support infantry during the bloody stalemates of World War I. Through the 1920s and 30s they evolved to provide protection and mobility, which meant they tended to be lightly armed. By 1942, however, it was clear that tanks needed to provide fire support for infantry and engage other tanks, which led to the widespread adoption of larger-calibre guns.[1] This brings us to the core role of a tank, which has not really changed in the 109 years since the first British tanks were deployed during the battle of Flers-Courcelette in 1916. A tank is a vehicle built around a large-calibre gun, which is mobile enough to take it most places that infantry will go, and carries enough protection to survive most things thrown at it in battle. The idea is that the gun provides overwhelming firepower that can help the infantry achieve their mission, whether that is against enemy armour, infantry, or buildings. So, the gun will tend to drive much of the design of a tank, from its minimum size to its weight and its speed.[2] The way a force fights will have a significant bearing on gun, armour, and mobility selection. But, generally speaking, design starts with the gun. So, with that in mind, we will start by looking at the gun that armed Nordstrom's tank, the M1 family.

The main gun on the M4A3E8 was the M1 series 76mm rifled gun, which had been developed during World War II to improve the lethality of the Sherman tanks against Germany's later designs like the Panther.[3] It had a 52-calibre (L52) barrel, which simply means that the barrel was 52 times as long as the diameter – around 3.96m long.[4]

At the end of the barrel was a muzzle brake, which is an extension of the barrel with vents or ports cut into it. As the projectile passes out of the muzzle, the gas that is propelling it down the barrel is expelled from the ports, reducing the recoil that the gun has to absorb. This is an important design feature of a tank, because it is essentially designed to bring a large and very powerful gun into a battle unharmed, so that it can provide firepower in support of infantry and other forces. The tank's gun is meant to defeat most of the things that it is likely to encounter with a few shots. Doing that requires a few things, of which the first is muzzle velocity. This is achieved by deflagrating a large propellant charge behind a projectile, in a process very similar to that of a rifle or shotgun. The detonation creates forward momentum for the projectile and, according to Newton's Third Law of Motion, an equal reaction in the opposite direction. In other words, the barrel, breech, and other recoiling parts move backwards. The M1 family of guns could weigh up to 520kg and the entire gun would move, possibly up to 30cm.[5] The weight and force of the gun would be absorbed by two hydraulic recoil cylinders that returned the gun to its firing position. A muzzle brake allowed some of that energy to be expelled from the muzzle, creating forward movement, rather than absorbed by the recoil mechanism.

The propellant burns, producing gas that expands. Behind the propellant is the breech of the gun, which is cut from a large piece of solid steel. The breech block is opened to insert ammunition and then closed, using one of two primary mechanisms: the sliding block and the interrupted screw. A sliding block moves vertically or horizontally to open the breech to the gunner; the gunner inserts a round of ammunition and the block closes. An interrupted screw is a section of metal with parts of the thread removed; this allows the block to be opened and a round loaded, after which the breech is closed and turned partially to lock.

This matters because the gases generated by the burning propellant cannot escape to the rear. They can only go forwards, and in front of those gases is the munition. The M1 series 76mm rifled gun was designed to fire a new nature of munition called the M93 Hyper Velocity Armour Piercing – Tracer (HVAP-T).* The HVAP-T had a tungsten carbide

*Note that 'nature' has been deliberately used instead of 'type'. Type can mean machine gun or tank ammunition, but nature very specifically refers to whether it explodes when it hits the target, or is designed to the penetrate the target.

core, which was selected because of its very high hardness and density, which made it better at penetrating armour than other materials like steel.[6] It seems self-explanatory that a harder metal is better at breaking through a softer one, but understanding why this happens, and the physics that control these interactions, is key to understanding all of the firepower and armour solutions that this book covers. With that, let's explore ballistics.

There are a few different parameters that are used to describe the physical effects that happen when a projectile is fired from a tank gun. The way the projectile behaves inside the barrel of the gun is known as internal ballistics; when it leaves the muzzle of the gun, it transitions to external ballistics. Finally, when it reaches the target, it is described by its terminal ballistics. Within this, a few facts and figures help to understand how a projectile is likely to perform. In a nutshell, however, penetrating armour with kinetic (as opposed to explosive, i.e. chemical) energy depends on many factors, which include the speed of the projectile, the hardness and density of the projectile compared to the armour, and the ratio of the length of the projectile to its diameter. Muzzle velocity describes how fast the projectile is travelling as it leaves the muzzle of the gun. If Nordstrom's tank was carrying the HVAP-T, it would have left the muzzle of his 76mm gun travelling at around 1,000m/s. If it was fired at a target 1,000m away, it would have taken 1.07 seconds to reach the enemy tank, and would have been travelling at 848 m/s when it got there.[7] Achieving this speed depends on that breech design as well as the projectile. Ideally, a projectile, the propellant/casing, and the breech together will achieve good levels of obturation. This means that they form a tight seal within the breech so the gases can only go forwards. The casing for the HVAP was made of brass or steel, and would expand when the propellant was ignited, filling what space was left in the breech of the gun. The penetrator itself was made of an aluminium windshield with the tungsten carbide core inside. On the outside of the penetrator was something called a rotating band. Rotating bands, or driving bands in the US, are typically made of a softer metal like copper, and help improve obturation by wedging into the rifling inside the barrel. The driving band is also essential for imparting spin from the rifling inside the barrel onto the ammunition. Driving bands continue to feature on modern tank ammunition for rifled guns, despite the ammunition natures changing quite significantly.

The band grips the rifling, which imparts spin onto the projectile as it leaves the barrel. As a projectile flies through the air, forces such as drag and the wind will begin acting on it – typically ahead of the centre of gravity. This can cause a projectile to tip and begin to tumble, which makes it less aerodynamic, slowing it down. For tank ammunition, it may also mean that the projectile will strike the target side-on, and therefore probably fail to penetrate the armour. So, the spin stabilizes the round because it creates angular momentum, which resists those forces. The speed of flight and stability of anti-armour rounds give a number of advantages for tank gunnery that have come to play an important role through to the modern tank. High-velocity rounds have a very flat trajectory, which makes them much more accurate than a slower round. The short flight time also means that it is unlikely that the enemy tank will have moved far by the time the round arrives on target. Altogether this increases accuracy, and the likelihood of a successful first shot. We have already seen how important a quick and accurate shot can be, both in Nordstrom's engagement of North Korean tanks and in the failure of the North Koreans to land their own shots. Had the rounds that passed over Nordstrom's head found their mark, it is likely that the advance of the 27th Commonwealth Brigade would have been slowed or stopped.

So, muzzle velocity in tank-on-tank engagements matters. But it is not the only element of gun-fired projectiles that should be considered. The second is muzzle energy or kinetic energy. This can be calculated if you know the weight of the fired projectile and its muzzle velocity. Kinetic energy is measured in Joules (J), or more typically megaJoules (MJ) for tank rounds, and you can calculate it by multiplying the muzzle velocity by itself, then multiplying the result of that sum by the mass of the projectile in kilograms. Finally, divide that number by two: the resultant figure provides the kinetic energy of the projectile at the muzzle. You can also calculate the terminal energy if you have the velocity of the projectile at a given range. For the HVAP-T, the weight given in a US Army data booklet from 1945 is 4.24kg. Using the formula for kinetic energy, the M93 HVAP returns a muzzle energy of 2.12 MJ, falling to 1.5 MJ at a range of 1,000m. I apologize for the maths, but I promise this is leading somewhere.

The next characteristic that matters is the hardness of the projectile. The HVAP was carrying a tungsten carbide core, which can have a Vickers hardness rating of 1,200–1,500 – more than double that of a typical hardened steel. In fact, it is so hard that the Brinell hardness test, which measures how hard a steel is, is not really suitable for it. This means that the core of the HVAP is much harder than the typical steel used in the hull of a tank and it will not deform when it hits. One way to think of this is to imagine trying to hammer a wooden nail into another piece of wood. You might make some progress but the wooden nail would not survive long and it would eventually crack and break. However, a steel nail will have no problem penetrating the same piece of wood as it is much harder. This is an imperfect representation of terminal ballistics, but it captures the essence of what is happening.

There are now two key elements to consider: the kinetic energy of the round, and its core material. The core is very hard and travelling very fast; its hardness means that it will deliver more of its energy into the target armour without the projectile deforming than would be delivered by a softer projectile that is the same shape, size, and same velocity.[8] It also means that the projectile could travel more slowly than a softer material and still penetrate a target, whereas the softer material might fail. This effect was experienced by US Army tank crews fighting against Germany's Panther tanks in Europe in 1944, for instance.[9] In Nordstrom's case, if he carried the M93 in his Sherman, much of the round's energy – 1.5 MJ at 1,000m – would be deposited over the surface area of the projectile into the target armour. At that point there are two possible results: either the armour will fail and some form of penetration will occur, or the round will fail and the crew will remain safe. If the armour is hit hard enough by a projectile that is at least as hard as the armour, then it may fail, assuming of course that it is not too thick.

When steel armour is defeated, it can fail in a number of ways. One of them is plugging, which is where the armour around and ahead of the projectile fails and is essentially pushed out of the rear face of the armour plate. Another mechanism is penetration, where the projectile passes all the way through the armour and into the vehicle and unfortunate crew inside. In both cases, it is likely that spalling will also occur; this is where small fragments of armour around the area with which the projectile made contact spread out in a cone inside the vehicle. This is probably the fate that befell the North Korean tank crews facing Lieutenant Nordstrom and his battalion as they moved down through the valley. The HVAP proved to be a significant overmatch for the North Korean armour, which is not surprising given that it was designed to defeat the armour of Germany's tanks.[10] But the US and other allied troops did not have it all their own way. North Korean T-34-85s were also well armed, and comparable to the M4A3E8 Sherman tanks, though unable to defeat the larger M26 Pershing.

The T-34-85 was a development of the original Soviet T-34 that had been the work horse of the Red Army during World War II. The original turret was replaced with a larger one allowing an 85mm ZiS-S-53 main gun to replace the 76mm model that had fought through most of the war. Its development was spurred by the appearance of Germany's Panther tanks in 1943, which required a larger gun to defeat their thick armour. A few hundred of the T-34-85s were deployed by the North Korean forces in 1950 and in July that year came head to head with the US 78th Tank Battalion equipped with the M24 Chaffee. The M24 was a light tank armed with a 75mm gun, and despite scoring several direct hits on the first T-34-85 that they encountered, the US battalion failed to penetrate its armour. M24 losses were heavy over the following two weeks, leading to a loss of confidence in tanks amongst US Army commanders.[11] Even against the better-protected Shermans, the 85mm ZiS-S-53 gun was equally capable of penetrating the frontal armour, as Lieutenant Nordstrom and his crews found out. However, it is worth noting that the North Koreans were poorly trained and would rarely hit US tanks with their first shot, a fact borne out by the account of the action as Commonwealth forces raced to the Yalu River. The result of this poor gunnery performance was that many more US tanks were actually lost to North Korean mines than to tanks. A US report on United Nations (UN) tank losses between July 1950 and January 1951 noted that 64 tanks were lost to mines, representing 64% of those lost to enemy action. Just 17 were lost to enemy tank fire – five fewer than were lost to infantry engagements.[12]

There are two observations to draw from this data that are relevant to all tank development that has followed. The first is that there has always been a competition between lethality and protection which has meant that seeing an enemy tank first, and hitting it first, often results in victory. This is not always the case, but it is clear throughout all conflicts that there are benefits to having a well-trained tank crew capable of accurate shooting. The second is that tank-on-tank engagements rarely define combat outcomes. Tanks certainly do define combat outcomes, but their role in engaging tanks is not always as prominent as some would like to think. For example, US and Commonwealth forces relied on their tanks to survive the Korean War. The US Army started the war with its armour in poor condition, and hurriedly scrambled a force together from gate guardians* and reserve forces in Japan in a desperate bid to stem the North's armoured advance.[13] There were many notable tank battles including a series of actions now known as the Battle of the Bowling Alley, which took place in August 1950 with M26 Pershing medium tanks from the US 73rd Tank Battalion inflicting heavy casualties on North Korean forces. Both of these aspects – seeing and shooting first, and the relatively modest impact of tank-on-tank engagements – were highlighted in that battle. *Time* magazine noted that North Korean tanks would 'drive down the road to within 100 yards of the first US foxhole and open flat trajectory fire with their 85-mm. guns; a good many of the shells went screaming down the road, hit the first small elevation in their path and bounced into a nearby hillside.'[14] This speaks to the accuracy element. Tanks are a very effective direct fire weapon in support of infantry operations, providing that their shots actually land on enemy forces. The M26 Pershing played a role in stopping the North Korean advance, as did shoulder-fire Bazookas. But it was primarily the artillery under the command of the US forces, combined with mines, that broke their advances over four days.[15]

*A gate guardian is a tank that has been retired from service and mounted on a concrete pedestal, typically at the entry to a military base.

Chapter 2

Simple protection

Why does seeing first and shooting first matter so much? Well, the reasons have changed depending on the weapons and armour in use. But at the time that Nordstrom was advancing down the Chongju Valley, there were really only two types of vehicle armour: cast armour and rolled homogeneous armour (RHA). Cast armour requires iron ore to be mixed with alloying metals – for example, nickel, chromium, and molybdenum in the case of the T-34's cast turret – which increases the hardness and corrosion resistance of the steel.[1] Once the iron ore and alloying materials have been melted in a large furnace, they are poured into a mould in the shape of the turret or hull and allowed to set before they are heat treated. Heat treatment is common to forging metal; it regularizes the grain structure of the steel so that all of the grains arrange themselves neatly. This increases the strength of the steel; it is then quenched in a cooling medium such as oil, or sometimes water, which rapidly reduces its temperature and freezes the grains in the position they were in while heated.[2]

RHA initially follows a similar process to that of cast armour; however, the resultant steel is forged into billets rather than the finished turret shape. The billets are then rolled under immense pressure into a sheet of steel; they may be heated or cold-rolled, but in either case the goal is to combine the layers and make them homogeneous. This simply means that each resulting sheet has the same properties throughout and is not weaker at one end than the other. Compared with casting, the alloying components of both provide the hardness; however the rolling process of RHA improves its toughness. Then, the resultant steel plate is heat treated, quenched, and tempered. Tempering is designed to return the toughness to the steel so that it can be welded or bent into shape.

Armour is heat treated to a desired level of hardness, and the relationship between hardness and strength is inverse. This means that the harder a steel is, the more brittle it becomes. Think of the difference between a drink can and a drinking glass. It is relatively easy to pierce a drink can with a nail, and much harder with a glass. However, you could pierce a drink can over and over again without it breaking, whereas a glass would fracture and potentially shatter with one successful penetration. This is essentially how armour works: a very hard armour will be more difficult to penetrate than a softer one; however, it will be less effective as a part of a tank's structure, and may even need to be replaced if it gets hit. Lower-hardness armour has the benefit of being easier to weld; it can also be used to make up the structure of a tank, as it is tougher and will still provide protection. However, if that armour is expected to withstand serious threats, and, by this, I mean heavy machine guns, medium-calibre cannons, or shaped charges, it will need to be either very thick or fitted with some form of additional armour. The hardness of a steel is measured: there are a few different measures, but the one often used for steel is the Brinell hardness rating (BHN or HB). The BHN refers to a test where a tungsten carbide ball is pressed into the armour until it creates a dent, and the diameter of the dent is measured. The smaller the diameter of the indentation left by the ball, the harder the armour.[3] RHA has a Brinell hardness between 250 and 410 BHN depending on its intended application. The cast armour of the T-34 turret was very hard, at 450–500 BHN, which was likely much harder than the turret armour on Nordstrom's M4. And this brings us back to the HVAP-T and its tungsten carbide core.

Tungsten carbide is very hard; in fact, it cannot be accurately measured using BHN, so another system called the Vickers Hardness (HV) rating is used. A 500 BHN steel would be around 544 HV. A tungsten carbide penetrator will typically have a hardness in excess of 1,000 HV, depending on the composition of the materials used in it.[4] Hardness is not the only thing that matters to armour penetration; thickness is also key. However, there are limits to how thick armour can be, which are imposed by the ability of the engine and transmission to move the vehicle, and the ease with which that armour can be produced and handled. There are also challenges around maintaining consistency throughout very thick pieces of steel, which altogether make protecting against large-calibre armour-piercing rounds a challenge with conventional steel armour alone.[5] For example, a piece of steel that is 1m² and 100mm thick will weigh around 785kg.* The M26 Pershing glacis was 100mm thick and angled to 46 degrees, which gives a line-of-sight thickness of 143mm. So, it was strong enough to withstand the 85mm shot from the T-34-85, but unlikely to absorb the impact of the 122mm D-25T gun fitted to the Soviet IS-2 tanks. All of this is to say that steel armour as a stand-alone form of protection was approaching the limits of what it could usefully achieve. It continues to be used as a base armour, and would protect the generation of tanks that followed the Pershing and T-34, but new forms of protection would soon become essential.

The reason for this brings us to the engineering spiral of an armoured vehicle and the design constraints that had come into place towards the end of World War II. One of these design constraints could be traced back to Roman times. How could the Romans have shaped modern tank design? Well, the gauge of the UK's railways (the distance between the tracks) was set at 4ft 8½in by the Railway Regulation Gauge Act of 1846.[6] That distance is often said to be the distance between the wheels of carts that were used as far back as when the Romans occupied Britain. Whether or not this is true is open to debate, but that statute from 1846 has shaped tank design regardless. Transport by rail is key for tanks: they are large heavy pieces of equipment and will generally be moved by rail or truck unless they are close to combat. This means that they cannot be wider than the rail infrastructure of the country developing them. As a result, it *could* be argued that if the width of Roman cart tracks was used to set the standard gauge railway track, then the Romans influenced modern tank design. Furthermore, the width of the UK's railway, the standard gauge as it came to be known, was adopted by most countries around the world. This means that design of many modern tanks has been shaped by the constraints of railway tracks before their designers ever put pen to paper.[7]

*Steel is often attributed a density of 7,850 kg/m³. Combined with the reported 100mm thickness of the M26 Pershing glacis and an arbitrary figure of 1 square metre, the weight of the glacis plate alone would be 785kg.

This measurement limits the width and height of a vehicle; it is then combined with the size of the gun and ideally the desired elevation and depression of the gun to give an indication of turret size. The bigger the gun, and the greater the elevation or depression required, the bigger the turret will have to be. The length of the hull is decided by its ratio to the track of the tank. The track is a measurement connected to the tracks, it means the distance between the centre of the two tracks. Make the hull too long in relation to that measurement and the tank will be difficult to steer. The hull also has to accommodate an engine, the turret and turret crew, a driver, the wheels, and suspension. Generally speaking, designers try to fit all of these things into a small space because this reduces the area that must be armoured. Every additional square metre of tank requires another square metre of armour, which quickly adds to the overall weight of the vehicle. For example, around 44% of the 50-tonne British Centurion (which entered service in late 1946) was armour, 11% the armament and ammunition, 30% the transmission, tracks and road wheels, 5% the engine, and another 10% in the crew and fuel.[8] This principle will return in every section of this book. But for the time being, it is enough to state that the design of the Sherman, combined with the available engines and transmissions, was reaching the limits of what could be achieved in terms of protection, as Nordstrom and his soldiers fought North Korean forces.

Chapter 3

'Anywhere a tank can go, is tank country: even the tops of mountains'

Tanks are often described in terms of their balance within something known as the iron triangle. Defining this triangle depends on which side of the Atlantic you sit. US definitions may refer to lethality, survivability, and mobility, while those in the UK tend to use firepower, protection, and mobility. The idea behind the triangle is to illustrate the design trade-offs mentioned above. For any increase in protection, mobility is likely to suffer. Increasing firepower will impact both protection and mobility, and so on. In an ideal world, tanks would represent a balance among these three characteristics, but that is rarely achieved. It is also the case that there is arguably a fourth characteristic: mission systems. Mission systems are often a part of the other three design elements. A stabilization system will make a tank gun more accurate, for example, and a radio will enable it to coordinate with other vehicles and avoid anti-tank obstacles, improving protection. But over the 73 years that followed Nordstrom's engagement with North Korean armour, the role of mission systems has come to define tanks and their capabilities. We will go into this in much more depth later, but for the time being, I'd like to introduce a fourth tank, the Centurion.

Not long before Lt Nordstrom's action in October 1950, the Chinese People's Volunteer Army (PVA) had joined the Korean War. They eventually pushed the UN forces back, leading to some desperate stands and counter-offensives by UN troops to retake lost territory. In April 1951, the PVA launched an attack against UN positions on the Imjin River with the goal of retaking Seoul. The area they attacked was defended by British and Belgian troops, including Centurion Mk 3 tanks from the 8th King's Royal Irish Hussars. The terrain was very difficult for tanks but the Centurions were able to find positions, climbing up steep hills to support the British infantry with direct fire.[1] Lt Brown, an officer from the Royal New Zealand Armoured Corps (RNZAC) wrote a report on the Centurions in service with the Hussars, noting that, 'a properly driven CENTURION will climb any hill it can get a grip on', at speeds up to 2 miles per hour.[2] The Centurion's mobility led US General John O'Daniel to reportedly state, 'anywhere a tank can go, is tank country: even the tops of mountains'.[3] The M26 Pershing, contrary to widespread reporting, was also capable of reaching difficult areas in Korea. In one instance in the winter of 1950, four Shermans skidded on an icy road as they rushed to support US Marines during the battle of the Chosin Reservoir. The Marines took their M26 Pershings the next day and succeeded in passing the road; they were then able to help their fellow soldiers during their fighting withdrawal to Hungnam.[4]

There are two aspects of the Centurion and M26 design to cover here: the powertrain and the mission systems. As noted by Lt Brown of the RNZAC, the ability of a Centurion to cover almost any terrain (within reason) was vital. It meant they could go where needed and support infantry during their operations. Both tanks had their issues when it came to mobility. The M26 had an unreliable transmission, and both were fuel hungry with a relatively limited range. However, both tanks helped set the standard for the main battle tanks that would follow. Their powertrain enabled them to go most places that infantry would, and their mission systems made them frighteningly effective when they got there. But what is a powertrain, and what makes a tank a good off-road vehicle?

Well, the powertrain is everything that makes a tank move. It includes the engine and transmission (which would come to be called a power-pack when offered as a unit in later tank designs), the suspension, roadwheels, and tracks. There are two sets of characteristics used to describe a tank or armoured vehicle's ability to move over ground. You are probably familiar with mobility, which describes the vehicle's ability to move. This has a surface-level set of specifications that are now fairly standard including top speed, driving range from internal fuel, acceleration, and whether or not the vehicle can climb a 60% gradient. You will find all of these statistics and a few more on the websites of any modern tank manufacturer. But there are many that they do not cover. For instance, ground pressure is an important one, and the power to weight ratio is another. We will go over them in a moment, but there is one more characteristic to introduce and that is trafficability. Trafficability does not describe the vehicle, but the ability of terrain to support the movement of one or many vehicles. Tank drivers and crews will assess trafficability as they manoeuvre, often by simply walking over terrain and testing how firm it is. There is a separate field of engineering called terramechanics, which provides a theoretical understanding for how and why a soil will or will not support a vehicle. Terramechanics can be quite dry, but it introduces several principles that are really useful for understanding the mobility of the M26 and the Centurion, so bear with me.

There are two concepts from terramechanics that will help. The first is traction, or tractive performance. The tractive performance of tracked and wheeled vehicles is influenced by the strength of the soil being travelled over. Weak soils with a high moisture content will be damaged more when travelled over than drier, stronger soils. The greater the level of shear stress (damage) caused to the soil by the vehicle, the greater the effort required to keep the vehicle moving.[5] This makes sense if you think about it; the damage here essentially means the vehicle is sinking into the soil as it drives. The second element is the thrust created by the vehicle's tracks or tyres. Put very simply, tracked vehicles typically have a much larger contact area than wheeled vehicles, because their tracks are both wide and long. This equates to thrust applied over a greater surface area, which means tracked vehicles can overcome soil slippage and deformation, whereas wheeled vehicles – especially those that cannot adjust their tyre pressures – will tend to create more damage to the soil and lose traction.[6] In a nutshell, very wet soil or soil that is not very cohesive (think a freshly ploughed field) will deform more quickly as a vehicle drives over it. If the deformation of the soil exceeds the vehicle's ability to generate thrust, the vehicle will eventually become immobilized.

Trafficability and terramechanics apply to all vehicles, but the mobility characteristics of a vehicle dictate how well they can move off-road. This was quite starkly illustrated by one video from the war in Ukraine, which shows an MT-LB, which is a Soviet armoured personnel carrier (APC) weighing around 11.9 tonnes, essentially swimming on soil that is completely water-logged. It overtakes a truck which has become stuck in the same place.[7] A tank interacts with the soil through its tracks, which serve to disperse its immense weight over a wide area. The road wheels are also important as they help distribute the weight over the tracks. The track area essentially decides the vehicle's ground pressure, which dictates how far a vehicle will sink into a given soil. To get the ground pressure of a vehicle, you divide its weight by the total area of both tracks. The M26 Pershing, at a combat weight of 41,891kg, had a ground pressure of 0.88kg/cm^2 (12.5 pounds per square inch (psi)), whereas the M4A3E8 came in at 0.77kg/cm^2 (11psi), despite weighing 33,656kg (74,200lb). Essentially, this means the M26's ground pressure was not significantly higher than the Sherman's, despite the fact that the M26 carried a lot more armour.[8] The Centurion's ground pressure was higher still at around 0.91 kg/cm^2 (13psi), but it was still able to travel over difficult terrain.

The ground pressure is much more than the track area and weight of the vehicle. It also includes the number and pitch of the road wheels. Fewer road wheels mean a higher peak pressure under each one, and the pressure varies from wheel to wheel. But the ground pressure is the best measure that tank designers have to understand how their vehicles will perform. And as far as tank design goes, it is quite difficult to reduce ground pressure.[9] The length of the vehicle is determined by the length-to-track ratio and the width is also limited by the railways (both discussed above). This means that most Western tanks have a width between 3.5 and 3.7m, and are between 7.5 and 8.2m long. The result is that the tracks can only be so long, and so wide, limiting the space for the weight of the vehicle to be dispersed over. Assuming that a vehicle is able to move over a given soil (trafficability), then the defining characteristic is known as the power-to-weight ratio. This is just the power output of the engine in hp or kW divided by the weight of the vehicle, usually in tonnes.* Broadly speaking, there is a sweet spot for the power-to-weight ratio, with the optimum performance being gained from the 25–30hp/tonne zone.[10] This defines how quickly a tank can accelerate and the top speeds that it can reach. The M26 Pershing had

*Power figures are cited as provided by the original manufacturers; readers should note that Continental European designs may use Metric Horsepower (PS) or kW, while British and American designs use Mechanical Horsepower (hp).

a power-to-weight ratio of just 11.9 hp/tonne and the Centurion Mk 3 reached a mighty 12.8 hp/tonne. This is not the whole picture, as is always the case with tanks. The engine is attached to a transmission and as energy is passed from the engine to the transmission, energy is lost. The end result is that while the engine can technically provide 11 hp/tonne, the hp at the drive sprocket will likely be lower than that. Regardless, the combination of ground pressure and the power-to-weight ratio of the M26 and Centurion in South Korea meant they were able to achieve some remarkable technical feats, but future tank designs would sweep clean past these achievements. The reality is that these tanks went places that tanks had rarely gone before in support of infantry. As the Cold War continued, concepts of operations changed with the introduction of more APCs, and consequently the mobility demands placed on tank design changed too.

Chapter 4
Dominating no-man's land

'We had this idea of dominating no-man's land, and if you saw an enemy, you would just fire a 20 pounder shell at him.'[1] Captain (Capt) Jim Selway was a commander with the British Royal Tank Regiment known for aggressive action. By December 1952 when his troop of Centurion Mk 3s was deployed to the Hook – an important ridge near the confluence of the Sami-Chon and Imjin rivers – the frontline was largely static. The Centurions focused on providing fire support to infantry and holding the line. They would occasionally let the infantry climb into their tanks and watch the Chinese lines through the tank sights. 'It gave the infantry a lot of confidence, the speed and accuracy of our fire. I remember one infantryman who said we saved his life. He came on the radio one day saying he needed support and within 20 seconds we had shells down to support him,' Jim recalled.[2] Lt Brown, the RNZAC officer, supports Jim Selway's account, claiming that the 20-pounder (20-pdr) gun on the Centurion was very accurate. 'My troop spent a week sniping individual enemies at a range of 3,600 yds [3,290m] with a most satisfactory degree of success … It will put a shot into a bunker mouth at 4,000 yds [3,657m], once ranging has been completed, although it may take up to three shells to put one right in.'[3]

Lt Brown's figures are interesting: 3,600yd is 36 American football pitches, or around 32 European football pitches. It is a very long distance at which to engage a single human or group of humans. The Centurion carried improved mission systems over its predecessors, although some of the technology – or at least the intent behind it – was carried by the more advanced German tanks. The Centurion Mk 3 was armed with a gun called the Ordnance Quick-Firing 20-pdr, from England's Royal Ordnance factory. It was an 83.4mm gun with a very long barrel at L64.* But the focus here is the Centurion's mission systems, the components built into the design to make it more accurate and effective. It starts with the turret. The Centurion had an electrically rotated turret with a manual backup, in contrast to most other tanks of its era, which used hydraulic turret controls. Hydraulics are useful, but tend to release hot and highly pressurized oil if the tank is penetrated. There had been electric drives before, but they lacked the accuracy needed to lay a gun onto target. This changed with the Valentine infantry tank in 1940, and an electric drive developed by Vickers Armstrong. The Centurion used an electric turret traverse that was suitable for gun laying, and meant that Lt Brown and Capt Jim Selway would have been able to make small adjustments to the position of their guns in Korea.[4]

Perhaps most importantly, the Centurion's gun was stabilized and so was the turret. The Centurion was one of the first tanks to have a stabilized turret and main armament. The Sherman had carried vertical stabilization for the main gun, but it seems that this was often deactivated. And, according to historian Professor Ogorkiewicz, US, French, and German tanks would not be fitted with stabilizers until the 1970s.[5] Stabilization is important because it helps to hold the gun steady and account for movement of the vehicle. If you have ever fired a rifle, you will appreciate the impact on accuracy of a sudden movement to the butt of the rifle. If you have not, you can replicate the effect by throwing a stone at a target. Try throwing it standing still, and then try running sideways and throwing at the same target. It is very likely that in the second scenario it will be much more difficult to hit the target.

The Centurion's stabilization relied on a number of components that could be activated or deactivated as desired. At its core were two gyroscopes, one for the turret and one for the gun. A gyroscope is a device used to measure movement. It typically consists of a rotor or spinning wheel mounted on a special frame called a gimbal. The rotor

*Calibre length was covered in Chapter 1, but in brief, it is the length of the gun divided by its calibre. The Sherman's M1 was L52; the Pershing's M3 was L50 (Christopher Chant, *World Encyclopedia of the Tank*, 2nd edn, Sutton Publishing, UK (2002), p.256).

spins while in use and any changes to the orientation of the gyroscope – like a tank bumping over terrain, for example – cause a reaction force on the gimbals, which is measured. The gyroscope then sends a signal to a common amplifier that in turn controls one of two electric motors: one for traverse and one for elevation. The signals cause the electric motors to apply torque in a direction that counteracts the detected movement. The end result is that the bearing and elevation of the gun remain constant, even when the tank is moving. The gunner will still have to manually track moving targets, but this stabilization is really key to the accuracy of Centurions when on the move.*

Tests by the US Army indicated that there was no real benefit to stabilizing the gun for shots when halting to fire, stating that it took longer to fire when using the stabilizer. Those tests showed that the Centurion could deliver up to eight rounds without halting in the course of an engagement, with around 60% or more achieving an effect on the target. It also meant that the Centurion could clear the given course a minute faster than a tank that was halting to fire. This all contributes to the survivability of the vehicle, ensuring that it can move into and out of action very quickly.[6] The stabilization is not the only thing that Centurion carried; the commander's and gunner's sights were also important. The commander had a cupola (a small dome-shaped structure on top of the turret) fitted with nine No. 7 Mk 1 periscopes around the perimeter that he could use for immediate situational awareness. The cupola also included a binocular sight with a 10× magnification and the commander could rotate the cupola and look for targets separate to the traverse of the turret. The gunner had his own monocular sight with an 8× magnification and range settings for the ranging machine gun. In theory, the gunner would estimate the range to the target, adjust the elevation of the sight, place the crosshair on the target, and then fire the ranging machine gun. The machine gun was loaded with tracer rounds so that he could see where they went. If the machine-gun rounds landed accurately, then he would load and

*This video provides a demonstration of the stabilization on the Centurion (although it does not appear to be a Mk 3 tank, it is still useful for understanding the role of stabilization): 'Testing a tank turret stabilizer', Lottie The Tank Whisperer, YouTube video (6 January 2024). https://www.youtube.com/watch?v=I4IFRehGeDE accessed 29 September 2025.

fire the main gun.[7] However, the anecdotal evidence from the Korean War and US Army tests indicate that the range was estimated, but that crews would fire the main gun until they had the desired effect on the target. This is yet another trend that will re-emerge; despite a designer's best efforts, the crew will always tend to use their tanks in the way that suits them.

The Centurion came to be a widely used and well-regarded tank for its balanced armour, mobility, and lethality. As discussed previously, the Centurion's first operational deployment was in Korea, but its true test came in Israel, which we will cover shortly. First, however, we must make a detour to Hungary.

PART 2

1954–65: Buttoned up – tanks and the nuclear era

The Centurion had performed well during the Korean War, demonstrating its mobility and firepower against the T-34-85. The M26, in contrast, had lost favour, spurring production of a tank called the M46, as well as the M47 Patton, and eventually the M48 Patton, which entered production in 1952 to replace all of the previous tanks in US service. The Soviet design bureaus meanwhile had been working on a new design that would eventually replace the venerable T-34-85 and the heavy IS-2 and IS-3. The IS-2 had been introduced into service towards the end of World War II. Its massive 122 mm gun and thick armour set it apart from previous Soviet designs. The IS-3 came later, and made use of unique geometries in its armour, including two angled plates on its glacis. While the IS-3 was living rent free in the heads of NATO planners, thanks to its appearance at the 1945 Victory Parade through Berlin, Aleksander Aleksandrovich Morozov was reviving an old design in his office in Kharkiv.[1]

The Soviets had been earlier adopters of the tank and worked on several interesting developmental tanks throughout World War II. However, the pressures of surviving Germany's onslaught led to a focus on the T-34 that was difficult to disrupt with new designs or updates. The T-34 had been designed by a team at the Tank Design Bureau of Plant No. 183, which was based in Ukraine, and led by a man named Mikhail Ilyich Koshkin. Koshkin and Morozov worked together on the design of the T-34 until Koshkin's death in 1940; Morozov continued its improvement during the war.[2] The design bureau had been forced to relocate beyond the Urals to evade the German advance, and gradually returned after the war, becoming the KB-60M Design Bureau. One design that Morozov had worked on was called the T-44; it included several innovative features for tanks of its day, like torsion bar suspension, and a transverse engine. This basically means that the engine was positioned sideways with cylinders running from left to right. It is most likely that the car you drive has a transverse engine mounting, but it was very unusual for tanks in the 1940s. The T-44 aimed to improve on the protection of the T-34 and retain the mobility by reducing the protected volume of the tank; the transverse engine contributed to this. The result was a 32-tonne tank with good mobility and protection, and the 85mm gun of the T-34-85.[3] It went into production in 1945 but the Soviets knew the gun was a problem, and attempts to fit the much bigger 122mm gun had failed. So, Morozov and his team of engineers got to work designing a new turret that could carry the 100mm D-10T rifled gun.

The result was a new turret and tank that was presented for the first time in 1945, and entered production in 1947 as the T-54-1. However, things did not go well for Morozov's new design and the output for the vehicle was reduced while Aleksander returned to the drawing board. A refined turret was introduced in 1949, which gained more popularity and allowed production of the new variant, T-54-2, to be increased. By 1951 Morozov's team had developed a third turret, which would become the final iteration for the T-54. This new variant, the T-54-3, entered production – along with many modifications to the rest of the vehicle – from 1952.[4] However, Morozov was growing tired of the iteration process and wanted to work on something new and revolutionary, which we will return to later.

Responsibility for the iteration of the T-54, which was rapidly becoming the Soviet Union's preferred tank, was transferred to a new design bureau at the Uralvagonzavod (literally Ural Wagon Factory). The new head of the team, L.N. Kartsev, took over and immediately looked to America and Korea. China had captured US tanks in Korea and the Soviets had their own M4 Shermans to examine from American aid provided during the war. The M4 was vertically stabilized and the Soviets found that stabilization could improve hit probability on the move, and that the bore evacuators of US tanks in Korea reduced the build-up of toxic fumes in the turret. These innovations were applied to the D-10TG gun and integrated into the

T-54, leading to the T-54A which entered production in 1955.[5] The die was cast: the Soviet Union and Warsaw Pact started production of the T-54A, which would eventually become the T-55. But, first, events in Hungary took a turn for the worse, and played an unexpected role in Western tank development.

Hungary's population had suffered under a brutal dictatorship led by Mátyás Rákosi since 1948 and the Hungarian Worker's Party. Rákosi was a communist and modelled his policies on Stalin's, imprisoning hundreds of thousands of Hungarians. However, he was removed from power in July 1956 by Nikita Khrushchev, the new leader of the Soviet Union. Just three months later, the Hungarian revolution began.* The Soviet response was characteristically brutal and ham-fisted. Newly produced T-54As trundled into Budapest, only for many of them to be disabled by the Hungarian resistance. It was no fault of the tank's design; they were not well-protected by infantry or artillery, which allowed the Hungarian fighters to get around them and even immobilize some by greasing the roads.[6] The UK's military attaché in Budapest at the time was Lieutenant Colonel (Lt Col) James Noel Cowley, and as the legend has it, he managed to bring one of those immobilized T-54As inside the UK's embassy compound.[7] British staff examined the vehicle extensively, which was supposedly enough to come to the conclusion that the 20-pdr arming the Centurion and the 90mm M3 of the M48 would not be able to beat the T-54A.[8] It is not really clear how the British were able to learn about the frontal armour of the T-54A from that brief inspection – especially as they supposedly returned the vehicle. But it has been so widely claimed that this event led to the development of something truly game-changing in the world of Western tank design that it is rarely questioned.

That something is the Royal Ordnance, L7 105mm tank gun, which would eventually become a NATO standard armament and still arms some South Korean tanks today. The L7 is a remarkable weapon for its anti-armour lethality, but it is worth noting that a paper published by

*It is important to note that many other events contributed to the revolution, as covered by this text: Paul E. Zinner, 'Revolution in Hungary: Reflections on the Vicissitudes of a Totalitarian System', *The Journal of Politics*, Vol. 21, No. 1 (1959): pp.3–36. https://doi.org/10.2307/2126642.

the British Army's Operational Research Group in 1954 had already reached the conclusion that the Centurion could not defeat the IS-3 from the front. The much larger 120mm gun of the Conqueror, introduced into service by the British in the 1950s, could deal with the IS-3. However, the Conqueror was not built in the same numbers as the Centurion and was quickly replaced by later developments.[9] The two tanks served in a mixed fleet, which was common before the main battle tank concept took off. In short, there would be different tanks for different roles. The Conqueror, for example, was capable of sitting at range and engaging heavy Soviet armour. The Centurion would advance with the troops, engaging medium armour. Moreover, Ogorkiewicz notes that development of the L7 started in 1954 by reboring a 20-pdr.[10] Reboring simply means that the bore of a 20-pdr was increased from 83.4mm to 105mm and then used for tests. It stands to reason that the British were already concerned about their ability to counter Soviet tanks when Lt Col Cowley arranged for a T-54A to be examined in the British embassy in 1956. Regardless, development of the L7 accelerated and it was accepted into service in 1958 by the US and 1959 by the UK. It is arguably the most successful tank gun outside of the Soviet Union, and may have accounted for more tank-on-tank kills during the Cold War than any other. We will return to the L7 shortly, but first I want to set the scene just a little more.

By 1954, where this part of the book begins, NATO had formed and was in the midst of disagreements with the Soviet Union over the role of West Germany. The US felt that if NATO were to defend Europe, and if most of NATO's power were to come from the US, then West Germany should be contributing to that defence.[11] This conversation was fuelled by the Soviet backing of North Korea, which had demonstrated its willingness to go against the interests of the West. West Germany was admitted to NATO in 1955 and the Warsaw Pact was formed shortly after.[12] Khrushchev had given a speech about Stalinism and the regime's wrongs in 1956, which was known as the 'Secret Speech'. He had wanted to forge a more harmonious relationship with NATO, which he called 'peaceful coexistence', rather than Stalin's approach, which assumed war was inevitable.[13] However, not long after this speech, the Hungarian revolution started and the Soviet response unfolded, as we have already covered. There was a change in relations to some extent, but the Soviet Union's forming the Warsaw Pact, crushing the Hungarian revolution so violently, and then working to counter US influence in Vietnam all contributed to increasing tensions. All of this was happening under the growing shadow of nuclear weapons, and budgetary challenges. The US in particular, under President Eisenhower, was facing significant pressure to reduce its defence spending. At the same time, it was widely acknowledged that Soviet forces in Europe would outmatch NATO in numbers. In 1953, this led to a doctrinal approach that came to be known as 'massive retaliation'. In short, the Soviets were informed that nuclear weapons would be used from the outset of any war, and extensively.[14]

Suffice to say, things were not looking good for Europe's land forces, and this environment led to several developments in the technology of tanks that can still be seen today: namely, nuclear, biological, and chemical (NBC) protection systems, larger-calibre guns sporting new types of armour-piercing ammunition, and early attempts to install night vision equipment on tanks. In this era, new doctrinal elements began to inform the designs of the next generation of tanks, primarily represented by the Chieftain, Leopard 1, and M60 for NATO, and the T-64 and T-72 for the USSR. For NATO designers, it was clear that their tanks would be likely to start in a defensive role, requiring tanks that could be dug in and fire their guns from a depressed position. The Soviets began establishing a tiered force, with some units employing the most modern tanks, and others the generation below – a trait that was carried on by Russia. Additionally, Soviet tanks were expected to fight through battlefields saturated with radiation. All of this, as well as the established survival pressures (armour and firepower), drove tank development in the mid-1950s. But let's start by returning to the L7.

Chapter 5

The L7 105mm vs D-10TG 100mm

Sunday 4 November 1956 was a mild day for the time of year, with a touch of frost and fog. Our story begins at around 4.00am, with Hungarians huddled in their basements in Budapest. Many had awoken in the dark to the ground and their apartments shaking. Some no doubt wondered if they were experiencing another earthquake – Budapest had been struck by a significant quake earlier in the year. They quickly realized the truth: Soviet forces had invaded and were bombarding the city with artillery and air power. This would be the T-54's combat debut, serving with Guards Tank Divisions attached to the Special Corps. The Special Corps had been established in 1955 to defend Hungary from a NATO incursion through Austria, and to ensure that any internal unrest would be dealt with quickly.[1] Two other Soviet armies were stationed in Hungary, the 38th Guards Army and the 8th Army. Together, these forces constituted a force of tens of thousands, with up to 4,000 tanks including T-34-85s and T-54s.*

Fighting had raged in the city between 24 October and 2 November. Hungary's brave revolutionaries had taken advantage of the lull to find more ammunition and food. Citizens in some parts of the city carried

*Note: A UN report on the revolution states that estimates placed the Soviet force numbers between 75,000 and 200,000, and 1,600 and 4,000 tanks. United Nations, 'Report of the Special Committee on the Problem of Hungary', General Assembly Official Records: Eleventh Session, Supplement No. 18 (A/3592), United Nations, New York (1957), p.56.

on with their regular lives, as seems to happen in most wars. But when the Soviets came back, they followed a pattern that is now familiar, with a similar gambit employed in Ukraine in February 2022. The tanks approached the city from different sides and headed straight down major roads, trying to find major centres of resistance and bypassing lone snipers and other, less-capable threats. In the earlier fighting in late October, children had joined the fray – smearing jam on the periscopes of Soviet tanks before dropping Molotov cocktails down the hatches.[2] Few would venture out as the Soviet forces stormed into Budapest on 4 November.

The new T-54s led the charge, firing at any point of resistance from close range, destroying buildings and strongpoints with abandon. They moved quickly, deliberately trying to overwhelm the Hungarian resistance, which had initially been instructed not to fight by Premier Imre Nagy. Realizing his folly, Nagy implored the Hungarian Army and resistance to fight back at 5.20am. But there was very little that they could do in the face of overwhelming firepower. 'When the first Soviet tank column appeared on Üllői Avenue at the defence perimeter of the school, they swept away some of the anti-tank weapons which we had placed there,' one fighter remembered.[3] He was not alone: while there are many accounts of Soviet columns being delayed and destroyed during the first stage of fighting, the second assault on the city fared much better and most resistance had ended by midday, with the rest of the strongpoints defeated by 7 November. It was not the technical specifics of the T-54 that paved the way for a Soviet victory during the second assault on the city. Across all of the available accounts, it appears that the sheer firepower brought to bear, the scale of the attack, and the apparent lack of warning were contributing factors. However, it was the D-10TG that shattered thousands of windows throughout the city, and destroyed hundreds of buildings.

The D-10TG was developed from the B-34 naval gun, which had been in service with the Soviet Navy since 1940. It has an L54 barrel (5.608m) with a horizontal sliding wedge breech block. The original D-10Ts were unstabilized, but the D-10TG carries vertical stabilization and a bore evacuator, which helps to offset the additional weight added to the breech of the gun for the stabilizer. A bore evacuator is a very useful addition to a tank because when a tank fires, the burning propellant creates harmful gases. The exact gases released by the D-10TG are

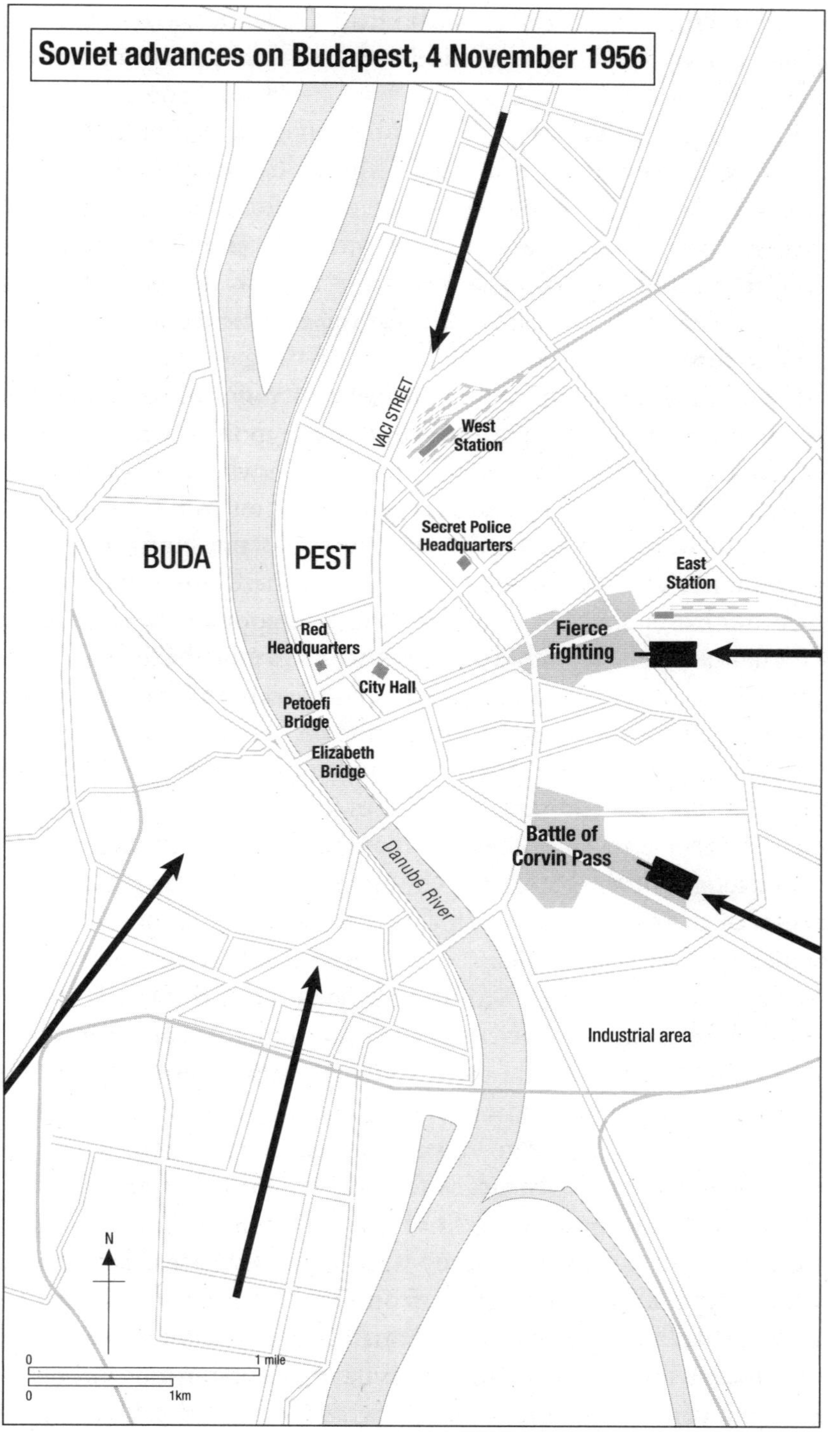
Soviet advances on Budapest, 4 November 1956
VACI STREET
West
Station
Secret Police
Headquarters
East
Station
BUDA
PEST
Red
Headquarters
City Hall
Fierce
fighting
Petoefi
Bridge
Elizabeth
Bridge
Battle of
Corvin Pass
Danube River
Industrial area
N
0
1 mile
0
1km

unknown, but tests of the M777 and Carl Gustaf anti-armour weapon in 2006 detected hydrogen cyanide and formaldehyde in the resulting smoke.[4] The main gun and machine guns fitted to most tanks can also produce dangerous amounts of carbon monoxide, with one test from 1943 showing that turret crews in an M7 tank accumulated dangerous levels of the gas in their blood.[5] None of these fumes are particularly beneficial to a soldier's health, and when fired repeatedly inside a closed turret, they build up. So, a bore evacuator is typically represented by a bulge on the barrel; for the T-54 it was right at the end. The bulge is a reservoir that covers holes in the barrel. As the gases generated by the propellant push the round down the barrel at very high pressure, some of them enter the bore evacuator via the holes in the barrel where they are then trapped in the reservoir. As soon as the round leaves the muzzle, the pressure drops, pulling the gases out of the reservoir through ports that face forwards – towards the muzzle. This expels most of the toxic fumes out of the end of the barrel, rather than back through the breech. However, that is not to say that the bore evacuator solved all problems on Soviet tanks. Israeli reports of captured Egyptian and Syrian T-62s indicate that fumes were a considerable problem for their crews, causing fatigue that led some crews to abandon their vehicles altogether.[6]

When it first entered service, the D-10TG could fire its armour-piercing projectile through 185mm of steel armour at a range of 1,000m.[7] This was a result of its chamber pressure of 3,000kgf/cm^2 and the length of the barrel, which together enabled the gun to fire its projectiles at 895m/s. However, this represents the capabilities of the original solid shot projectile; the T-55 would later be armed with the 3BM-8 Armour Piercing Discarding Sabot round, which significantly improved penetration. For now, however, and the comparison with the L7, the most effective armour-piercing round available to the T-54 in 1956 was the BR-412B, which fired a solid projectile 404mm long with a diameter of 100mm. This creates a length-to-diameter (L:D) ratio of 1:4, which simply means the projectile is four times as long as it is round. You may have heard of this figure before, but it is worth touching upon as it will come up again. The L:D ratio is important because, generally speaking, the greater the surface area at the tip of the projectile, the wider the area that the kinetic energy is distributed over. Modern armour-piercing rounds have an L:D ratio of 30:1, which means the penetrator's length is 30 times its diameter, and the kinetic energy is applied over a very small surface area. A low L:D ratio means that the pressure on the armour is dispersed, and penetration efficiency is reduced. To help visualize this difference, you can test the different penetration characteristics of things like wooden spoons against a nail by pressing them into soil or cardboard. The wider cross-sectional area of the wooden spoon will make it more challenging to push into most materials, while the nail should not struggle.

The BR-412B penetrator was made of hardened steel, with the nose of the projectile coming in at around 600 BHN. The base and core of the projectile were softer. There are two reasons for this: the first is that the hardness at the tip of the projectile is necessary for it to penetrate high-hardness armour. The second is that the BR-412B was filled with 65g of an explosive called A-IX-2. A-IX-2 is a Russian explosive that consists of 73% RDX (a high explosive), 23% aluminium powder, and 4% wax as a phlegmatizer, which is used to stabilize the RDX and make it less sensitive.[8] When the projectile penetrated the armour of a tank, it would pass out of the other side and the explosive would detonate, shattering the base of the projectile into five or six large pieces. The BR-412B was supplemented from 1951 by the BR-412D, which was a similar round fitted with an armour-penetrating cap.[9] This cap was made out of a softer material than the penetrator so that when it struck the armour of a vehicle, the cap would absorb most of the initial shock, rather than the hardened penetrator. This comes back to the hardness vs strength factor that also applies to armour. A material can be very hard and brittle, or very strong and not as hard. At high velocities, steel will tend to shatter when it hits face-hardened armour, especially if that armour is sloped.[10] So, the cap was designed to absorb that initial shock, allowing the penetrator to make it to the vehicle in one piece.

The BR-412 rounds were designed so that the gunner could set his sights at 1,220m before going into combat. If a NATO tank was spotted, he could place the sight at the centre of mass and fire. If the tank was at that range, the shot would be likely to land at the base of the turret. If it was closer or further away than 1,220m, the shot would strike higher up on the turret or lower down and hit the hull respectively. This helped to speed up engagements rather than waiting for range finding to be done.[11] When they hit the armour, the rounds would either fail, leaving a dent in the armour, or penetrate. The penetration mechanisms are quite daunting for these full-calibre shells. If the diameter of the shell is much greater than the thickness of the armour – so anything less than 40mm thick for the BR-412 – the round can cause something called dishing.

Quite simply, dishing occurs when the round overmatches the armour to such an extent that it is bent out of the way. If the armour is slightly thicker and the round is blunt when it hits but still overmatches the armour, it will lead to a mechanism called plugging. In this case, the round literally knocks a plug of armour out into the tank's interior. A third mechanism is called 'ductile hole enlargement'. In this case, the armour is thicker than the diameter of the round and the round has to push the armour out of the way, creating massive amounts of friction and heat as it does so. The armour may in fact melt, lubricating the path for the projectile and expanding the size of the hole as it does. In all three failures, penetration will be accompanied by extensive spalling, which is where shards of metal from the rear of the armour plate break away and travel – usually in a cone shape – into the crew and equipment inside the tank. The projectile will also travel through the armour and into the hull. Most tanks are cramped inside, which means that most penetrations will lead to the crew being killed or wounded. The round, and the BR-412 in particular, may also detonate ammunition, ignite hydraulic fluid and fuel, and break apart into fragments. In short, penetration with a kinetic energy round is usually the end of a tank and its crew.

Soviet tank doctrine saw the tank company as an important unit that could act independently or as an attachment to a motor rifle brigade. It could perform in the anti-tank role, as a reconnaissance platform, or to provide fire support amongst many other battlefield tasks. Tank companies were also expected to lead the attack. The Soviets really thought only in terms of the attack, with defensive operations expected to be a temporary expedient until an offensive could be resumed.[12] This context is important because the T-54 and later T-55 were designed for tank-on-tank engagements, but also provided crucial fire support to infantry. For this, the T-54 would generally carry more high-explosive ammunition than armour-piercing ammunition. The primary high-explosive round was the UOF-412 high-explosive (HE) round, which was fired from a steel case. The total round, including the case and munition, weighed 30.2kg and the projectile (designated OF-412) constituted 15.6kg of that. For comparison, the high-explosive round fired by the Centurion weighed 7.8kg. The OF-412 was filled with 1.46kg of TNT and had a point detonating fuze, which meant that it could detonate immediately upon impact, or the detonation could be delayed so that it would explode shortly after landing. It could be fired up to 16km, which might sound quite far for a tank, but all Soviet tanks are built to provide indirect fire support in one way or another, which means they are expected to be used against targets that the tank crew cannot see.

In all, the D-10TG was reasonably effective, and it would eventually be fitted with a new two-axis stabilizer which improved its accuracy. The BR-412B could defeat a lot of the armour of an M48 at around 1,200m, but could not penetrate the upper glacis. The BR-412D likely improved performance against the upper glacis, and both rounds serve to illustrate the extent to which the T-54 changed the calculus for NATO tanks. They may not have known how much armour the D-10TG could penetrate before Lt Col Cowley arranged for one to be examined in 1956, but they would have had a good idea of what it could do. Tanks are all about the guns and getting the gun into a position to damage the enemy. If your tanks carry guns that are inferior to the enemy's, then your tanks may find themselves out-ranged and their armour overmatched. And if your gun is not able to penetrate the enemy's armour, then your forces will likely suffer disproportionate losses. The T-54 and eventually the T-55 introduced a gun that could penetrate the armour of most Western tanks, and a level of armour that was quite capable of resisting the existing armament. The 105mm L7 was, therefore, a timely intervention.

The L7 was originally developed from the 20-pdr, as already mentioned, but it retained the chamber volume of the 20-pdr, which theoretically would limit the amount of propellant that could be used. Nevertheless, the L7 could fire an L28A1 armour-piercing discarding sabot (APDS) round at 1,480m/s.[13] The APDS is what gave the L7 and the tanks that carried it the edge for some time. As an ammunition nature, the APDS had been around since World War II, but it was not very widely used – the D-10TG being a case in point. It was originally developed as a concept by French engineers at a company called Edgar Brandt. As German forces swept through the French countryside in 1940, they escaped to Britain taking their early work with them, which was taken up by the UK's Armament Research and Development

Establishment. The first tank to receive the round was the Churchill, which had a 57mm, 6-pdr gun.[14] While effective, the UK would become unreasonably attached to the APDS, even when newer, more effective natures became available. So, what is an APDS, and why was its development so important?

We have already touched on the role of a projectile's cross-section in penetrating armour. The smaller the cross section the better, basically. Together with the hardness of the penetrator, the muzzle velocity, the engagement range, and the properties of the defending armour, you have all of the ingredients needed for target penetration. However, a full-bore projectile like the BR-412D faces several challenges. Its weight and shape will mean that it is slower than a sub-calibre projectile, and that it slows down because of drag more quickly. And although it is made of high-hardness steel, it is nowhere near the hardness of tungsten carbide. These factors limit the penetration that a full-bore projectile can achieve. An APDS aims to resolve and improve upon most of these characteristics. The core of the round is a penetrator, which in the case of the L7 was made of tungsten carbide. This is the same material used in the HVAP rounds carried by Lt Nordstrom from Part 1. Its high hardness and density make it well suited for increasing kinetic energy and for overmatching the relatively soft steel armours. To improve velocity and reduce drag, the penetrator is made to be smaller than the bore of the barrel – or sub-calibre. This means that it will be able to travel faster than a full-bore round and with a flatter trajectory, but it also creates a design challenge. As we covered in Part 1, high-performance ammunition requires good obturation to ensure that the right level of energy is imparted to the projectile. If the penetrator was much smaller than the barrel, it would not create a seal and would rattle around the inside of the gun. So, the penetrator is fitted with a sabot (the French word for a wooden shoe), which matches the bore of the gun. APDS rounds often come with a sabot that is shaped like a pot at the base of the projectile.

With the sabot providing obturation, the propellant is ignited and sends the round down the barrel of the gun. As it leaves the muzzle, the forces imparted to the sabot peel it away from the penetrator, leaving it to make its way towards the intended target. Because of these forces, sabots have to be quite robust and are relatively heavy as a result, which means they absorb a lot of the energy generated by the propellant rather than the penetrator.[15] Even so, the APDS and L7 combination provided British, American, German, and Swiss forces with the lethality to outmatch Soviet armour. The first APDS for the L7 was the L22, but it would go through several iterations until the L52 was introduced in the 1970s. This round could penetrate 120mm of steel armour set at an angle of 60 degrees, from a range of 1,830m.[16] This effectively means that the L52 could penetrate a line-of-sight thickness of 240mm, and the earlier APDS iterations were not far from this, albeit at around half the range. The T-54 carried a 100mm-thick armoured plate for its glacis, which was set at a 60-degree angle, providing a line-of-sight thickness of 200mm.[17] Its turret was also around 200mm thick at the front. This means that the early APDS rounds – introduced in the 1950s – ensured that the Centurion or Leopard 1 could defeat a T-54 or T-55 at typical combat ranges. By the time that the L52 was introduced, NATO tank crews could be reasonably certain of their ability to hold older Soviet tanks at risk from very long ranges. That is not to say that older tanks were powerless against newer designs, however. South Vietnamese forces equipped with M48A3 Pattons – armed only with the 90mm M41 guns – reportedly accounted for dozens of North Vietnamese T-54/55s during the 1972 offensives.[18] Over this period, NATO's previous focus on technical capability was increasing as the only reasonable counter to the Soviet mass. But an increase in range required an increase in visibility and accuracy. It's time to look at mission systems and suspension.

Chapter 6

Stability starts with the tracks

Stability is a big deal for tanks, especially when they are looking to engage moving targets at long range. A slight movement of the hull can lead to a lack of stability at the gun, which can easily translate to a missed shot. When all tanks were on an equal footing, i.e. unstabilized, this might be survivable. However, with effective engagement ranges approaching 2,000m, a missed shot could mean the end of the crew. We have to start by understanding what is being stabilized and why. For that, we have to look at vibrations. The hull of a tank is subject to vibrations in three axes as they drive:

1. Vertical vibrations around the centre of gravity. Quite simply, the tank will bounce up and down as it travels, especially off-road.
2. Pitching vibrations around its horizontal axis. You can think of this as being like a boat in a rough sea. The front of a boat will rise with a wave, pointing the rear down, and then over the crest of the wave the front of the boat will point down. A tank may be subject to hundreds of small pitching vibrations as it drives, and without good suspension and gun stabilization, it would be impossible to fire on the move.
3. Torsional vibrations around its longitudinal axis. Now imagine a line from the front to the back of the tank, and think of twisting motions around it. This may represent itself as the suspension on one side compressing while the other side is extending.

These effects may have been known since the first tanks crossed the Somme in 1916, but they were certainly an element of tank design by the late 1950s and described in engineering formulas.[1] Although gun stabilization was becoming more widespread, it cannot account for everything as it requires power, and power is a precious resource in tanks. So, minimizing the vibration through the running gear has become essential to stabilization by reducing the movements that the stabilizing equipment must account for.

There was also a growing realization that these vibrations affected the crew, as well as the vehicle and its accuracy. As the vehicle passes over rough ground, the vibrations are passed through the hull and into the crew, who may be sitting, standing, or reclining. It has been found through many scientific studies that high-frequency vibrations lead to fatigue and even sickness. The size of vibrations that a human can handle also increases with a lower frequency. The frequency of vibrations is measured in Hertz (Hz); 60 Hz means that there are 60 vibration cycles every second, 1 Hz means one cycle every second. In a nutshell, the frequency generally increases with vehicle speed, and the size of vibrations (amplitude) increases the rougher the ground. A tank crew will not be able to physically handle a tank moving at high speed over rough ground, especially hard, broken ground. This is because the frequency and amplitude of the vibrations will be too high.[2]

Regardless of which country a tank comes from, and the design philosophy that underlines it, it is the job of the suspension, tracks, roadwheels, and drive sprocket to minimize the vibrations imparted to the vehicle and crew. The tracks are key: they are how a tank interacts with the world. There are a few design considerations to bear in mind: the first is the surface area. As touched upon in the chapter 'Anywhere a tank can go, is tank country: even the tops of mountains', the surface area of the tracks is key to spreading the weight of the tank, which in turn is essential for mobility. In general, designers have tried to maximize the width of tracks, but this is limited by the hull and width constraints. During World War II, German Tiger tanks were provided with wider tracks that made them too big to be carried on a railway wagon. So smaller tracks were fitted for transport and the crews had to go through the job of replacing them before combat. The second consideration is weight. Tank tracks are very heavy: a single link may weigh as much as 35kg, and the Centurion's tracks weighed

132.5kg per metre.[3] Tracks can add considerably to the weight of a vehicle, and heavier tracks create more rolling resistance that has to be overcome.

However, another consideration is track life. Tracks go through a lot in their life. Technically, they disperse the weight of the vehicle over a wide area, but realistically a lot of that vehicle's weight will pass through a single track link, especially on hard ground. Tracks are also meant to be tensioned, which helps distribute the vehicle's weight, but also results in them being stretched over time. If they become too loose, then tracks can be thrown off the drive sprocket, immobilizing the tank. All of this together means that tracks will need replacing after a few thousand kilometres; the M60 could have a track life of 6,000km, for example, while the M1 Abrams came in at just 2,900km.[4] Track life can be increased by making the tracks more robust, but that will also increase the weight. The final design factor is pitch, which is the measurement from one point on a track link to the identical point on the next track link. There is a sweet spot for track pitch: too long and it will impact the design of the drive sprocket leading to a louder vehicle and greater vibration through the hull; too short and it will impact the ground pressure and distribution of the vehicle's weight. Lighter vehicles can have a shorter track pitch, but tanks must compromise to a much greater extent.

Now that we have a baseline for tracks and track performance, let's take a look at the technology of the time. The Centurion, M48, and T-54/55 tracks were primarily built of steel; some included rubber. The Centurion used a single-pin track design, which is where the front of one track link is connected to the back of the next with a pin. The teeth of the drive sprocket propels the track by engaging with holes in the track link, which are worn over time and can eventually lead to the track being replaced. A double-pin track differs because each track link has two pins, one at the front and one at the back. The links are joined together using separate connectors with rubber bushings built in. This was a major advantage of double-pin tracks over single-pin at the time. British tanks, like the Centurion, tended to carry single-pin tracks because they were too heavy and imparted too much force to have rubber bushes inside the lugs. Double-pin tracks have the rubber bushes built in and they also rotate less than with single-pin tracks, so that they can be used by heavier vehicles. The Soviets, however, had much lighter vehicles such as the T-54, which could be fitted with single-pin, rubber-bushed tracks. The rubber increases track life, but also weight and cost. In addition, both styles of track have a horn in the centre of the track which runs between the road wheels. This helps keep the track on the vehicle, especially when turning. Turning a tank pushes a lot of force towards the side of the hull, which would push the track off the road wheels if the central horn were not present.

Hopefully you can see that there is a lot of friction involved in a tank's track, which rapidly leads to changes in length and tension. The pitch of the track is measured to get an idea of how much the length has changed. Crews can account for this by moving the idler, which is an unpowered wheel at the opposite end of the hull to the drive sprocket. Eventually they may also have to remove a track link to get back to the appropriate tension, or replace the entire track. The final element is the rubber track pads. Some tracks have the rubber built into them, which is useful for protecting roads from excessive damage, but provides less grip on soft soil. Others are just steel, which provides the opposite effect.

The tracks are an important part of reducing vibrations and, as we will see later, some modern technologies promise quite drastic reductions. When the Centurion, T-54/55, and M48 were roaming the fields of Europe, however, the primary concern appears to have been track life and mobility. The suspension of all three vehicles also showed some signs of divergence. The M48 and T-54/55 carried torsion bar suspension, while the Centurion carried Horstman bogey suspension.

Suspension means that the vehicle body is resting on or suspended from something with give – i.e. a spring. Suspension does this by allowing a degree of wheel travel to happen against resistance, which reduces the amount of force passed onto the vehicle hull. This is because increasing the distance over which a force is applied reduces its acceleration. At its most basic, then, suspension is a spring designed to absorb shock. And that is just what a torsion bar is. Torsion bars have been used in civilian cars since the 1930s, and were used in several of Germany's tanks during World War II. They have come to be the primary form of suspension for tanks and armoured fighting vehicles despite the introduction of other systems, like the Horstman system used by the Centurion.

Torsion bars are made of steel and lie along the bottom of the vehicle hull inside the armour. The bar is anchored on the opposite side of the hull to the roadwheel it is supporting. At the other end, the bar is attached to a trailing arm that carries the roadwheel. It is called a trailing arm simply because the pivot point – where it connects to the vehicle hull – is ahead of the roadwheel. The roadwheel is trailing behind the pivot point. As the roadwheel moves over terrain it moves up and down with bumps and holes, which in turn twists (torsions) the bar. The bar, which is essentially a long spring, provides resistance to the bump and reduces the shock that gets transferred to the vehicle. This means that one of the key design considerations for a torsion bar is its shear stress, which describes the amount of force that it would take to break it. Additionally, the front two roadwheel stations of any tank will tend to have the most extreme duty requirements because they absorb the pitching of the vehicle.[5] For that reason, they will often be fitted with additional dampers to absorb the shock, and in some cases – like later variants of the Leopard 2 – the front torsion bars have to be upgraded to a higher strength so that they can handle the weight added to the vehicle. The length of the trailing arm also impacts torsion bar performance: a shorter trailing arm leads to more stress on the torsion bar, so it must be stronger. Increasing the number of wheels can also reduce the strength of torsion bar required, as can reducing the required travel. These are important considerations because they will impact the diameter of the torsion bar – generally between 50 and 70mm – as well as the weight. They are a cost- and design-effective solution to the increasing weight of tanks and the need for them to travel faster on and off-road. However, installing torsion bars means that the height of the vehicle has to be increased. This is an interesting juncture to bring the T-54 and T-55 back to the conversation.

Soviet designers attempted to keep the size of their vehicles down, both to minimize the size of target that they presented, and to reduce the overall vehicle weight. But they also tried to minimize complexity while maintaining certain performance standards. Soviet tanks like the T-34-85 had employed a form of spring suspension that is reported to have been designed by John Walter Christie, an American engineer. The roadwheels were mounted on a trailing arm in a similar fashion to a torsion bar, but inside the tank was a coiled spring, instead of a bar. Christie suspension took up a lot of room inside the tank, making conditions cramped and increasing the height of the hull. However, it did allow the large roadwheels a good amount of travel. But without a bump stop, which limits roadwheel travel to a sensible amount, the T-34s experienced a considerable amount of pitch. The torsion bar suspension in a T-55, however, provides 218mm of travel, which is essentially limited by the strength and length of the steel used. There are ten torsion bars in total in a T-55, one for each roadwheel.[6]

Soviet tanks often get a bad rap for their ride comfort, but it is worth noting that the Israelis saw them differently, according to Lt Col Eshe, an Israeli armour officer and one of the founders of the Israeli Armoured Corps, who later became a journalist: 'The ordnance experts agreed unanimously that the basic T-55 was a good tank with excellent automotive capabilities riding on one of the world's best suspension and track systems ... The tank had an extremely low silhouette, and was fast even over rough terrain and sand.'[7] The Israelis should know: they had captured several T-55s from the Egyptians during the Six Day War in 1967 and put them to use with their own armoured formations in 1969 during Operation *Raviv*. Operation *Raviv* can only be described as a daring raid: the Israelis landed six T-55s and three BTR-50s on the Egyptian coast, hoping that the use of Egyptian armour would confuse their opponents. They spent 10 hours – often offroad – destroying coastal air defence radars before they were collected again and returned home.[8] But we are getting ahead of ourselves. Let's return to the Centurion and its unique suspension.

There are several instances throughout this book where British tank designers adopt technologies that buck the trend. Some, like the rifled 120mm main gun that will feature in Part 3, failed to gain any real traction. The Horstman suspension used by the Centurion, however, was the beginning of a strong legacy for the company and its designs. At the time of writing (2025), the various Horstman suspension systems equip dozens of armoured vehicles, including the Challenger 2 tank, the K9 Thunder self-propelled howitzer, and the Puma infantry fighting vehicle. The company started out providing the Horstman Bogey, which provided the suspension for the Bren Gun Carrier. The Centurion also carried Horstman bogey suspension which, unlike torsion bars, could be mounted outside the vehicle hull. This meant it took up less space inside the hull, leaving more room for important things like ammunition or the crew. Bogeys were also easier to access and replace than a torsion bar or internally mounted suspension, which is a benefit when mines were a threat, which they often were.

The most immediate difference between bogeys and torsion bars, besides the external mounting, is that torsion bars provide individual suspension for each roadwheel. Bogies mount two wheels onto the same suspension system. This means that whatever happens to one wheel translates into a response from the other. As one wheel is pushed up by a rock, for example, the other wheel will be pressed down into the ground. This can be a good thing. Tanks rely on their tracks staying in contact with the ground to move, and a bogey can help ensure that happens. The up-and-down motion of the roadwheels is translated into horizontal motion by bellcranks inside the bogey. Bellcranks are typically two arms connected at an angle with a pivot joint at their junction. They are used to change a vertical motion into a horizontal one. When the wheels go over an object, the bellcranks compress the springs inside the bogey, allowing the movement to occur and reducing the force passed onto the vehicle. However, this arrangement limits the wheel travel, a lot. If both wheels on a Centurion bogey were moved, they could only travel 86mm. A single wheel could travel up to 146mm. This meant the vehicles were good at crossing low-frequency obstacles like rocks, and helps to explain why they could cover such challenging terrain in Korea. However, the short wheel travel and limited damping meant that the Centurion was prone to pitching (remember the section on vibration?) and that something called resonance could exacerbate this effect.[9] Resonance is where the bounce of the suspension matches the bounce of the terrain, and the vehicle can become extremely uncomfortable for the crew at that stage, which could happen if it drove at speed over undulating terrain or roads.

The need for increased speed and mobility, as well as the growth in tank weight, would eventually spell the end for the Horstman bogey suspension, but not before the British selected it for the Chieftain main battle tank. However, the two designs help illustrate the design choices that were shaping tanks in the 1940s and 50s. Over time, torsion bars have come to be the dominant choice for tank suspension. The US M48, which was in service at the same time as the Centurion and T-54/55, used torsion bars; the M60 that replaced it would do so too; and the M1 Abrams that replaced the M60 carried them on. The Leopard 1 used torsion bars, as do Leopard 2s, including the most modern variants, and Russia's T-72B3M and T-90M both use torsion bars. They are relatively simple but effective devices and equip what are arguably the most effective and successful modern tank designs. Tracks have also remained relatively constant, so we will not return to them in detail, but this chapter should show how the tracks, roadwheels, and suspension all work together to provide a stable platform, both for the sake of the crew, and for the accuracy of the main gun. And they would need it, because both sides were beginning to imagine a world in which nuclear and chemical weapons were the only way forward.

Chapter 7

Buttoned up and fighting dirty

> Two minutes before the 0930 shot, the Exercise Director ordered all participants to crouch, cover their faces with their hands, and lean against the forward wall of the trenches. Three seconds after the flash, the troops were allowed to stand and observe the rising fireball. About 15 seconds later, the shock wave reached the trench area, temporarily obscuring vision.[1]

This somewhat plain description described the experience of tens of thousands of regular soldiers from NATO and the Soviet Union in the early 1950s. They were brought to remote areas for several days and briefed on nuclear weapons and the way that they worked. New equipment was issued, and it was explained that they would be deployed in trenches during a nuclear test. Then, on the morning of the tests they were ferried to the testing ground and into trenches. Some Soviet trenches were fitted with double doors and some foxholes were covered, but other soldiers recounted simply hiding behind mounds of earth to save themselves.[2] In other tests, unfortunate sheep were equipped with radiation-resistant suits and left to graze within the irradiated area of Soviet blasts; some were even bundled into tanks to see how they would fare. US soldiers were similarly instructed to crouch down until after the immense flash had passed them. They then toured the blast sites and equipment that had been left within close range of the bombs to examine the damage. Some even conducted exercises, led by US Army 'rad-safe monitors', who were responsible for ensuring that the intensity of radiation did not surpass the supposedly safe limit of 500mr/hr.[3] This is a measure of radiation in the air; meaning in this case that anyone in that area could be subjected to up to 500 millirems of gamma or X-ray radiation every hour.In theory, short exposure to this dose of radiation would not be immediately harmful, but the Soviets and Americans weren't thinking about short doses at all; they wanted their troops to fight irradiated.

During the Cold War, both the Soviet and NATO forces developed tactical nuclear weapons. Unlike the nuclear weapons that most people probably think of, these were not intended to end the world, although some maintain that their use would have led to that anyway. From 1954 the US Army had started deploying a tactical nuclear 'artillery rocket' known as Honest John, reportedly named after a Texan making hard-to-believe claims.[4] Honest John carried a 20-kiloton nuclear warhead, and initial variants had a range of 32km, which was later increased to 48km. Nuclear weapons are ideally detonated off the ground, which provides space for the full effects to take place. Those effects are thermal radiation, also known as heat, blast and overpressure, and radioactive fallout. Nuclear weapons are equated to the high-explosive or TNT equivalent. A 20-kiloton warhead is said to be equivalent to 20,000 tonnes of TNT in energy, for example, but the blast and overpressure effects can be much greater than even the equivalent TNT. Overpressure is essentially what it sounds like: the weapon creates a shock wave that travels out from the epicentre of the blast. As it travels, it disturbs air molecules and increases the air pressure. This can knock buildings over, turn vehicles, and kill people if they are exposed. When that pressure is at its greatest, it is called peak static overpressure (PSO). This provides a useful point of comparison between conventional high-explosive weapons and nuclear: a 500kg warhead loaded with TNT would create a PSO of 12.5psi, or 87 kilopascals (kPa), 30m from the blast. This means that the pressure on a building or vehicle would have increased – almost instantaneously – by 12.5lb on every square inch of its surface. Residential buildings will collapse at 5psi, and most people would be killed at that same psi.[5]

A 1-kiloton nuclear warhead would generate the same amount of overpressure at a range of 300m, and a 1-megaton warhead at 3,000m. But that is not all: a 20-kiloton warhead would also generate a fireball with a radius of 222m, which means it would cover an area of around

21 European football pitches. The fireball would produce certain death: no humans or vehicles inside that zone would survive. This is in part because of the radiation, as well as the blast and the heat generated. The lethal radiation dose would extend out to 3.94km^2, meaning that most people within that area – 552 European football pitches – would die, and 15% of survivors would die of radiation-caused cancer. Finally, the moderate blast damage would extend to an area of 11.4km^2 and the full extent of thermal radiation would reach 13.9km^2 (1,947 European football pitches). Humans within that area that were exposed would immediately suffer burns to their clothes and exposed skin, leading to extensive third-degree burns that would be immediately or eventually fatal.* Properly built trenches and defences would provide some protection from the worst of the blast effects and thermal radiation. And nuclear, biological, chemical (NBC) suits were designed that would also help mitigate some of the burning effects. But you should be able to see that the effects of even 'small yield' tactical weapons like Honest John could be devastating. However, it is interesting to note that one book, *Nuclear Weapons: Principles, Effects, and Survivability,* published in 1994, states, 'when low-yield weapons are used against well-equipped and well-trained troops, the immediate nuclear radiation is the immediate governing effect'.[6] The author goes on to state that the effects of radiation would cause casualties at a greater distance than the blast or thermal effects.

This is supported to some extent by some of the trials mentioned at the start of this chapter, which included men using trenches to minimize their exposure to those elements, and emerging after the blast and heat had passed. Tanks, by and large, were relatively immune to the blast and thermal effects as long as they were not inside the immediate fireball. The thick armour would also provide some resistance to the radiation, but the Soviets planned to drive through irradiated areas of the battlefield. And NATO planned to irradiate those areas for them. Indeed, NATO's policy around tactical nuclear weapons was quite aggressive, and anticipated that things like Honest John and the W33 nuclear shell fired by the 8-inch M110 howitzer would be used to stop Soviet advances

*You can explore the effects of nuclear weapons yourself by visiting NUKEMAP here: https://nuclearsecrecy.com/nukemap/.

by surrounding them with nuclear effects.[7] The Soviets had their own tactical nuclear weapons and envisaged using them to create openings in NATO's defensive lines that their troops could pour through.[8]

The T-55 and the T-54 were developed before the Soviet Union or NATO had tactical nuclear weapons, and tests showed that the overpressure alone was enough to displace the turret. An NBC protection system was developed, which used a gamma radiation sensor to indicate when a nuclear bomb had been detonated, and automatically close all external openings to the tank, including the engine, supposedly before the blast wave reached the vehicle. At the same time, an overpressure device was installed, which would increase the pressure inside the vehicle to prevent particles getting inside.[9] Eventually (in the late 1960s) T-55s would be fitted with an anti-radiation lining inside the vehicle and on top of the turret hatches, which was made of a lead-impregnated polymer. This was designed to increase the vehicle's protection from gamma radiation. The M60A1 carried a similar system called M13A1, which is actually still in use with US forces today. It passed air from outside the vehicle through a chemical, biological, radiological, and nuclear (CBRN) filter before warming it if cold and feeding it directly into a crew member's respirator through a hose.[10] CBRN filters work against different agents in different ways. Radiological and biological weapons were countered by filters made of dense, fibrous materials like fibreglass. Those filters essentially catch and trap harmful particles like anthrax spores. Another element focuses on gas and vapor adsorption, using something like activated carbon, which has a very significant internal surface area that also traps the agents used in chemical warfare.

The chemical warfare aspect is, depending on whom you talk to, as frightening as the nuclear. For that reason, it is worth unpacking a little further. In early 2025, I interviewed some former Cold War artillery officers from the British Army. One of them told me, 'We were expecting to be hit with hydrogen cyanide or some thicker nerve agent that would fix you in place and then you'd receive counter-battery fire.' Hydrogen cyanide is a blood agent, which works by preventing the body from extracting oxygen from the blood. It would be delivered as a gas from artillery shells or air launched munitions, which means it would disperse relatively quickly and the weather would shape its impact. However, even mild exposure can lead to headaches, nausea, and dizziness for a long enough time to disrupt a unit's ability to function.[11]

Large-dose exposure to hydrogen cyanide leads to death within a few minutes and there was the likelihood that these lighter agents would be mixed with heavier agents. Heavier nerve agents are more persistent: they stick to vehicles and clothing and include weapons like Sarin and VX, which attack the nervous system and can cause death in minutes, again depending on exposure.[12] The Novichok nerve agent used by Russia against British citizens and the Skripals in the UK in 2018 is a heavy, persistent nerve agent. This means it does not decompose or easily wash away. Twenty-four of the emergency response vehicles that were used by the UK in 2018 were all buried or otherwise destroyed, such was the risk of contamination with the agent.[13] During the Cold War, Soviet forces fully expected to use chemical weapons including nerve agents from the outset, a disturbing fact confirmed to one of the officers I interviewed by Russian peers in the early 1990s. Troops that were contaminated with CBRN weapons would be expected to 'fight dirty'. This essentially meant they would be kept separate from the main, hopefully uncontaminated force, until the commanders could figure out what to do with them. All the while they would continue to fight, assuming they could, which is why the need for CBRN protection became so important for Cold War tanks. Notably, the Centurion did not include an overpressure system, but later British tanks would.

It also became important to harden circuits and microchips against the electromagnetic pulse (EMP) of a nuclear weapon. The EMP is generated by the interaction of the gamma radiation with particles in the air. As the gamma rays pass air molecules, they strip electrons from them, which are then deflected by the Earth's magnetic field, creating a massive and brief pulse of energy. That energy primarily damages the points at which a microchip connects to another component.[14] This can lead to destruction of the device or altering its performance. Armoured vehicles actually provide some shielding from EMPs, but external apertures like radio antennae and sights create vulnerabilities that can expose all electronics inside a vehicle. This problem became marked as NATO in particular moved from vacuum tubes to solid state technology. To explain why this is the case, let's start with a brief explainer of computing. Computing essentially uses the control of electrical currents to set a transistor to a 0 or a 1. Basically, it is either open or closed, and a series of transistors set to 0 or 1 leads to a response in a visual display or some other element. A vacuum tube is similar to a lightbulb, and works by passing current at high voltages through a wire in a vacuum. Compared to emerging microchips, vacuum tubes were large and made of quite robust components; they also worked at much higher voltages, so an EMP would have less impact on them. However, NATO was working to introduce more complex mission systems and sights into its vehicles, which took advantage of the solid state (i.e. no vacuum needed) microchip. A single microchip in the 1950s and 60s could have thousands of microscopic transistors on it; a modern chip will have billions. This essentially represents its computing power, and they operate at a fraction of the voltage of a vacuum tube. Altogether, this means that an EMP could easily overpower the transistors, damaging them and the vehicle's ability to function.

Over time, the imperative for hardening electronics seems to have waned for Western forces; it is rather expensive after all. But most modern vehicles carry a CBRN system despite the fact that this threat has changed. And this is perhaps why fighting dirty and buttoned up is so important for the modern tank. Buttoned up refers to closing all hatches and openings, activating the protective CBRN filters and potentially staying inside the tank for days. Fighting through the worst possible conditions has resulted in design considerations that are still relevant, perhaps now more relevant, today. However, fighting through a nuclear warzone covered in chemical and biological weapons was not the only problem that tank designers were looking to solve. As the T-54s of the USSR's Special Corps finished mopping up resistance in Budapest, there was a growing realization that it would be useful if tanks could fight at night. But to do that, their crews would need to be able to see in the dark.

Chapter 8
Fighting at night

Imagine, if you can, sitting in the commander's seat of a Centurion, on the right-hand side of the turret. You are somewhere in the German countryside, manoeuvring your tank to resupply in the dark. Poking your head out of the cupola you can see as much as you expected to, nothing. The dark shapes around you could be anything, and a wrong turn could have you exploring that countryside all night. You duck back inside the cupola and close the hatch; it was too cold to have your head out anyway. Turning to one of your periscopes, you press your head against the padding above the eyepiece, and turn on the switches at the bottom and side of the cupola. As you wait for the parts inside to power up, you rub your hands in a vain attempt to warm them, and wonder if it is time for a cup of tea. Now, looking through the eyepiece, the darkness turns to a grainy green circle – like looking through a toilet tube – but the world around you starts to make a little more sense. Over to your right, some trees, the outlines of an FV432 APC just visible against the background. It becomes clearer as your infrared searchlight passes over it. To the left and 20m away, a barn – you quietly congratulate yourself for turning the night vision on, rather than driving through it. In front of you stretch the fields leading to the inner German border, broken occasionally by hedgerows. Or, at least, you assume that is what is in front of you; the search light and periscope only let you see out to a few hundred metres. Now, you can give the driver instructions on what to do and where to go. He follows your orders to head over to the 432 for resupply.

This fictional scenario gives some idea of the capabilities that were added to tanks in the late 1950s. The night vision devices of this era built upon early systems used in World War II, and would have limited utility in combat, but they paved the way for systems that truly altered the story of the modern tank. Let's start with the early technology involved, which is called active infrared; but first we need to take a brief but helpful diversion into astrophysics. Light is part of the electromagnetic spectrum, which basically means it is energy moving through space as waves of oscillating magnetic or electric fields. We rely on the electromagnetic spectrum (EMS) for all sorts of things. The differences between the phenomena in the EMS are defined by their frequency and wavelength. The wavelength describes the distance between wave peaks, and frequency explains how often the wave oscillates. The longer the wavelength, the lower the frequency and energy, and shorter wavelengths lead to a higher frequency and more energy. This effect will become important in later sections when we look at radios and battle management systems. But, for now, at one end, the EMS consists of X-rays and gamma rays, with very short wavelengths. At the other end you have the frequencies used for radio communications, microwaves, and the internet.

This book was written through a browser-based word-processor through a 2.4 GHz internet connection. This means that there are 2.4 billion cycles per second, and each wave is around 12.5cm long. Compare this with visible light, like the colour red. Red has a frequency of 400 THz, and one Terahertz means it cycles one trillion times per second – so the frequency is very high compared to WiFi. The wavelength of the colour red is around 750 nanometres (nm), which is millions of times shorter than my router. You can see these colours because there are special receptor cones in your eyes that are adapted to the different types of colour and their wavelengths. Your night vision is dependent on a different vision system within the eye, which is still very sensitive but unable to see colour. Ok, are you ready to get back to night vision?

So, when it is dark we lose the ability to see colour and detail. This is a problem for armed forces because fighting at night, especially when your opponent cannot, and conducting resupply and other tasks at night is a very valuable skill to have. The main problem is the darkness. Obviously, a torch, or searchlight in the case of a tank, can solve this problem quite easily. But a searchlight powerful enough to provide meaningful engagement ranges would be a bad idea on the German plains as it would give your position away for miles around. That is because the light of a torch is in the visible part of the spectrum, like the colour red. So, early night vision devices went to the infrared spectrum, which is next-door to visible light and consists of near-infrared, medium infrared, and thermal infrared energy. We only need to think about near-infrared at the moment, with wavelengths measured in microns – a few hundred billionths of a metre. Early night vision devices, such as the commander's periscope fitted to the Centurion Mk 9/1, used an external source of near infrared light, essentially a large flashlight fitted to the turret that emitted infrared light. It was invisible to humans without an infrared optic, but could be seen by adversaries and other vehicles with a similar optic, and provided some vision out to around 450m.[1] The optic consisted of a lens and an image-intensifier tube, an incredibly sensitive piece of engineering which could be damaged if exposed to daylight.[2] The tube works by making the most of the light that it can gather to create an image. Inside the tube is something called a photocathode. The photocathode absorbs the light particles (photons) and releases corresponding electrical particles (electrons) and electricity at very high voltages to accelerate them. The accelerated electrons then hit a screen coated with phosphor, which is a material that absorbs energy and turns it into light. This screen is viewed by the gunner or commander of a Centurion as an image of what the optic is viewing and the infrared searchlight is illuminating. So, in a nutshell, the image-intensifier takes invisible light, and increases its energy to excite the photons so that they can be received as visible light.

Infrared night vision was introduced into Centurions from 1965, usually with the upgrade to Mk 9/1 and Mk 10/1 variants of the tank, which also carried the L7 and additional armour to counter the punchy D-10TG carried by the T-54 and T-55. The Soviets had introduced infrared vision from the T-54B, which entered service in 1957.[3] And by the early 1960s production had transitioned to the T-55, which incorporated many of the changes implemented in production of the T-54 as well as an anti-radiation lining. The American M60A1 also featured infrared periscopes and entered service from 1962.[4] If you read across the many different encyclopaedias and books that cover the history of armour up to the early 2000s, the focus is often on the guns, armour, and engines, in that order. These are all important changes that took place between 1954 and 1965, but fighting at night could be argued to have set a much more important precedent for the modern tank.

Let me explain. The T-54, which eventually became the T-55, increased the calibre and lethality of the primary Soviet battle tanks considerably with the D-10T 100mm gun and its family of ammunition. The introduction of the L7 also dramatically increased the lethality of NATO tanks compared with the M4A3E8 Sherman that had carried Lieutenant Nordstrom into battle in 1952, as well as the 20-pdr that had enabled Centurions to suppress North Korean and Chinese troops later in that war. With the notable exception of the Centurion, tanks in this era increased protection and maintained mobility through larger engines and torsion bar suspension. Table 1 provides a comparison of late World War II tanks with those from the early Cold War to show just how far they had come in capability.

But why does fighting at night matter more to the modern tank than increased armour, firepower, and mobility? Well, by 1964, developments were already under way that would take tanks far beyond simple steel protection and APDS ammunition: developments that would demand dramatic increases in engine power and the way that tanks were able to cross terrain. All of this means that the tanks that were lining up to fight each other in Europe and the Middle East in the mid-1960s would bear very little resemblance to the tanks that followed them. However, the demand to fight at night has remained constant, and the ability of a tank crew to see and make sense of their surroundings is now key. The introduction of infrared imagers started a long development process that has led to modern tanks now carrying systems that allow their crews to remain under armour at all times while maintaining a good awareness of what is going on around them. In fact, many of the more modern tank designs feature dramatically improved optics, rather than similar changes to their armament. So, the introduction of infrared imaging to the T-55, Centurion, and M60 was a critical moment in the development of the modern tank, one that deserves greater appreciation than it has received to this point.

TABLE 1 Late World War II vs Early Cold War Tanks

Tank	*T-34-85*	*Sherman M4A3E8*	*T-54/55*	*Centurion Mk 10/1*
Main gun	ZiS-S-53 85mm gun	M1A1/A2 76mm gun	D-10T 100mm gun	L7 105mm gun
Penetration	102mm at 1,000m	Approx 160mm at 1,000m	185–200mm at 1,000m	Approx 240mm at 1,000m*
Armour	Up to 75mm thick	Up to 76mm thick	Up to 210mm thick	Up to 200mm thick after the up-armouring programme
Weight	32,000kg	32,285kg	36,000kg	52,000kg
Range	300km	161km	500km on roads	102km on roads
Speed	50km/h	48km/h	50km/h	34km/h
Engine	V-2-34 500hp engine providing 15.6hp/tonne	Ford GAA 450hp petrol engine providing 13.9hp/tonne	V-2-54 570hp engine providing 15.8hp/tonne	Meteor Mk IVB 650hp petrol engine providing 12.5hp/tonne

Overall, this era served to set the path of development for the future tank. The concepts of mixed fleets, which were dominant at the start of 1954, had died by 1965. The idea that heavy tanks would provide the anti-tank power and lighter tanks would support infantry gave way to what became known as the main battle tank (MBT). In theory, NATO and the Soviets set out to design tanks that could perform all roles well, including tank battles, engaging fixed positions, and holding ground. They would be shaped by the emerging need for improved optics, which

*This is based upon an assessment of what would be reasonable. The figures provided in Chapter 5 cover penetration of the L22 round at 1,000m against a 60-degree plate. All other figures in this table are for 0 degrees. It is reasonable to assume that at 1,000m, the L7 could penetrate 240mm of armour at 0 degrees.

gave crews better options to use their new, more potent ammunition. Better armour began to replace steel, and new more compact engines gave these new beasts greater mobility than ever before. By 1965, the design philosophy of all nations involved had also become clear. The Soviets favoured a lighter platform that put mobility and protection on an equal footing, with firepower a clear design driver. The British placed protection and firepower on a par, a trait that continues to this day with the Challenger 3, with mobility being something of an afterthought. The US was similar, although it would later attempt to improve mobility through an innovative new engine. Germany, which we have not yet covered, would generally set out to balance all three characteristics, and the French would favour speed and firepower over protection.

However, it is worth noting that to this day (October 2025), Ukrainian soldiers complain of the comparatively poor performance of Western tanks in the infantry support role. They prefer the design of their Soviet MBTs, which more explicitly allows for fire support against buildings and targets that they cannot see, as well as their reduced weight, which means damaged tanks can be recovered more easily.[5] This is in part because Western tanks never really relinquished the primary role of tank-on-tank engagements. They have adapted to do other things, as we will see in later chapters, but their primary utility, both in design and doctrine, was always to kill other tanks. The Soviets took a different approach, as did the Israelis; this was informed by a series of brutal wars in the Middle East, which is where the next part of this book will start.

PART 3

1965–73: The die is cast – MBTs take their final form?

Lt Col Zeev Eitan had stopped his battalion of AMX-13s at B'ir Gifgafah along the Ismailia road, which comes from an Egyptian city called Ismailia on the edge of the Sinai Peninsula. The date was 8 June 1967. Israel's armoured forces had been advancing against varying Egyptian resistance for three days in what would come to be known as the Six Day War. His force, around a brigade, occupied a difficult position. They had advanced so quickly that there were Egyptian units behind them, as well as in front of them. The unit, like most Israeli forces by this time, was exhausted, but Zeev pushed them to clean the finicky guns in their French tanks and positioned his armoured infantry to defend against a possible night attack. By midnight the position was as ready as it could be and Zeev's men settled down for some sleep, which would be disrupted at 3.00am. Egyptian tanks were approaching to the rear of his position; fortunately for Zeev it was two trucks of Egyptian infantry, readily engaged by guard posts. But clear noises of tanks were heard from the other direction.[1]

Up until this point, the Israelis had been the ones advancing. They had overcome many defensive positions and pulled through close-range tank-on-tank engagements. Defensive positions were where Egypt's large army was most comfortable. It had received help from German advisors prior to the 1956 Suez War, and sought out Soviet help prior to 1967. However, it had made several errors of judgement, such as the assumption that sand dunes at Umm Qatef, a major Egyptian position, were impassable to tanks: an assumption that Israel's General Sharon proved wrong when his forces used them to encircle, and ultimately destroy, the defending 2nd Infantry Division in just 12 hours.

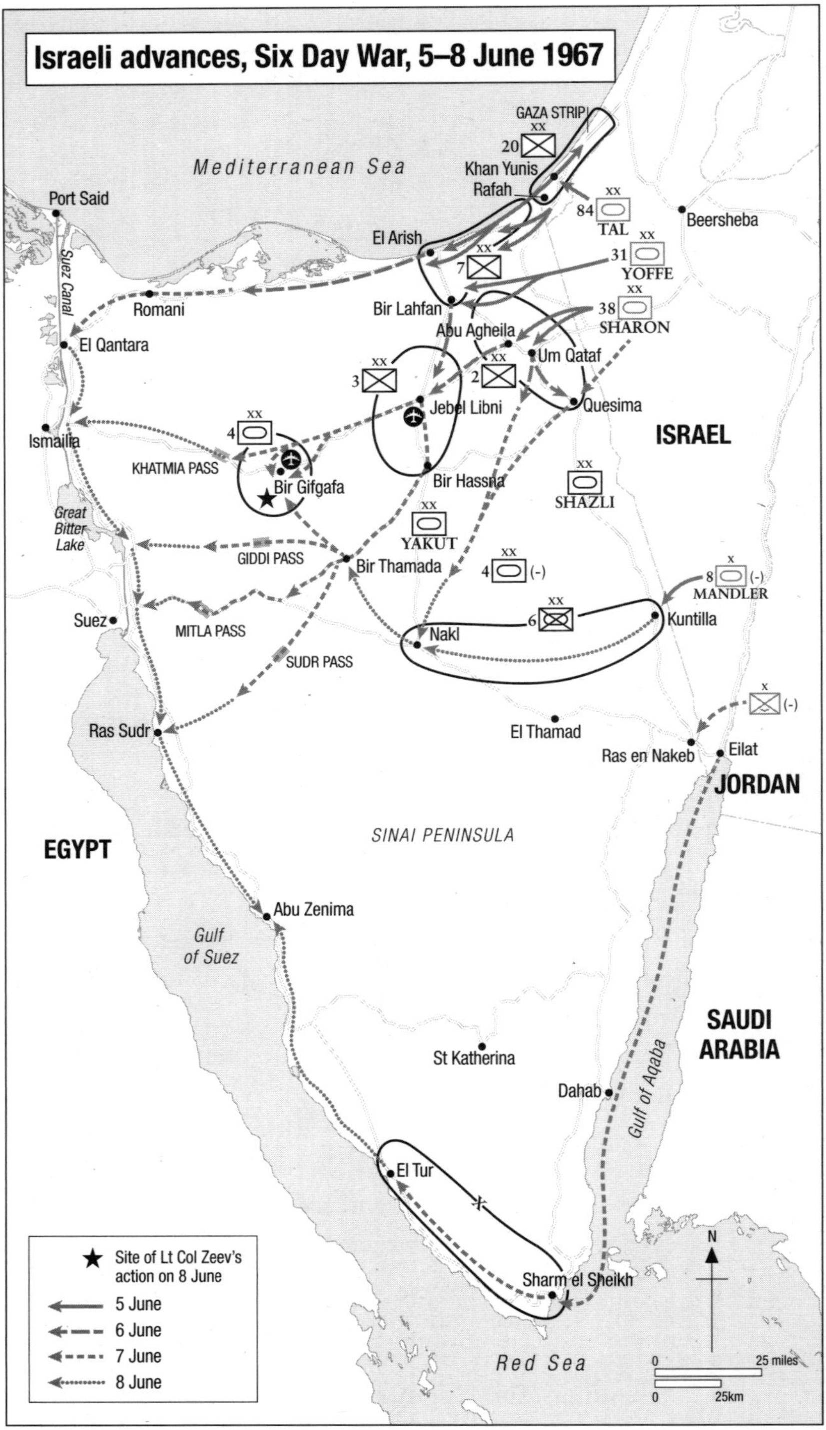
Israeli advances, Six Day War, 5–8 June 1967
Mediterranean Sea
GAZA STRIP
20
Khan Yunis
Rafah
84
TAL
Beersheba
El Arish
7
31
YOFFE
38
SHARON
Port Said
Suez Canal
Romani
Bir Lahfan
Abu Agheila
Um Qataf
El Qantara
3
2
Jebel Libni
Quesima
ISRAEL
Ismailia
4
KHATMIA PASS
Bir Gifgafa
Bir Hassna
SHAZLI
Great Bitter Lake
YAKUT
GIDDI PASS
Bir Thamada
4 (-)
8 (-)
MANDLER
Suez
MITLA PASS
6
Nakl
Kuntilla
SUDR PASS
(-)
Ras Sudr
El Thamad
Ras en Nakeb
Eilat
JORDAN
EGYPT
SINAI PENINSULA
Abu Zenima
Gulf of Suez
SAUDI ARABIA
St Katherina
Dahab
Gulf of Aqaba
El Tur
Sharm el Sheikh
Site of Lt Col Zeev's action on 8 June
5 June
6 June
7 June
8 June
Red Sea
N
0
25 miles
0
25km

This map shows the positions of the Egyptian and Israeli forces at the beginning of the Six Day War on 5 June 1967, and the subsequent Israeli movements on each of the following days from 5–8 June, reaching the Suez Canal in the early hours of the morning of the 9th. It is apparent from this map that although there was an Egyptian armoured reserve held back around B'ir Gifgafa, much of the Egyptian force was pushed into the eastern half of the Sinai, meaning that it was able to offer little defence in depth during an inevitable IDF counter-attack or, as it turned out, an Israeli offensive. Note also the position of Major-General Avaham Mabler's 8th Armoured Brigade in the far south, a deployment that served to pull key Egyptian formations away from the *three-ugdah* (division) thrust in the north.

When assaulted from the intended direction, however, Egyptian defences were strong and the units usually held their own, firing on Israeli tanks until they were overrun or killed.[2] Egypt deployed a mixture of T-34s, Su-100 anti-tank vehicles, and T-55s, while Israel was putting the Centurion, M4 Sherman, AMX-13, and M48 Patton to work. You might think, from the technical descriptions, that the T-34-85 would be no match for the Centurion. However, the Centurion's gun range and frontal armour made them hard to kill, but not invulnerable. This was demonstrated in the lead-up to and during the Six Day War, when several Israeli Centurions were knocked out by Egyptian and Syrian T-34s.

But Centurions were not the only tanks being deployed, and Lt Col Zeev must have been all too aware that the 75mm SA 50 gun his light tanks carried was no match for the T-55, from the front at least. He may not have known that he would be the defending commander against one of Egypt's two counter-attacks, a somewhat unique but unenviable position. As the lead elements of the Egyptian formation approached, Zeev sent his half-track with a 120mm mortar forwards and ordered his 81mm mortars to fire illumination rounds. They could see the T-55s approaching through the dark, their small headlights switched on. The T-55s engaged the half-track, killing most of the crew, and other half-tracks were engaged in quick order. Zeev's position would have been filled with thick acrid smoke at this point, as ammunition, fuel, and bodies burnt. Some of his men abandoned their positions, unwilling to face the onslaught, but Zeev and his tank commanders held firm. The Centurion and its L7 could engage Egyptian armour from a few thousand metres away, such was its penetrating power. But the AMX-13 could not offer its crews the same safety; they would have to wait.

And wait they did; with the lead T-55 just 100m from their position, the Israeli tanks finally opened fire. According to Shabtai Teveth, a journalist attached to General Tal's formation, Zeev was able to watch two armour-piercing shells bounce harmlessly off the frontal armour of the lead T-55. It is not clear what ammunition the Israelis were firing, but the SA 50 could employ the PCOT-51P armour-piercing shell, which could penetrate a maximum of 170mm of steel armour at 1,000m, and the POT-51A, which could penetrate 110mm of armour at the same range. Neither would cut it against the thick frontal armour of the T-55. Zeev's tanks would have to get to the sides of the Egyptians. He had already informed General Tal of the advance, and Tal – who will feature in the next section – sent a company of Shermans and Centurions forward to relieve Zeev, but they had some 40km to travel. Zeev ordered his tanks to fire at the sides of the T-55s, where the armour was much thinner, and they began to achieve some success, but the Egyptian crews took their toll. When the Shermans finally arrived, they found a scene of heavy destruction: burnt Israeli vehicles and crews littered the battlefield. Eight Centurions arrived later, and pushed through the position towards Suez. They were battle-scarred from several successive engagements; the skirts over the tracks were perforated and the turrets scarred. They were under the command of Major (Maj) Shamai Kaplan and soon encountered T-55s in the hull-down position. This is a common tactic for tank combat, and simply means that a hole the size of the hull, or a berm the height of the hull, is dug, leaving just the turret visible. When Kaplan's Centurions crested a hill and saw the tanks, they were able to engage them accurately, destroying them before they could return fire. Shamai would not have it all his way, however, and an ambush soon claimed his life as a shell from a T-55 hit his cupola. The Egyptians managed to disable another Centurion with two direct hits in the same engagement, but ten T-55s were ultimately destroyed by six Israeli tanks.[3]

The Six Day War wasn't the best introduction for the T-55, but Egypt's losses did little to dampen its export success. The Soviet Union would eventually sell them to more than 50 different countries, and until Russia's invasion of Ukraine in 2022, some T-55 variants remained in service with Croatia, Finland, Poland, and Romania – all NATO states.[4] The Israelis also found the vehicles to be well designed for their intended purpose and would go on to employ captured

Egyptian armour in Operation *Raviv* in 1969. The Israel Defense Forces (IDF) eventually modified the T-55 into the Tiran-5Sh, which carried a licence-produced version of the 105mm L7, and even added a computer-based fire control system to the tanks. The Tirans were then further modified into the Achzarit heavy APC by removing the turret and replacing the engine in the early 1980s following heavy losses in the Lebanon War, in part a result of the use of M113 APCs.[5] Generally speaking, the T-55 has had a rough time whenever it has been required to face off with Western armour. When it first entered service, this was often a result of the way these tanks were used. The accounts from the Six Day War indicate that they were certainly capable of causing heavy losses to the Israeli forces, but the rigid Syrian and Egyptian doctrine left the tanks and their crews vulnerable to quick-thinking manoeuvres and combined arms warfare. At the same time, the Centurion's weight included an impressive amount of armour that made them survivable vehicles; Israeli officers have recounted how some tanks took multiple direct hits and were able to keep fighting, even after driving over mines and being hit with large-calibre mortars.[6] Nevertheless, the T-55 has been used as a heavy combat platform in almost every war since and has been extensively deployed in urban environments in support of infantry forces.

Overall, the Six Day War shows some of the challenges of tank engagements that remain relevant to the modern tank. Engagements could be very short-range, as well as at the extreme distances of what the tanks could physically achieve. In short-range engagements, even the relatively weak guns of the AMX-13 could punch through the side armour of a newer vehicle. This means that seeing and shooting first is often a key requirement for tank crews. At long ranges, mission systems, training, and experience all become key. Israeli tank gunnery, which had been honed in the various Golan Heights incidents leading up to 1967, proved decisive, against both the Egyptians and the Syrians.[7] It was also apparent that the Centurion and the L7 could outmatch Soviet armour, and that Western concepts of combined arms manoeuvre warfare could overwhelm even well-prepared defensive positions. The Soviets, by this time, had several irons in the fire when it came to new tanks.

Chapter 9

Enter the smoothbore

According to military historian Steven Zaloga, the T-62 was the result of much political in-fighting between the Soviet tank design bureaus.[1] Nikita Khrushchev, the Soviet premier, also played a role in shaping its development. But the politics of the T-62 are less important for the modern tank than their outcome. What is clear is that by 1959 the Soviets needed a tank with a bigger gun. As set out in Chapter 1, tanks are all about the gun, and the gun needs to be able to achieve the things its user needs it to do, otherwise the tanks are likely to fail in their mission. The Soviets needed a gun that could compete with the L7 and the increasing armour of NATO tanks.

By this point, the Uralvagonzavod was the design authority for the T-55; the Kharkiv Design Bureau was focused on the mysterious Object 430, which we will return to shortly. A more powerful rifled gun called the D-54 had been developed to replace the D-10TG, but it was too much for the existing T-55 hull and turret. This was a consequence of several elements of gun design, which included higher chamber pressures resulting from increased propellant that was more energetic than previous designs. There are several routes to improving the energy that propellant produces, some of which can be achieved through design. The goal with propellant is to achieve an equal and fast burn rate – for high-velocity ammunition at least. There are two approaches to propellant shape: sticks and pellets. Some cartridges will blend both, with sticks at the base of the projectile and pellets at the neck. Either way, the propellant is typically made of nitrocellulose, which is manufactured by nitrating cotton pulp. Put simply, cotton pulp is harvested from cotton plants – the same plants used to make clothes – and treated with a controlled mixture of nitric acid and sulfuric acid which increase the energy stored in the cotton fibres. The degree of nitration, i.e. the number of nitrate groups added from the nitric acid, results in a product that is used either in lacquers or in ammunition propellant. For propellant, higher nitration is needed, but that also makes the nitrocellulose unstable, so it has to be washed and further treated to neutralize the instability and make it safe for storage and use.

Nitrocellulose is then transported as a fibrous material that is kept damp and handled as little as possible. To turn that product into propellant, it is condensed and dehydrated using alcohol and turned into its final form, which might be the sticks or pellets used in a tank shell. The surface area of the propellant is key to its burn rate and the evenness of its burn. So, designers introduce holes into the pellets and sticks, which means that more of the propellant can be burned at any one time.[2] Increasing the amount of propellant and the energy that it produces means that it will generate more recoil, and may also mean longer ammunition. Recoil can be managed with recuperators and buffers, hydraulic pistons that compress as the gun and breech recoil, and return the gun to its original position. But longer ammunition creates problems for a tank's design as there is only so much space inside a turret, and only so much hull to accommodate a larger turret. It is not clear which of these plagued the D-54, but the problem eventually led to the design of a larger turret; this turret was also mated to a longer T-55 hull, which had been designed to appease Khrushchev, according to Zaloga.[3] At the same time, the Soviets introduced the T-12 Rapira, a towed anti-tank gun, which really changed the game for our modern tank.

The Rapira was designed to give Soviet anti-tank teams some serious capability against Western tanks and infantry. It did this through a combination of a smoothbore barrel and a new type of ammunition – the armour-piercing fin-stabilized discarding sabot (APFSDS). To understand this round, think back to the L7 and its APDS. The APDS is intended to increase muzzle velocity by using a sub-calibre projectile and a sabot to hold it in place inside the barrel. Remember also that the ability of a round to penetrate armour is shaped (at this point in the story of the modern tank) by its length:diameter ratio (L:D), by the material used, and by the muzzle velocity. APDS allows this to happen by creating a lighter projectile (than a full-bore round), and by applying a higher pressure over a larger bore area than a gun of the same calibre as the penetrator. If, for example, the bore had a diameter of 28mm and matched the projectile, it would not be possible to put much propellant behind it and the velocity would be limited. However, by putting a 28mm projectile in a 105mm bore, you can put an awful lot of propellant behind it. Finally, the L7 provided a longer barrel so that the pressure could act on the round for longer, imparting more of its energy. The Soviets didn't really have an APDS round, but the technology was approaching its limits in any case.

This is because of the internal and external ballistics involved – yes, it's time for more physics. You may already know that the rifling inside a tank gun, howitzer barrel, and assault rifle is there to make the projectile spin when it leaves the muzzle. Not sideways – that is bad for ballistic performance – but along its length. This helps to stabilize it so that it flies straight and is more accurate. The rifling inside the barrel has a degree of twist that is represented as a ratio, such as 1:40, for instance, which means the round would rotate once every 40 inches. The rate of spin needed to stabilize a sub-calibre projectile increases quite dramatically the smaller the diameter and longer the length of the penetrator. This is not good for the development of rounds with a long L:D ratio. A long rod fired from a cup sabot and a rifled gun would have to spin at impossibly high speeds to prevent it from tumbling. The spin rate also increases relative to the difference in size between the bore and projectile. If the bore is twice the size of the projectile, the projectile would need four times the spin to be stable in flight.[4] Some attempts were made to create rifling that could provide this stabilization (up to a spin rate of 1:12), and the materials used in Western APDS were also improved to provide increased density. The penetration of the rounds did increase, but not at the rate of improvements in armour. In short, it was not physically possible to increase the penetration of the APDS type round fired from the 105mm guns beyond a certain point.

So, let's return to the T-12 and its smoothbore barrel. A smoothbore is a barrel without rifling. The interior is completely smooth, which means the ammunition must find its own way to stabilize after leaving the muzzle. The possibility of the APDS being spin-stabilized was naturally eliminated. The Soviets instead settled on the APFSDS, which has since become the primary anti-armour nature used by tanks around the world. An APFSDS solves many of the challenges that an APDS cannot. It allows for a very long and thin sub-calibre dart to be fired from a much larger bore. The dart is carried down the barrel by a sabot, but instead of sitting at the rear of the dart as in an APDS, it will sit towards the front. The sabot comes in different varieties like the double ramp, ring, and saddle. A saddle sabot is shaped like a saddle, with a dip in between two peaks. A double ramp sabot has a bulge in the middle of the projectile, which is usually its centre of gravity. The sabot leading up to that bulge is ramped, allowing the propellant gases to concentrate behind the bulge, which holds the obturating band. The section after the bulge is ramped in the other direction. A ring sabot consists of a ring that is, again, around the centre of gravity of the penetrator. This configuration relies on the fins at the rear of the round to ride the bore and keep the rod centred in the barrel. Keeping the round centred is the reason that the obturating ring of all sabots is located at the centre of gravity.[5]

So, as the round leaves the muzzle of the gun, the sabot, which is made of sections, peels away from the penetrator. The long penetrator then continues on its way to the target at very high speeds, typically in excess of 1,500m/s. It is stabilized by the fins at the rear, which work a lot like the fletchings on an arrow. If the nose of the projectile starts to pitch or yaw, the fins restore balance and keep it flying straight, leading to a stable flight. All of this combines to create the APFSDS, which flies at very high speeds and enables much of its energy to be concentrated over a very small area. It is not perfect: a lot of energy is spent on propelling the sabot, which is why so much effort goes into its design. And there are immense shearing forces imparted to the penetrator by the sabot and sabot separation. But the end results are hard to dispute. The T-12, which was the same calibre as the D-10TG used by the T-55, could penetrate 230mm of armour at 1,000m using its BM-2 APFSDS. This is 30–45mm more than the D-10TG at the same calibre and would have given the T-12 gunners a fighting chance against a Centurion from the front at typical combat ranges.

The Soviets had a competing design, the D-54, which would come with its own APDS. But even that could not out-perform the T-12. According to Zaloga, Khrushchev was quite pleased with the T-12 and ordered it to be fitted to the next model of tank under design at that time, only for the head of the Uralvagonzavod Design Bureau to realize that it would not fit, because the ammunition was too long. Instead, the decision was taken to rebore the D-54 to 115mm, turning it into a smoothbore, and modifying the BM-2 to be fired from the newly created gun.[6] This was then mated to the new larger turret built for the D-54 and the longer T-55 hull to become the T-62. The new gun was known as the U5-TS Molot, with an L52 (6.05m) barrel, a horizontal wedge breech block and a recoil length of 350–415mm. A new stabilizer called Meteor was developed to help the heavier weapon fire more accurately on the move, and it reportedly had a 50% chance of hitting an M60A1 at 1,500m.[7] In Soviet parlance, the projectile receives its own designation and the complete round, including propellant and projectile, another designation. One of the early APFSDS rounds available to the T-62 was the 3UBM4, which fired the BM-4 and BM-6 APFSDS. Both were made of a steel alloy, which was not exceptionally hard compared to tungsten, but was considered good enough for the time, especially when fired by its large propellant charge. The charge was made of a mixture of nitrocellulose and another explosive called nitro-diglycol, which helps to stabilize the burn rate and increase the energy output.[8] Altogether, the BM-4 round could penetrate 248mm of armour at a range of 1,000m, which meant it could defeat tanks like the Centurion and M60A1. The BM-6 could penetrate 120mm of armour with a 60-degree slope at 1,900m, which made it roughly as capable as the L52 APDS fired by the L7.[9] The 105mm L52 APDS could penetrate around 240mm at 1,800m, but the L52 employed a tungsten alloy core, which is significantly harder than the steel used in early Soviet APFSDS, which should confer greater penetration against most targets.

But that was not all that the T-62 brought to the table. Its U5-TS Molot (which received the Grau code of 2A20), could also fire the BK-4 high-explosive anti-tank (HEAT) projectile. HEAT as a concept had been around for a while and development is typically attributed to a chemist called Charles Munroe while working at the US Navy's (USN) Naval Torpedo Station in 1888. Munroe demonstrated that an explosive charge with the letters USN imprinted on them when detonated against a steel plate would imprint the letters on that steel. He also observed that a cavity formed in an explosive would increase the depth of penetration against steel targets. This phenomenon became known as the Munroe Effect in the US and UK. You may also see it referred to as the Neumann effect, after two German chemists who discovered it around the same time. Put simply, the Munroe Effect states that the depth of a crater formed in a target can be increased by utilizing a line-shaped charge, and that this effect can be further improved by detonating the charge at an optimal distance from the target.[10] The Munroe Effect was put to use in World War II to penetrate tank armour, and is the basis for the warheads fired by US Bazookas and German Panzerfausts.

Distilling the idea down to its most basic principles, a HEAT round consists of a cone of metal with explosives arranged around the peak of the cone. When the fuze is triggered by striking the target, the explosive detonates, concentrating all of its energy on the peak of the cone. Technically speaking, the cone then collapses and the apex passes through the middle of the metal and stretches out from where the explosion starts. It does this very quickly, but the speed is impacted by the design of the cone: the smaller the angle at the tip of the cone, the higher the velocity at the tip of the jet.[11] That velocity can be as fast as 10km per second (km/s), which means the jet will have immense kinetic energy as it strikes the target. You can actually replicate this effect – safely – at home, using a yoghurt. The small pots of fromage frais that you might give to children work best because the yoghurt holds its shape. Use a small spoon to carve a cone into the middle of the yoghurt, taking care to make it as symmetrical as possible. Then, slam the bottom of the pot down on a flat, firm surface. The shockwaves should ripple through the yoghurt, collapsing your cone and creating a jet of yoghurt. Be prepared to stand on a chair and clean your ceiling afterwards!

The downside to a HEAT round is that the jet can be relatively thin, especially when compared to an APFSDS and there is also less material to cause damage behind the armour. Nevertheless, some later versions of the BK-4 could penetrate an average of 499mm of rolled homogeneous armour (RHA) in test conditions.[12] Replicating this in the real world would depend on a lot of things like the projectile actually hitting the tank (it was much slower than an APFSDS), and hitting it at the right angle. But the increase in this type of warhead effectively spelt the end of tanks built from RHA alone. The Soviets were not alone in deploying HEAT rounds from their tank guns; the French included the Obus G HEAT round as the main anti-armour munition of the AMX-30, which entered service in 1966. And other forces were beginning to make greater use of infantry anti-tank teams armed with HEAT weapons.

The North Vietnamese Army was making extensive use of the RPG-2, also known as the B-40, against US forces, which was the predecessor to the ubiquitous RPG-7 used so widely today.

The smoothbore gun of the T-62 and its ammunition natures really helped change the trajectory of tank armaments. With only a few exceptions, the vast majority of modern-day tanks have smoothbore guns firing APFSDS as their main anti-tank ammunition, and that looks unlikely to change. However, for all its technological trailblazing and shaping of the modern tank, its introduction into combat was far less impressive. The T-54's first operational deployment was against Hungary, which is a reflection of the fact that the Soviet armed forces were as much oriented towards suppressing internal dissent as they were expected to fight NATO. It should be no surprise then that the T-62's first outing was against reformists in Czechoslovakia in 1968. A lot happened in 1968: Martin Luther King and Senator Robert Kennedy were assassinated, and extensive protests in America, both the Civil Rights Movement and against the war in Vietnam, were consuming the administration's attention. The Vietnam War itself was consuming men and equipment at a frightening rate and even leading to protests in the UK. In London, the British pound was suffering from its devaluation in 1967 and increasing national debt. A run on the UK's gold reserves further worsened the situation, and immigration designed to support the economy had created political division. In France, the May 1968 protests paralysed Charles de Gaulle's government, and West Germany was rocked by its own student protests against the Vietnam War. All of this meant that as Soviet and Warsaw Pact forces took their T-55s and T-62s out of their garages and moved them to Czechoslovakia's border in August 1968, there was very little chance that the West would notice.

The T-62's first deployment was less violent than the T-54's. In a very well-coordinated operation, Russian paratroopers in plain clothes secured Ruzyne Airport and used it as a hub to land an entire airborne division. Czechoslovakia was also surrounded, and invaded by forces from Hungary, Bulgaria, East Germany, Russia, and Poland. The combined forces amassed hundreds of thousands of troops across 17 divisions, with 2,000 tanks, and 500 aircraft.[13] The Czechoslovakian army did not resist the invasion, and it ultimately ended the country's reform efforts. The T-62 did not have to fight in the way that the T-54 did in 1956, but its presence was noted. The 1969 border war between

Russia and China was different, however. Tensions had risen between the two powers over which country had the right to expand and represent communism. Things came to a head around an island called Zhenbao (also called Damansky Island), which is in the Ussuri River. Following an ambush of Russian forces on 2 May 1969, the Russians moved the T-62 – a secret at the time – and its BM-21 multiple rocket launcher (also a secret) into the area. When fighting broke out again on 15 May, the Soviet forces responded with overwhelming firepower, which drove the Chinese forces back across the river. In the process, however, a T-62 was somehow disabled and captured by the Chinese forces.[14] A mere five years later, a new tank would enter service with the People's Liberation Army called the Type 69. It borrowed heavily from the T-62, including infrared sights and a stabilized gun.

Chapter 10

Armour vs mobility

While matters were coming to a head in Czechoslovakia, US and Australian forces were grappling with the Tet Offensive in Vietnam. Starting in late January 1968, the offensive is the background for the film *Full Metal Jacket.* North Vietnamese Army (NVA) and Viet Cong forces had conducted a massive and coordinated offensive throughout the country, seizing key cities including Hue. US Marines, including the 1st and 3rd Tank Battalions, were sent to retake the city with their M48s.[1] As they entered the city, the tanks were showered with B-40 anti-armour rockets, a domestically manufactured version of the Soviet RPG-2. The RPG-2 and B-40 are shoulder-fired weapons with an 80mm warhead propelled by a 40mm charge. The rocket carried a HEAT warhead and was accurate out to a range of 150m against a stationary target, depending on the user's capabilities, and in all probability, their bravery. Having entered service in 1954, the RPG-2 had been around for over a decade when the US Marines manoeuvred their M48s to retake Hue, but Vietnam was really the rocket's first use at scale.

Capt Batcheller, who led Alpha Company, the 2nd Battalion of the 5th Marine Regiment, had been woken early as the North Vietnamese forces overran Army of the Republic of Vietnam (ARVN) troops defending the city. He was told to head out, link up with other ARVN troops, and re-enter Hue. The rendezvous with additional ARVN forces did not happen, but he did meet Lt Col Edward J. Lamontagne, who was accompanying four M48s from the 3rd Tank Battalion. Lamontagne and the tanks had been separated from their company by the offensive, and so supported Batcheller and his unit as they entered the city.

Once they had reached the city, after passing through a small NVA blocking force, things were quiet. Batcheller and the rest of the US Marines in the area had very limited intelligence at the time, and the extent of the offensive was not widely known. Some of Alpha Company dismounted from their trucks and climbed onto the M48s, something that is often practised by infantry supporting tanks. As they crossed the An Cuu Bridge, which spanned the Phu Cam Canal, the tanks and marines were engaged by small arms and B-40s. They managed to clear those positions, only to be hit by a larger hail of fire just 200m further on.[2] The tank commander of the lead M48 was killed by a B-40 in that engagement and Batcheller would be wounded and evacuated shortly after.

This was just the beginning of the Battle for Hue. The NVA had moved recoilless rifles such as the Type 52, a Chinese copy of the US Army's M20 into the city. A recoilless rifle is essentially a large-calibre weapon used to fire projectiles over short distances. Think back to Newton's Third Law of Motion (every action has an equal and opposite reaction). This means that when a sealed gun, like that of a tank, is fired, the gun moves backwards with as much force as it generates to fire the shell forwards. A recoilless rifle is not sealed, however, which allows the gases generated in firing its munitions to be vented out the back of the tube. This is bad for anyone standing behind it, but allows the weapons to be deployed in difficult environments and hard to reach places by infantry. The Type 52 could penetrate at least 100mm of RHA. Not enough to bother the front of a tank, but in urban combat the sides, rear, and roof of a tank are all much more vulnerable. Several M48s were lost to the Type 52 and B-40 during the Battle for Hue. One commander recalled an M48 that was hit 120 times; another M48 would go through five or six crews during Hue.[3]

Nevertheless, the tank became a key part of the Marine tactics in retaking Hue. When a strong point was identified, the infantry would try to suppress the position using small arms and 3.5in rockets – often known as the 'Super Bazooka'. This was another shoulder-fired anti-armour weapon, reportedly capable of penetrating around 280mm of RHA; it was technically far more lethal than the B-40. It would allow time for an M48 to approach the position and fire three or four concrete-penetrating, high-explosive shells into the position. A concrete-penetrating shell typically has a different fuzing mechanism, allowing the round to pass through a wall before it is detonated. This may be more effective if an enemy is in a building than a point-detonating fuze, which would make the shell explode on the surface of the wall. During the Battle for Hue, the M48 fire was often followed by recoilless rifle fire from an M50 Ontos, a strange-looking and lightly armoured tracked vehicle that carried six M40 106mm recoilless rifles. Once this was complete, the infantry could storm the position using CS gas and small arms once more.[4]

The fighting in Hue and the role of the M48s has an important bearing on the modern tank for several reasons. Firstly, it helps to reinforce that core point: a tank is all about the gun. The armour of the M48 was essential: without it, the tanks could not have supported the Marines against withering fire in the way that they did. For comparison, the much lighter Ontos had to take cover as soon as it had fired. The tanks also took a lot of punishment from the B-40 and recoilless rifles. There is sometimes the impression that a weapon's armour penetration decides whether or not it will defeat a tank. For example, this logic seems to imply that if a tank has 200mm of armour and a weapon can penetrate 230mm, then the tank will lose. But the reality is far more complex. The defeat mechanisms of shaped charges are far from certain. Time and again, tank crews have taken hits from HEAT rounds and suffered casualties, only for the tanks themselves to keep fighting. In other circumstances, the crews have survived as well as the tank, and in others still, the HEAT round has caused a catastrophic kill against the tank. But the point remains that the level of armour is central to getting the gun into a position to achieve a given task. So, the question that presents itself is how – given all of the fighting that was going on around the world at the time – did NATO countries arrive at such different conclusions in their tank design?

The T-62 does appear to have had an impact on the story of the modern tank. The smoothbore barrel and APFSDS are defining characteristics of pretty much every NATO main battle tank, even though NATO would not adopt its own APFSDS until the late 1970s, and even then with some resistance. The British, ever alternative in their approach to tank design, introduced many features that were completely new in the form of the Chieftain and that are also found today. Chieftain is a tank that tends to be recalled with a mixture of fondness, admiration, and frustration. It is, by most accounts, the first true main battle tank, having replaced the Centurion and Conqueror; its large 120mm L11 rifled gun, combined with a new level of protection and mobility that exceeded that of the Centurion, meant it could adequately replace both types in service. The Chieftain had a two-stroke engine that could run on most fuels per a NATO requirement issued in the 1950s. It produced a lot of smoke that could be seen from some distance, and required a lot of maintenance. However, the thing that is worth observing with this tank's power-pack is its dimensions and what that tells us about the design philosophy, because that is really what this chapter is about.

The power-pack was under-rated for the Chieftain. It could only provide 585hp for the Chieftain Mk 1 when it entered service as a training vehicle. The Mk 2 followed in 1966, providing 640hp, but the tank weighed in at around 55,000kg, which translated to a power-to-weight ratio of 11.8hp/tonne at the drive sprocket. Somehow, the British had taken a step back from the Centurion. But the Chieftain engine was picked for the volume within the hull that it occupied, which meant the profile of the tank could be reduced. At the same time, the 2-stroke design was expected to produce more power than a larger 4-stroke engine, because the L60 generates a power stroke with every revolution of the crankshaft, whereas a 4-stroke engine produces one power stroke for every two revolutions. If you're not familiar with engine mechanics, the crankshaft is the part of an engine that takes the up and down motion of the pistons, and turns it into rotation for a vehicle's wheels, or drive sprocket in this case. The power stroke is what happens when the engine pistons compress the fuel (diesel) and air, leading to combustion. The force of the combustion drives the piston down the engine cylinder to a connecting rod that is attached to the crankshaft. In a 2-stroke engine, the pistons compress fuel and air every time that the crankshaft rotates. In a 4-stroke engine, the first rotation will empty the cylinder, drawing fuel and air into the vacuum, which is then filled by the piston on the compression stroke. As the fuel is ignited or combusted, the piston is driven back down, cycling the crankshaft once more, before the piston returns to the cylinder again to clean it. So, by using a different type of engine, the British designers were able to reduce the area that it took up inside the hull.

Another design element that was different in the Chieftain was the reclining driver's position, which allowed the hull to be very well sloped, and much lower than previous designs. At the same time, thick armour was used on the turret front and glacis so that the tank could soak up punishment from the front. The L11 fired two-piece ammunition, which means the projectile and propellant are separated from each other. This allowed the propellant – which is very vulnerable if hit and likely to cause a catastrophic kill – to be stored below the turret ring, where it is best protected. The design appears to have been heavily influenced by the Korean War and prevailing wisdom around Soviet doctrine. In short, the British were expecting to sit and absorb a Soviet attack. That led to protection and lethality being prioritized above mobility. These are traits that most British tanks have carried since the late stages of World War II through to today. Several of the Chieftain's design aspects have been carried through to other tanks. For instance, the drive to reduce the volume taken up by the power-pack is key for most tanks. This led to the development of increasingly powerful but compact engines like the MTU883, which was introduced in 1979, and provides 1,500hp at a total volume of 1.31 cubic metres.[5] This is very small, and the manufacturer, Motoren- und Turbinen-Union (Motor and Turbine Union or MTU) continued to work on maintaining output and reducing the volume of its diesel engines. In theory, the reduced volume of a complete power-pack should allow for a lighter vehicle as it means that a smaller space needs to be armoured. In most cases, however, the user will simply opt for more armour, as we shall see when we come to the Leopard 1 and AMX-30 in the next few pages

Lieutenant Nordstrom's platoon, fighting in Korea, had found out the hard way what happens when your tank does not carry enough armour. Maj Shamai Kaplan and his Centurions demonstrated what could be achieved when a tank does carry enough armour. And US Marines fighting to retake Hue knew that the job would be deadly if their M48s could not weather the storm of B-40 rockets and recoilless rifles brought down on them. At the very least, it is fair to state that there is a minimum level of armour required for a tank to achieve its job. Sooner or later, that tank will have to stand and receive fire; its ability to do that defines success. Germany and France, however, had reached the conclusion that mobility was key, and could offer enough protection to succeed.

When I first started out as a defence analyst, somebody remarked that the main battle tank designs in Europe reflected experiences from World War II. Neither the UK, US, Germany, France, or Russia had deviated far from the design principles that worked for them during the 1940s, that person explained. It's an appealing conclusion – with the exception of the Leopard 1. The Leopard 1 from Krauss-Maffei entered service in 1965 weighing 40 tonnes. It had just 70mm of armour at its thickest – the glacis and turret – and as little as 10mm elsewhere.[6] For reference, the NATO-calibre M993 7.62×51mm armour-piercing round from Norwegian ammunition manufacturer NAMMO can penetrate 18mm of armour at a range of 100m. It is, in fairness, a relatively modern round that can be fired from a general purpose machine gun, but it helps to illustrate just how little armour the Leopard 1 carried.[7] The Soviet 57-BZ-542 cartridge fires the 12.7mm B-32 round, which has a steel core and can penetrate 20mm of steel armour at 100m, and was produced from the 1930s. It is also designed to be fired from heavy machine guns and sniper rifles. The upper glacis carried the thickest armour, a 70mm welded steel plate, the hardness of which is unknown. It appears to have been sloped at around 60 degrees, which gives a line-of-sight thickness of 140mm. This means that German crews would have had a difficult time facing Soviet T-55s, and even more so if they encountered the T-62.

The Leopard 1 was built to withstand 20mm cannon rounds, and probably could withstand artillery fragmentation as well. It is widely reported that HEAT rounds were deemed to have made conventional steel armour irrelevant. This is another appealing conclusion, but the lethality of APDS rounds – especially when measured in terms of behind-armour effects – was comparable at the time.[8] What we can say is that mobility was key for the Leopard 1: it could reach an impressive 65km/h on roads, and even reach 25km/h in reverse. It could cross a 3m trench, and had a range of 600km. Its MTU MB 838 engine provided 833hp, giving a power-to-weight ratio of 20.8hp/tonne. However, the original versions came with an unstabilized gun, which would be retrofitted and production standard from the early 1970s – as would a few tonnes of additional armour. For comparison, the Leopard 1 was around 15km/h faster than the T-55 and M60, and around 30km/h faster than the Centurion, with three times the range.

The French AMX-30 came into service shortly after the Leopard 1, with first production in 1966 and the tanks entering service the following year. Its armour was thinner, no more than 80mm thick at any point, and it carried a CN-105 105mm rifled gun, designed and built in France, rather than the L7 that armed the Leopard 1. Like the Leopard 1, the AMX-30 came without stabilization, which meant that the crew would have had to stop to fire their main guns, somewhat negating any benefits they could gain from being able to move quickly. Like its German equivalent, the AMX-30 was very light, just 37 tonnes and its HS 110 engine from Hispano-Suiza provided 700hp and a power-to-weight ratio of 18.9hp/tonne at the sprocket.[9]

What are we to make of these designs and the German/French approach? Well, first and foremost, note that both were up-armoured fairly quickly after the first production batches entered service. The idea that mobility can compensate for heavy armour is also tenuous. Conceptually, it would require moving fast enough that a guided missile crew, soldier armed with an RPG, or T-55/T-62 crew could not track the tank and engage it. The road speed may have allowed this, but roads also tend to be in straight lines, which would have made it easier to predict the vehicle's movement. Secondly, if the vehicles were moving in an offensive, they would probably drive straight forwards, rather than across an enemy's position, which would mean that the challenge of hitting them was similar to that of a Centurion, except that the enemy crews may have had less time to do it. Thirdly, off-road speeds are always slower than road speeds. Cast your mind back to Chapter 6 and the impact of vibration on a crew, vehicle, and its stability. Moving off-road increases the vibration cycles, which reduces speed. And, in many circumstances, the mud of Eastern Europe would have further impaired the top speeds of the Leopard 1 and AMX-30, so it is unlikely that they could have moved quickly enough to usefully improve their survivability. Again, bear in mind that the BM-6 APFSDS fired by the T-62 left the barrel at 1,600 m/s. It would have taken around 1 second to reach an AMX-30 at typical combat ranges, and could penetrate 120mm of armour set at 60 degrees – this round would likely have passed through the front and rear of the AMX-30.[10]

There is one more element to consider, which is Cold War doctrine. The absolute primacy given to the mobility of the AMX-30 and Leopard 1 would make some sense in this context. NATO was and is a defensive alliance; its purpose and plan during the 1960s and 70s was to defend West Germany during a Soviet invasion. But there were three primary armies involved (France withdrew from NATO's integrated command structure in 1966): Germany, the US, and the UK. All had slightly differing views on what it meant to defend. Germany's armed forces favoured mobile defensive operations and delaying battles if possible, which were intended to set the conditions for counter-attacks. The idea was that by moving forces around, a commander could repeatedly engage the Soviets as they advanced, delaying them and inflicting losses. Static positions were expected to be defended by infantry with anti-armour weapons and artillery in support, and tanks as a counter-attacking force.[11] Using tanks in this way may have favoured mobility and speed, especially if there was a lot of ground to cover. However, it is worth returning to the lessons of Hue and the Six Day War; but let's start by thinking about the numbers involved.

NATO deployed fewer tanks than the Soviets, and was expecting the range and lethality of the L7 to balance things out. The battlegroup was a standard combat formation, consisting of infantry and reconnaissance elements and potentially up to 12 tanks.[12] However, the Soviets might attack a battlegroup with a motor rifle regiment. A motor rifle regiment generally included a tank battalion and three motor rifle battalions in BTRs – an 8×8 wheeled APC. The tank battalion included around 40 tanks, which would have led the offensive effort.[13] If the commander of a motor rifle regiment was successful in finding a weakness in the NATO lines, he would have been reinforced by additional regiments configured in a similar manner. Moreover, any Soviet attack would have been preceded by a daunting amount of artillery fire support. What does this have to do with Hue and the Six Day War? Well, those two wars showed that well-armoured tanks can take a fair amount of damage and keep fighting. In both cases, damaged tanks were proved pivotal at given moments. Of course, the weight of armour means nothing if the tank is decisively overmatched, but that has always been the case. Instead, the M48 and Centurion could withstand blows from the B-40 rocket propelled grenade, heavy machine guns, and Egyptian artillery, as well as some of the smaller guns on the battlefield. Egyptian T-55s were even observed to shrug off 75mm armour-piercing rounds at close range. This speaks to the staying power of heavily armoured tanks, which can take multiple blows and keep their crews protected. It is unclear how the Leopard 1 would have fared with the same level of damage, but with just 10mm of armour in some parts – which again could be penetrated by Soviet heavy machine guns – it seems unlikely that it would have held up as well as the heavier tanks.

The German and French design approaches changed with time and now most modern tanks – with the notable exception of Japan's Type 10 – have placed protection on an equal footing with lethality. Increasing protection through additional armour has reached a point of diminishing returns in that vehicle weights are widely considered excessive and there is an apparent drive to reduce the weight of future tanks – in the European Union at least. However, the core driver of protection remains the maintenance of staying power. Most tanks are designed to take multiple hits during a single engagement and stay in the field; none are vulnerable to small arms fire like the AMX-30, and most can shrug off even the best medium-calibre ammunition on the market. So, despite its many short-comings, the Chieftain was the start of a trend that would prevail to the modern day. Its design was heavily shaped by the fighting that the British Army of the Rhine expected, which included the presumption that allies to their flanks would break, leaving them to die heroically in the face of the Soviet advance. It also rested on the first factor identified in this book: tanks are about the guns, and getting the guns into position to do what is needed. The first eras focused on guns, a trend that continued until the 1990s, but the period from 1965 saw the start of improved protection and design trends on which later tanks converged.

The Leopard 1 did set the standard in terms of mobility, and today most tanks are built to reach some of its capabilities despite weighing at least 50% more. The compact and powerful MTU MB 838 was the start of a long lineage of tank engines that are dominant on the international market today. And the entire power-pack, which consists of the engine, transmission, and cooling, can be removed in around 20 minutes. This is another design practice that continues to this day, and is a stark contrast with the tanks that came before it. The focus on mobility is perhaps a result of the tank commander's belief in manoeuvre. Western forces often hold manoeuvre up as a sort of Holy Grail of battle, as if simply moving around creates problems that an enemy cannot handle. It was certainly the case for Israel in 1967, but it is worth noting that manoeuvre on that scale is comparatively rare. It is far more common for tanks to be dragged into a city or defensive position, where the weight of their armour and accuracy of the gun is what matters more than anything else.

So, what is the legacy of the Leopard 1 and AMX-30? Can we trace anything from their development to the modern day? As mentioned above, the mobility standards are now the baseline for most tanks, regardless of their protection. However, based on the competing designs of the 1960s, and every tank that has come out of NATO since, it is safe to state that firepower and protection have been the defining design factors. Mobility is typically defined by national preference and doctrine. And there does not appear to have been any drive to enhance mobility characteristics, such as top speed or gap crossing, as part of a design process beyond what was possible for the Leopard 1. The British have continued to favour heavy armour at the expense of mobility. The Challenger 2 with its Dorchester Level 2H standard armour weighs in at 74,840kg, for example, giving it a power-to-weight ratio of 16 hp/tonne. The US M1A2 Abrams also places a premium on armour, but its complex gas turbine engine compensates for the added weight over short distances. Germany's Leopard 2 is generally considered to represent the best in terms of balanced characteristics, but the latest iteration, the Leopard 2A8, still adds considerably to the tank's protective layers. Even Russia, which maintained relatively light vehicle designs throughout the Cold War, has increased the weight of its T-90M to at least 48 tonnes, making it around two to four tonnes heavier than the T-72B3, and two tonnes more than the T-80BVM.

As NATO forces debated the relative merits of mobility and armour in Berlin, Comrade Morozov was working hard at the Kharkiv Design Bureau, some 1,600km away. Morozov and his team were putting the finishing touches on Object 430, a new type of tank that would decisively change Soviet design practices, leading to a profound influence on China's tank design, as well as NATO's. It's time to take a look at the T-64.

Chapter 11

'They will pay for this for years to come'

The T-62 had been designed by L.N. Kartsev, the lead designer from Design Bureau No. 520 in Nizhny Tagil, the design bureau at Uralvagonzavod. There was growing competition between Nizhny Tagil and Design Bureau No. 60 under Morozov at the time. Morozov and his team had continued modernizing the T-55, but they were also working on something designed to be altogether new, which started out life as Object 430. Initial work in the form of drawings and concepts was already under way by 1953, when the US announced its doctrine of massive retaliation. The goal appears to have been a tank that could combine the firepower and protection of heavier tanks like the IS-2 with the mobility of lighter platforms like the T-55. The first prototypes were produced in 1957 and tested the year after alongside a competing design, Object 140, from Kartsev's team. Ultimately neither tank was adopted, but work continued on Object 430, leading it to become Object 432. The main changes from the original prototypes included a larger gun, the D-68 115mm gun, as well as improved tracks and the 5TDF 700hp engine and significantly improved protection – especially against HEAT rounds and nuclear weapons. Technical work on the design was complete by 1961 and first production came in 1963, but the tank would not be accepted into service until 1966.[1] It was given the designation T-64 and became the high-capability element of the Soviet armed forces. The Soviets, and later the Russians, essentially maintained a fleet of high- and low-capability tanks. The T-64 and eventually the T-80 came to represent the high capability, with the T-72 and T-55 the low capability.

The U-5TS was a powerful addition to the Soviet arsenal, and includes several design features that can be found in Russian tanks today, such as its relatively high muzzle velocity. However, despite its efficacy, the Soviets had launched another set of requirements in 1961 for a gun with a muzzle velocity of 1,800m/s. The OKB-9 design bureau proposed a 125mm gun shortly after. OKB stands for *opytnoe konstruktorskoe byuro*, which translates to experimental design bureau. These were (and still are) specific Soviet research establishments with their own manufacturing and testing facilities. OKB-9 is partnered to Factory No. 9, which is still the primary producer of tank guns for Russia today. The bureau developed the 85mm gun for the T-35-85, as well as the D-10T family, and the 115mm U5TS for the T-62. But its work in the early 1960s was to set the foundation for every Soviet tank that followed, as well as modern Russian tanks, and a version of it arms China's primary MBTs too. Design work on the new 125mm gun started in 1962, but it would take many years for the gun to reach service.[2] When it eventually came into service in 1968 it replaced the D-68 tank gun in production, the vehicles then becoming T-64A.

But it was not just the T-64A's gun that shaped the modern tank, it was also the way the gun was loaded. As noted earlier, Soviet designers had been working to reduce the size of their vehicles for some time. A smaller vehicle meant a lighter vehicle which could have improved mobility. However, one of the main limitations on achieving a smaller vehicle is the crew. People have to be inside the tank to make it work and the way the tank is loaded impacts how those people can be inside the tank. For example, the M156 High-Explosive Squash Head (HESH) round from Elbit Systems is a long heavy round of ammunition, 93.9cm long and weighing in at 21.2kg. This round would be stored in a rack and the loader would have to turn around and extract it from its rack and load it into the breech of the gun. Typically, this requires the loader to be standing, which sets the minimum height of the tank from the floor of the hull to the turret roof. In a country such as America or Europe, this requires a height of around 180cm, which must be measured from above the torsion bars for something like the M60. As a result, a lot of Western tanks were quite tall; for example, the M60 was 3.8m tall to the top of the commander's cupola. In contrast, the T-55 is just 2.4m tall. The result of Soviet tank design and the focus on reducing vehicle size and silhouette reportedly led to the deliberate selection of shorter crews.

The T-64 took this to another level with the introduction of an automatic loader. An automatic loader, sometimes called a carousel, is found in all modern-day in-service Russian tanks and even in the Chinese Type 99. However, the T-64A system is only found in the T-64 and T-80 tanks; the T-72 and most likely the Chinese tanks have a different type of carousel. The system consists of a mechanical circular rack underneath the turret loaded with 28 rounds and their separate propellant charges. It takes at least 7 seconds to load a round, depending on its location in the autoloader, and up to 19.5 seconds if a full rotation of the carousel is required. This gives the T-64 a reliable firing rate of 8 rounds per minute, as well as the ability to reload while driving over rough ground without the loader being slammed into the turret walls. Like the Chieftain, the T-64 uses a combustible charge case instead of brass or steel. The cases are made of nitrocellulose and cellulose, as well as binders and stabilizers. At the base of the propellant is a stub case made of steel, which provides obturation. When the round is fired, the cartridge case is burnt, almost completely, with the nitrocellulose contributing to the overall pressure behind the round, and the stub case is ejected. In a T-64, the projectile is carried horizontally in the autoloader with the propellant arranged vertically behind it. As the round is brought to the breech of the gun, the autoloading mechanism extends, lining the propellant up behind the projectile before driving both into the breech of the gun. Each round and charge combination is stored in its own autoloading mechanism, and these are loaded into the tank in the reverse of how they are fired. So, the empty mechanism is raised, and a member of the crew is passed the ammunition and charge to place them into the autoloader and secure them. The loading arm then returns to the base of the hull and the whole carousel rotates one place before the next arm is brought into the turret to be loaded.

The autoloader gave Morozov and his team a few advantages in the T-64's design. First, the crew could be reduced to three, which is very good for minimizing the area that must be protected. Secondly, without the need for a loader who might have to stand to handle large ammunition, the height of the vehicle could be reduced to 2.17m. Bear in mind that the T-64A's ground clearance is in the order of 500mm, so the true internal height is around 1.6m.[3] The resultant tank weighed in at 38.5 tonnes with a ground pressure of 0.86kg/cm^2, an acceptable power-to-weight ratio of 18hp/tonne, and a top speed of 60km/h on roads and around 45km/h on a dirt road. It was relatively capable but the engine proved to be unreliable in early variants, requiring constant maintenance and frequent rebuilds. The autoloader would occasionally 'eat Soviet tankers', dragging their arm into the hull or breech of the gun if clothing became snagged on it.[4] However, some 240 changes were made to the production design of the T-64 between 1969 and 1975, which are thought to have ironed most of those issues out.[5] In defence of the T-64 and the Chieftain, both tanks were attempting to achieve several technologically ambitious goals at the time, which built complexity into their designs. While many of the other tanks covered until now were essentially continuations of what had worked in World War II, the T-64 was a decisive and clean break.

The gun has arguably had the greatest influence. As noted above, the original variant was armed with a 115mm gun, which was swiftly replaced by the 2A26 125mm smoothbore gun. We will return to its capabilities shortly, but it is worth noting that the 2A26 became the basis for the 2A46, which has also remained the primary tank gun of Russian and Chinese-designed vehicles, including even the T-90M, Russia's most modern tank. So, the gun and loading mechanism that the T-64 introduced have stayed, shaping the design and concept of employment for armour in Russia and elsewhere today. The reason for this is that the 2A26 and 2A46 that came from it are punchy guns. The 2A26 brought a suite of APFSDS, HEAT, and high-explosive (HE) ammunition, all fired at relatively high chamber pressures. Ogorkiewicz notes that HE ammunition was a comparatively rare ammunition nature for tanks produced after 1970, with only the T-64/72, AMX-30, and several other minor European tanks carrying it. This was probably correct in 1991 when his *Technology of Tanks* was published, but there are many types of HE for the NATO 120mm smoothbore in service today, which suggests it may have been a temporary lapse. However, its inclusion in the T-64 is noteworthy because it helps illustrate how doctrine can shape design.

There have been several iterations of 125mm HE rounds for the 2A26/2A46 family, but one of the earliest is the VOF22, which fires the OF19 projectile out to a maximum range of 10km. The OF19 is filled with 3.15kg of TNT and carries a fuze that allows it to detonate either when it hits a target or after passing through it, which is quite useful for attacking buildings and fortifications. The later OF26 introduced a different explosive, AI-X-2, which is the preferred mixture in Russian munitions. It combines hexogen, aluminium, and a wax phlegmatizer, which is added to the explosive to stabilize it and prevent it from detonating because of a shock or impact. The word supposedly comes from the adjective 'phlegmatic', which means 'having an unemotional and stolidly calm disposition'. Together, this mixture provides a more energetic explosive when compared to TNT, which in turn is designed to produce a greater number of shell fragments moving at high speeds. This is how high-explosive fragmentation shells achieve their effects. Yes, the explosive itself is very dangerous, but the area that it can affect through over-pressure is relatively small. The fragments, however, create a 40×20m area that is lethal to infantry. The fragmentation comes from the shell body, which must be both strong enough to withstand being fired at 850m/s and brittle enough to shatter into very small pieces when the explosive charge detonates. Ideally, the fragmentation from a shell will weigh no more than a few grams. This helps them maintain a high speed out to longer distances and gives them greater penetrating power against humans and soft targets.* Lt Brown from the RNZAC lamented the poor fragmentation of the Centurion's 20-pdr in 1952, stating: 'The fragmentation of the HE round is poor. It appears to fragment in strips the length of the shell. I have seen two Chinese soldiers bisected nearly at the navel … but on the other hand I've also landed a shell about six feet from the heels of a fleeing enemy and he showed NO effect.'[6] Smaller fragments are therefore better in HE rounds, especially when suppressing infantry.

But why does the technology behind a HE shell matter? It's because tanks were seen as the leading edge of a Soviet assault and expected to provide the breakthrough force necessary to succeed. They were required to fire on the move, or from a short halt if the target needed more than one round. Tank formations would receive priority for supporting artillery fire, but were also expected to watch out for and counter anti-tank guided missile (ATGM) teams. In all of these roles, the HE round had a lot to offer; it had the firepower to engage defensive positions as well as lighter command vehicles, and infantry concentrations, which

*The term 'soft targets' is often used to describe vehicles and structures that are not armoured. It may include people, cars, and furniture.

we already know were expected to be the core of NATO's defensive positions. The prospect of suppressing ATGM teams is interesting because it touches upon a characteristic of tank fire support that is often overlooked, and that is speed. The British Swingfire ATGM was introduced into service in the 1970s as a large anti-tank missile that was hoped to help the British Army on the Rhine reduce Soviet tank numbers before they reached combat ranges. It reportedly had a maximum range of 4,000m, but travelled at just 185m/s. So, it would take around 21 seconds for the missile to reach its maximum range, during which time the gunner – who could sit separately from the vehicle – would have to maintain the target vehicle within his sights for the entire time of flight. If a T-64A crew managed to locate the gunner or the lightly armoured FV102 Striker that fired the missiles, their own OF26 munition would reach them in around 5 seconds at the same distance. Accounts of direct fire support provided by tanks, from Lt Brown in Korea through to Ukrainian soldiers receiving Russian tank fire, note that it is particularly disturbing because it arrives without warning. The round is travelling at 2.5 times the speed of sound when it leaves the muzzle, which means those on the receiving end will not hear the round tearing through the air, nor the sound of it being fired until it lands. So, the HE Frag rounds were an important part of the T-64A's armoury. However, that is not to say that all effort was focused on explosive natures; the Soviet Union also continued the development of the APFSDS.

The BM-12 was introduced in 1968, which suggests it may have become the primary anti-armour round for early T-64As. It had a frightening muzzle velocity of 1,800m/s, and released a 3.62kg, 51.8cm-long dart with a diameter of 44mm. This provides a length-to-diameter ratio of 11.7:1 and a muzzle energy of 5.86 MJ.[7] The body of the dart was made of steel and a tungsten carbide core was integrated into its tip to help increase penetration by essentially breaking the armour. This works because tungsten carbide is a ceramic component, which means it starts life as a powder that is sintered to form a solid that is very, very hard. With its high velocity and hardness, the tungsten core can help shatter or break the armour, making the penetration by the steel rod easier. The BM-12 APFSDS is mostly encased inside one of the propellant charges, which extends up to the rear of the obturating band. The charge is filled with rods of propellant and any space around the sabot is taken up with smaller pieces of propellant to help increase muzzle velocity. A second charge, called the 4Sh63, would also be used to fire the APFSDS and help reach those impressive muzzle velocities. The BM-12 was the start of APFSDS development for the 125mm family of guns, and it was continuously improved upon to increase armour penetration through the introduction of new materials for the penetrator.

Technically, a steel penetrator will always perform worse in terms of armour penetration than an equivalent made of a high-hardness alloy or depleted uranium. The Soviets would have known this – it is basic material science, and other alloys were available at the time – so why did they choose steel for their APFSDS rounds? One element, according to Ogorkiewicz, is cost and simplicity, which is understandable. Another is to do with the strength of steel compared to a high-hardness alloy, and the way that sabots work. Think back to Chapter 9 and the design of a sabot: the purpose of the sabot is to impart force to the projectile, and that force is quite significant, which means that the projectile itself is stressed by the interface with the sabot. The harder a metal, the more brittle it becomes and the greater the risk of it shattering under the firing force of the gun. So, this results in a longer thread and connection to the sabot to disperse that force over a wider area. Steel, however, is more ductile – which basically means it can bend more without breaking – which allows for a shorter, simpler connection with the sabot. The result has a few benefits, including reduced sabot weight, which in turn increases muzzle velocity for the penetrator. In any case, the primary armour of Western tanks at the time was also steel, which meant there was little need at the time for a heavier metal to be used. Also, Soviet doctrine emphasized the use of three tanks against a single target; they were only expected to shift fire after the target tank was killed.[8] Even the T-62 had a 50/50 chance of hitting a stationary US tank at 1,500m, and the probability of the second round hitting was estimated to be around 65%. So, three T-64s engaging an M60, Leopard 1, or Chieftain probably would have had the edge. Some sources indicate that the Chieftain's armour could not even protect the crew from the 115mm BM-6 fired by the T-62 at a range of 1,600m. If these reports, which are supposedly based upon Soviet tests of a Chieftain, are correct, it also means that the steel BM-12 fired by the T-64A would not have struggled.[9]

One more unique element of the T-64 was the heavy machine gun fitted to the turret roof, which could be operated remotely with the crew kept safe under the armour. Most other tanks of the era required the commander or gunner to expose themselves to operate these weapons. Even Soviet tanks like the T-80 would not carry this feature until the late 1980s. The T-64's designers did not stop there, and the BM-series would later be complemented by a gun-launched ATGM, which we will return to in the next section. But first, there is one more element of the T-64 to address: protection.

The Soviets and Americans had been working on composite armours since the 1950s at least, and were probably not alone in those endeavours. Those designers and scientists may not have realized it at the time, but composite armour was critical to the future of the tank. HEAT weapons were gaining lethality and reliability almost by the year, as Capt Batcheller and his men discovered during the Battle for Hue City in 1968. With APFSDS added into the mix, it was becoming close to impossible to protect a tank using steel alone. The Soviet 9M14 Malyutka ATGM, which we will learn much more about in the next chapter, could penetrate around 460mm of rolled homogeneous armour at ranges up to 3km. It would take a long time to get there, but it would require 230mm of steel at an angle of 60 degrees to protect the crew from that missile. This is not impossible, but increasing the thickness beyond that would add significantly to the weight of the tank, reducing mobility. At the same time, increasing the lethality – or at least the penetration – of an ATGM is a matter of adjusting the size or geometry of the metal liner.[10] So, steel armour was in a losing battle: another solution was needed. Composite armour does just that; it is a composite solution consisting of at least two materials that together generally provide more protection than steel for the same weight.

The T-64 introduced a form of composite armour in both the turret and the glacis. The glacis design, or a version of it, was adopted into the T-72. It consisted of an 80mm-thick steel plate, followed by two layers of glass reinforced fibre both 52mm thick, and a final 20mm sheet of steel. The steel was armoured steel and initial designs filled the gap between the plates with aluminium rather than glass reinforced fibre; the latter came into use around 1970. In total, the glacis was 204mm thick, but it was also angled at 68 degrees, which gives a line-of-sight thickness of 544mm. You might be wondering how a glass reinforced fibre could offer any sort of protection against HEAT that steel could not. In theory, the mechanism is described in terms of hydrodynamics.

In other words, scientists and engineers treat the HEAT jet and the armour it hits as if they behave like a liquid. This is because the tip of the jet is moving so fast that it can create hydrodynamic flow at the point of impact. The steel starts to move apart under the pressure almost as if it is water. A steel target will erode the jet, and if it could be made thick enough would provide protection but at a much greater weight. A material that is less dense, however, like the glass reinforced fibre in the T-64, allows the energy of the jet to disperse, and it may begin to unravel, turning into multiple fragments that are much easier for the armour behind the fibre to absorb. This provides mass efficiency because the lighter aerial density saves around half the weight of steel that would be needed for the same level of protection.

It was a clever and efficient design that allowed the T-64A to keep its weight to 38 tonnes while maintaining its protection against what was the worst threat at the time. The turret was also interesting. The Soviets designed the turret to have cavities in the cheeks either side of the gun. The cavities were filled with various materials during trials including high-hardness steel inserts, cast aluminium, and eventually rows of what are often described as 'ultra-porcelain balls' that were up to 70mm in diameter. At other times the balls are referred to as corundum, which is a very hard material that can be found naturally or man-made. Corundum is made up of aluminium oxide, which is known for its resistance to HEAT jets. Sintered aluminium oxide has a very high hardness and continuously presents new, hard material in the path of the jet, corroding it as it pushes through the armour.[11] These balls were arranged inside the cavities in the frontal arc of the T-64A, providing a good level of protection against HEAT rounds that was equivalent to 450mm of steel, but at a much lighter weight. It is also worth a pause here to reflect on the location of armour for main battle tanks. Experience from World War II had shown that tanks absorbed the most damage from the front, and so it was decided to position most of the protection at the front of early post-war tanks. This continued into the Cold War and remained relevant, despite multiple tank deployments in urban environments. Modern tanks, however, are far more concerned with protection from all angles.

Its production run was ultimately short; the finalized production design for the T-64A was officially accepted into service in January 1973 under Order No. 021 from the USSR's Minister of Defence.[12]

Letters between the Soviet design bureaus appear to recount significant tension between the chief designers. JSC Research Institute of Steel (NII Stali), which was responsible for the development of steel armours and other advanced designs, had proposed filling the turret's cheeks with high-hardness steel, which they argued was more robust than the ceramics put forward by Morozov. 'Despite the turrets being overweight, their resilience cannot be considered satisfactory. For instance, a hit from a 100mm AP shell near belts I-II (shot #17) resulted in a 370mm long tear in the lower section,' A.T. Larin wrote to the designers in Kharkov in January 1968. 'Damage of this kind on turrets with aluminium filler or with high-hardness steel inserts was not observed,' he continued. Larin's points were later contradicted by another bureau, VNII Transmash, which had carried out some of the production and testing, 'We were informed of a letter from … comrade A.T. Larin, in which he baselessly lists three drawbacks of Object 434 turrets with a ceramic filler.' The VNII Transmash letter, which came from director V.S. Starovoytov, dismissed Larin's claims entirely, concluding by saying, 'the letter from organization 2652 [NII Stali] contains not a single element of truth to it, and its goal is unclear'.[13] So, it seems that the drama between Soviet tank designers may have been partly responsible for the delays in getting the T-64 into production. The increased complexity of the turret likely also played a role.

Nevertheless, the tank had a relatively short production run, and the last T-64 (a T-64BV) was built just 14 years after the type was accepted into service, in 1987. The total number produced is unclear, but estimates range between 8,000 and 14,000 tanks, the vast majority of which stayed in Ukraine.[14] By the time the T-64 was officially accepted into service, the T-72 and even the T-80 were well under way. But the concept of the autoloader, 125mm main gun, composite armour and the resultant low profile was here to stay. The T-64A was not seen in public by Western observers until 1976. Intelligence agencies were aware of its existence, but could not appreciate how different it was until it was seen for the first time. They could not have known about the advanced armour array in the turret, or about the very high muzzle velocity of the main gun. But it was probably obvious that the tank had a much lower profile and a bigger gun, and was a significant departure from previous Soviet designs, one that would shape every other tank the Soviets produced. Morozov was far from pleased by this, and left a rueful note in his diary, shortly after the T-64A had been approved to enter service:

> Tagil [Uralvagonzavod] 'stole' our tank and is remaking it. There are no such examples anywhere in life. At one time, every design bureau in the USSR was working on a promising tank. Ultimately, LKZ [Leningrad Kirov plant], ChKZ [Chelyabinsk Kirov Plant], and Tagil never completed their projects and subsequently abandoned work. One tank, the '432', from the Kharkiv plant, remained, which LKZ and Tagil then began 'improving', changing the engine, chassis, mechanical protection, and everything else. To this day, not a single plant has created anything new, but is instead trying to 'refine' other plants' designs ... At the very least, this is theft. They will pay for this for years to come![15]

The T-72 and T-80 are indeed closely based on the T-64, and their introduction into service added complexity to the maintenance and production of tanks that was inherited by Russia and still appears to be challenging the Russians today. But Morozov's dismay appears to primarily have been one of pride. He had worked on elements of the design for over a decade only to see them 'stolen' by the other bureaus. That said, his work was a success in many ways. The T-64 outmatched the majority of Western tanks in service at the time and deserved the premium tank status that it was given by Western observers. This is perhaps why most of its design features were adopted by the other tank design bureaus, and the T-72 would go on to become one of the most widely used tanks in the world, whilst the T-64 would remain relatively obscure.

This era saw the introduction of the smoothbore gun, APFSDS ammunition, and HEAT warheads that could reliably be fired from the shoulder. Early Cold War tanks went to war in Vietnam and Czechoslovakia. They proved relatively capable, but simultaneously vulnerable, driving the development of new armour and bigger guns. For the Soviets, the Warsaw Pact, and the client states that emerged from the bloc from 1990, these years were formative. They established the tank design principles from which they have never moved away. The T-64s and T-72s that fought each other in Ukraine can all trace their history back to the 1960s, and Morozov's vision for the future tank.

For the West, however, the design ethos was still evolving, shaped as much by politics as technology, which is perhaps one of the key similarities between NATO and Soviet design.

The T-64 would not make its combat debut until 1992, and then only on a small scale. It would have to wait until 2014, and Russia's first invasion of Ukraine, to be fully tested. But in the interim, the majority of NATO and Soviet tanks went to war, some multiple times. And this brings us to the next section, where MBTs had their trial by fire and technology started rapidly evolving.

PART 4

1973–91: Trial by fire – tanks go to war

In early October 1973, Israeli regular soldiers manning the Bar-Lev defensive line, a set of fortifications in the Sinai Desert, had gone home to celebrate Yom Kippur. Their positions were filled by reservists. Tensions between Israel and Egypt had remained high following the Six Day War in 1967. Egypt's new president, Anwar El-Sadat, had resolved to address the lingering tension with action. So, at 2.00pm on 6 October 1973, 2,000 Egyptian artillery pieces opened fire on the unfortunate Israeli reservists in their fortresses, marking the start of the Yom Kippur War. More than 10,000 shells fell on the Israelis' positions in the first few minutes, effectively silencing them, and within hours, Egyptian engineers had built bridges across the Suez Canal. Men and vehicles crossed the bridges in their thousands; amongst them were some soldiers lugging bulky and heavy packs on their backs. Working as teams of three, they stuck together, quickly moving forward with other Egyptian infantry formations to set up large semi-circular defensive positions. This was happening along the entire line of the offensive, from the Gulf of Suez to the Mediterranean Sea, some 190km. It confused the Israelis: where was the main line of effort? Where should the 252nd Armoured Division that was holding the Sinai Peninsula focus its counter-attack?

This was all part of Sadat's plan. Those teams of three pushed on, moving ahead of the trenches and foxholes dug by the infantry; they settled down and put their heavy backpacks on the desert floor. It was time to work. Two of the soldiers would have carried the 9P11, which included a 9M14 Malyutka anti-tank guided missile on its launch-rail. NATO planners called this missile the AT-3 Sagger. The 9P11 pack weighed 18.1kg, and they had to carry that along with their personal weapons.

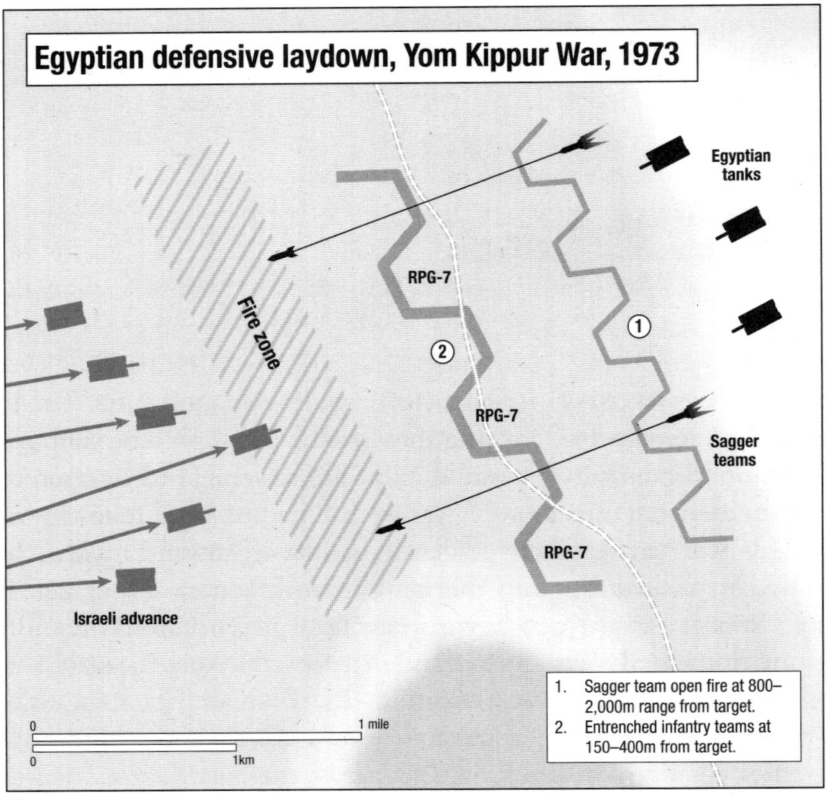

The third member of the team got off lightly; his 12.4kg pack was the 9S415 control panel for the missiles. They worked quickly, following the plans that they had been rehearsing since 1970 and had practised in multiple large-scale exercises. Sadat and his war minister, Isma'il 'Ali, had a thorough understanding of the Egyptian soldier and his shortcomings; there would be no mistakes this time, nothing left to chance. According to some accounts, the movements of individual sections and soldiers had been planned and rehearsed by Egypt's central command.

'Every day for years, all operators of Sagger anti-tank missiles lined up outside vans containing simulators and went through half an hour's exercise in tracking enemy tanks with their missile', Chaim Herzog, an Israeli officer who eventually became president, wrote of the Egyptian preparations. Estimates vary, but US intelligence reports from 1975 indicated that soldiers had to fire 2,300 simulated Saggers to qualify, and would fire 50–60 per week in training. So, they knew what they were doing as they set up their 'suitcase Saggers', but thundering towards them were packets of Israeli tanks, the venerable Centurion and the American M60. Israeli tank crews were experienced and aggressive, confident in their abilities after their success in 1967. Isma'il 'Ali knew that it made no sense to try to out-manoeuvre or out-think the Israelis; his men would not thrive in those circumstances. Instead, he hoped that his missile wall would blunt Israeli counter-attacks on the land and in the air, leading to unacceptable losses and the termination of the war on Egypt's terms. The Sagger teams were the leading edge of this wall; there were literally thousands of them in the attacking formations, but their role was key, so they took their time setting up. The senior gunner was responsible for firing the missiles, and would be supported by the junior gunner, who would make the missiles ready and protect the gunner or fire missiles if he was wounded. The third man was sent forwards with an RPG-7, the descendant of the RPG-2, which had caused so much damage to the US Marines fighting to retake Hue City just five years earlier. They camouflaged their positions, intending to hide from the Israeli tanks as much as possible. Their own armour was arranged behind them, beckoning the commanders of the 252nd Division to attack. And that is exactly what the Israeli commanders did, pushing forward to do battle with the newly arrived T-62s and T-55s, eager to repeat the successes of the past war. However, as they drew closer it became clear that something was not quite as expected.

> We were advancing and in the distance I saw specks dotted on the sand dunes. I couldn't make out what they were. As we got closer, I thought they looked like tree stumps. They were motionless and scattered across the terrain ahead of us. I got on the intercom and asked the tanks ahead what they made of it. One of my tank commanders radioed back: 'My God, they're not tree stumps. They're men!' For a moment I couldn't understand. What were men doing standing out there – quite still – when we were advancing in our tanks towards them? Suddenly all hell broke loose. A barrage of missiles was being fired at us. Many of our tanks were hit. We had never come up against anything like this before ...

That Israeli commander was surveying Egyptian senior gunners, most likely lying down behind their 9S415 control panels, looking down the 9Sh16 optic, trying to get a good sight picture of the approaching tanks. The missiles were set up on their launch rails, some tens of metres away from the gunners, the junior gunner moving between them to make sure they were ready to be fired. The view through the optics was probably blurry, but the shapes moving in front of them – up to 2,000m away – could only be tanks. Once he was confident, the commander would fire the missile; a loud roar and a gust of grey smoke announced the missile's launch. Now came the difficult part: the Sagger is a manual command to line-of-sight (MCLOS) missile, which basically means the operator has to tell it where to go. As the senior gunners released their missile, they would have peered through their optics looking for the tell-tale orange flare in the base of the missile. It was their job to watch the missile and correct its flight with a joystick on the control panel. Moving the joystick would send a signal down a thin wire attached to the back of the missile and bring it back onto a collision course with the Israeli tank. The senior gunner had to maintain his focus – the Malyutka was not quick, and would take 17 seconds to travel 2,000m. This probably isn't a long time to most, but is very probably nerve-wracking if an Israeli tank is firing at you. Some Israeli commanders said that they detected the missiles heading for them in-flight, and the most effective counter-measure was to try to shoot the senior gunner. If he lost concentration, the missile could crash into the floor, as many thousands are thought to have done.

As the missiles arched and wound their way towards the targets, Israeli tanks would have started to encounter Egyptian mines as well as fire from the supporting tanks, but the Saggers were the weapon on which most post-war analysis focused. Isma'il Ali's missile shield was so dense that it did not matter if most missiles missed. The missiles were often fired in salvos, with more than one missile fired per tank. As a result of the Egyptian defences, the 252nd Armoured Division lost 200 of its 300 tanks in just two days to these tactics. Having deployed their armour in penny packets to respond to the length of the offensive, the Israelis would find themselves in firing sacks with camouflaged Sagger crews behind them, wheeled armoured vehicles called BRDMs with more Saggers in front of them, and Egyptian artillery raining down on top of them. US intelligence assessments of the weapon after the Yom Kippur War make for sober reading: 'The warhead, capable of penetrating any known armour in the free world, gives it a very high degree of lethality. The probability of a first round kill against a stationary, fully exposed M60A1 tank at ranges from 1,000 to 3,000 meters is over 60%.' The lethality of the Sagger's HEAT warhead is exactly what NATO and Soviet planners had been worrying about for some time. The Sagger was not new: it entered service in 1963, and the Soviets were not shy about exporting it. Moreover, they understood what these weapons and their NATO equivalents could do, and that concern was eventually reflected in the corundum spheres in the turrets of the T-64A. Israeli forces knew that Egypt and Syria had them, and that Soviet trainers were assisting in their training, but it was reportedly the density of Sagger use that took them by surprise – estimates range between 6,000 and 8,000 missiles in the Sinai region alone.

The missile had also been employed in Vietnam the year before. In a single engagement with South Vietnam's newly established 20th Tank Regiment in April 1972, North Vietnamese soldiers killed or wounded all officers from the regiment's 3rd Squadron and destroyed three M48A3 tanks using Saggers. A few weeks later, the Sagger was used to attack the 1st Squadron from the 14th Cavalry Regiment, destroying its M41 tanks housed at the Tan Canh compound. In a sign of the ATGM's versatility, Saggers were also used against a reinforced bunker. Then, in May, South Vietnamese forces returned the favour, destroying a column of armour that was advancing on Kontum City with M72 Light Anti-armour Weapons and helicopters armed with TOW ATGMs. The TOW helicopters were a novelty, but they proved their worth in the defence of Kontum.

So, what should we make of all this, and how is it relevant to the modern tank? Well, the key thing to understand is that there was a lot of concern about the lethality of HEAT warheads at the time, and that concern was not unfounded. They had proven themselves to be capable and effective weapons that could outmatch 'any known armour', according to the US intelligence community. This threat landscape, as well as some political issues and technological advances, shaped the tank designs of the 1970s and 80s quite significantly. And this is important because, almost without exception, every one of the modern tanks that is in service today can trace its origins back to this era. They have essentially been adapting ever since. Encounters with Sagger in Vietnam and Israel served to reconfirm the importance of combined arms warfare, a lesson that is still repeated today. In short, both wars demonstrated that sending tanks into an offensive without artillery and supporting infantry to engage the enemy's infantry would end badly. They also demonstrated that Western armour was struggling to keep up with the threats arranged against them. NATO and its allies were working to counter this threat, and several new designs emerged between 1973 and 1990 that included systems specifically designed to counter HEAT warheads. So let's begin by looking at protection, and there are two key approaches to consider: Chobham and Blazer.

Chapter 12
Mass efficiency vs bunker mentality

There are two extremes when it comes to armouring tanks. At one end is Russia, and to some extent China, both of which appear to rely on mass efficient explosive reactive armour to provide the bulk of the protection for their tanks. At the other is the UK, which has a penchant for producing insanely heavy but well-armoured tanks. The US, Germany, Israel, Japan, and France all fall somewhere along this spectrum, and most picked their spot between the 1970s and late-1980s. To get started, think back to Chapter 11 and the composite armour for the T-64. At that time, the UK's Fighting Vehicles Research and Development Establishment (FVRDE) had also developed a new armour that provided increased protection against HEAT rounds; they called it Chobham.

The core challenge of HEAT warheads is the jet and the way it interacts with the world around it. A well-built warhead will produce a jet travelling at speeds up to 10km/s at its tip; the rear of the jet will travel at around one tenth of this speed. The jet is, contrary to popular belief, still solid. Some past reporting asserts that the jet is molten and very high temperature, that it can somehow burn through some of the hardest and most resilient materials known to man. None of this is true. It is simply a metal that has been stretched so quickly and to such an extreme that scientists and engineers treat it like a liquid using hydrodynamic theory to explain what is happening. But we can also return to our basic physics to understand these weapons. Remember the calculation for kinetic energy? Where the kinetic energy (KE) equals one half of the mass (m) times velocity squared. So, one study cites a liner material weighing 280g, which would equate to a kinetic energy of 14 MJ if it were travelling at 10km/s.[1] For reference, this is more than a lot of APFSDS rounds, even modern ones, and is equivalent to a Mazda MX5 travelling at 600km/h. That is not to say that all HEAT rounds will carry that much kinetic energy when they detonate, but it is to say that as a weapon, a HEAT round has the potential to deliver an incredible amount of energy to a very small area. The jet penetrates the vehicle's armour by basically pushing the armour material out of the way. As the jet does this, it is also eroded by the armour material and will eventually run out of liner to push into the hole in the armour. In fact, the liner material will be deposited on the inside walls of the cavity that it creates. This means that the depth of penetration is ultimately decided by the length of the projectile and the density of the projectile material and armour. Advanced HEAT warheads will produce a jet that can penetrate up to ten times the diameter of the charge, and they will often use copper as a liner material because it is ductile enough that it will not form into a shower of fragments, and also has a density of 8,900kg/cubic metre. The velocity is important for getting into the armour, but the depth of penetration is decided by the length of the jet (or APFSDS round), and the density of the materials involved.

This all matters because now we can begin to understand how a tank can be protected against HEAT warheads. Either you must put material and armour geometries in front of it that are harder to erode, or you must disrupt the formation of the jet. Composite armour uses materials and geometries to increase the material that the jet has to erode. Explosive reactive armour primarily uses geometry and movement to disrupt jet formation, and Chobham uses layers and differences in material resistance to disrupt the jet's formation. Take the composite armour in the T-64A and its corundum spheres, for example. Ogorkiewicz states that ceramics are effective against HEAT warheads because their high strength confines the diameter of the jet's penetration into the armour to a greater extent than RHA or high-hardness steels. This leads to greater erosion of the jet because it does not have as much room to displace ceramic material, which repeatedly comes back into contact with the length of the jet as the armour is comminuted (the ceramic material gets turned to sand).[2] These effects are amplified if the ceramic material is contained and the transfer of motion limited by non-ceramic materials such as steel. The result is an improvement in mass effectiveness, which describes how much steel armour it would take to match the performance of a composite armour. Some can reach a mass effectiveness of 1.6, which means you would need 16kg of steel armour to meet the same level of protection as 10kg of composite armour. This should have benefits for the weight of the vehicle, although that is not what happened with Chobham.

Around the same time that Morozov was arguing with Larin about the merits of ceramics against aluminium in armour solutions, the West was beginning to pour research into Chobham. Like the T-64's armour, Chobham was designed to counter the effects of HEAT weapons and the initial trials were aimed at demonstrating that it could be fitted to an MBT. It was developed by the Military Vehicles and Engineering Establishment (MVEE – previously the FVRDE) in the UK during the 1960s. The British were rightly concerned about the Chieftain's protection. The tank had been designed when the T-55 was the primary threat and the widespread adoption of HEAT warheads combined with the introduction of the Russian 115mm Molot gun meant that Chieftain was vulnerable. Their concerns were later proven to be correct when the tanks were eventually used in the 1980–88 Iran–Iraq War. There it was found that the armour was extremely vulnerable to Soviet weapons from the 115mm to the 125mm tank guns used by the Iraqis, with one Iraqi commander later claiming that a sabot round had penetrated the frontal armour of a Chieftain and made it through the back of the tank.[3] Later analysis by British diplomats and a representative of the MVEE 'under thin cover' found that 70% of the damaged tanks captured by Iraq had been penetrated by the 115mm APDS rounds fired by Iraq's T-62s. They studied 88 vehicles that had taken APDS hits and 44 hit by HEAT warheads. They noted that many of the APDS strikes had penetrated the hull, which was described as 'relatively vulnerable', but some had punched through the turret front, which was the best-protected part of the Chieftain. Upon penetration, some Chieftains had suffered ammunition fires, a result of the Iranian crews not properly maintaining the liquid ammunition bins, as well as the energy of the penetrating APDS round itself. 'A 20° high energy cone of spall was discharged from the point of penetration. Four feet from the penetration the cone was some 600mm in diameter', which came with an internal hole between 60 and 85mm in diameter, they added. The HEAT round penetrations had caused much less damage inside the vehicles, and produced smaller internal holes around 35mm.[4] Nonetheless, any concerns that the British had around the survivability of their Chieftains in the 1960s certainly justified the development of Chobham armour.

There were several efforts to replace Chieftain in the 1960s and 70s. This included an aluminium version of the Chieftain designed to carry the extra weight of Chobham armour. There was also a project with Germany called the Future Main Battle Tank, which came to an unsuccessful close in 1977. For various reasons, none of these projects resulted in a new tank, and a combination of worsening economic conditions left upgrading the Chieftain as one of the few options left. The FVRDE was across the problem and working on an armour known as Burlington, which would eventually become known as Chobham because of where the facilities were based.

For many years the nature of Chobham armour was considered to be top secret. However, a declassified report from 1969 in the UK's National Archives provides some insights. The report looked at the feasibility of fitting Burlington armour to the Chieftain in both a maximal and minimal configuration. In the former case, the new armour would be fitted to as much of the vehicle as possible, and in the latter armour would be fitted to the places that offered the most protection to the crew, mostly the sides of the turret and hull. The report provides a technical diagram that shows one of the armour packs, or 'biscuits' as the report refers to them. So, from this, which is believed to be accurate, the famed Chobham armour consisted of a box that was 30.48cm high and 20.32cm deep. The box was made of steel with a plastic liner and contained an array of spaced steel plates around 3mm thick that were backed by around 6.3mm of 'plastic'. The plate-plastic combinations were angled down towards the bottom of the box and the front of the box appears to be a few inches from the leading edge of the plates. The plates are around 25mm from each other and separated by brackets, providing space for seven full plates inside a biscuit. It is important to note that this report came from a time when the armour was at a pre-production standard, meaning that it may have changed in some regards when it was eventually produced for the Challenger 1. However, this drawing provides enough information to understand how Chobham worked. The design of the armour packs, for the sides of the vehicle at least, meant that the thin edge of the plate was facing the direction of attack with the large face of the plate at an angle. This means that if the armour was hit by a HEAT warhead, the jet would have to pass through at least two layers of the angled steel. In theory, as the jet penetrated the steel, it would be compressed, then as it passed through the other side of the plate it would spread out, the tip of the jet mushrooming to some extent. This would increase its surface area and, in theory, reduce its penetration against the next plate where the whole effect was repeated. Furthermore, transitioning from the steel to the air introduced a shock to the metal jet, which could disrupt its flow, leading to parts of the jet turning into particles, further reducing its penetration potential. It is also worth noting that the document recommended arranging the Chobham armour at a distance from the hull of the tank. It noted that the resultant design would be too wide for European rail gauges, but added that close fitting the armour to the tank would significantly reduce its protection.

The armour for the glacis of the tank pursued a similar configuration and would have added at least three layers of spaced armour to the glacis with a burster plate in front of them. The burster plate included two additional layers that were designed to increase the armour's ability to take multiple hits. In all, the complete Chobham armour kit that was designed to provide the most protection from Carl Gustaf shoulder-fired anti-armour weapons and some APDS rounds was expected to weigh 5.5 tonnes, leading to a loss of performance off-road for the Chieftain, as well as a reduction in its ability to drive on roads, difficulties accessing the vehicle for the crew, and a loss of visibility. Not to mention removal of the search light, which would eliminate what night-fighting capability the tank had. By 1971, a Chieftain had been fitted with the armour for trials, but political considerations and financial troubles came to the fore, leading the UK briefly down the path of a joint project with Germany to develop a new tank that ultimately failed. The British did, however, share the technology with the US, which was beginning to look at the XM1 (which would become the M1 Abrams), as well as with Germany for the Leopard 2. It would also eventually protect the UK's Challenger 1 tanks, as well as some of its lighter armoured fighting vehicles. So, this type of spaced armour became very important, and can be found on many modern tanks, making the development of Burlington a key moment in the story of the modern tanks.

Chobham armour addressed the main problem of a tank's protection: how do you counter a very lethal weapon, one that can be made more lethal by simply making it bigger, when the existing level of armour is too heavy, too cumbersome, and not good enough anyway? It did this in a mass efficient way – more efficiently than would be the case with lots of steel armour at least, but it still came with a cost in terms of weight. For NATO forces, this was an acceptable trade-off to make. They had a major adversary to face down and for the UK and the US at least, the plan was to dig their tanks into the reverse slope of a hill and go hull down. In this position, they hoped that the long range of their L7 guns and the additional armour would give them the survivability and lethality to face down the Soviet armed forces. Indeed, in 1977 the US Secretary of the Army claimed that the XM1 was 'immune to any currently known anti-tank missile'.[5] Ogorkiewicz asserts that this was a result of the British-developed Chobham armour. The bunker mentality would change in the 1980s, but tank development is often slow in peacetime, so as NATO's planners settled on a more mobile approach to counter a Soviet invasion, they were beginning to receive tanks built with a lot of armour and extra weight. Three NATO MBTs were built carrying Burlington or a version of it: the Challenger 1, which entered service with the UK in 1983, the M1 Abrams, which was first delivered to the US Army in 1980, and the Leopard 2, delivered in 1979.[6] The Abrams and Leopard are the de facto NATO tanks, although it took a while for all states to join their respective clubs. There are, or will be, 17 users of the Leopard 2 in NATO, and three users of the M1 Abrams, although that includes Poland, which happens to run the Leopard 2, M1 Abrams, and K2 Black Panther. Nevertheless, all three of these tanks were heavier than their designers set out to make them when they entered service. This is important because it is a trend that continues to the current day. The Leopard 2A8 is thought to weigh in at slightly less than 70 tonnes – close to 20 tonnes more than the Leopard 2A0, while the M1A2 SEP v3 comes in at a little over 67 tonnes, which is 13 tonnes more than the original M1 Abrams. When operationally deployed, the weight of these tanks has ballooned yet further. The UK's Challenger 2 tipped the scales at a staggering 74.4 tonnes, with its full Theatre Entry Standard-TELIC armour kit for use in Iraq adding 12 tonnes to the vehicle's base weight.

Hopefully this helps to reflect the process that Western tank designers were going through. The designs mentioned above can all trace their lineage back to several failed projects in the 1960s and 70s, such as MBT-70 (a US-German development) and MBT-80 (a British-German development). These developments tend to be well covered in most other books looking at this time period, and they seem to have relatively comprehensive Wikipedia entries if you are after something succinct. But the point here is to show that the challenge posed by Soviet tanks was real, and that NATO designers had no good response for close to two decades. Chieftain is often held up as the saving grace, the one NATO tank that could outmatch the Soviets, with its 120mm rifled gun providing the range to outstrip them and support the bunker mentality that it was hoped would win the day. However, the feedback from the Iran–Iraq War suggests that it was far from survivable enough, and in any case, it was deployed only with the British, who occupied a fairly small chunk of the inner German border. With the introduction of Chobham and three tanks built around it, as well as new larger main guns, to which we will return shortly, the tide began to turn for NATO, in terms of technological capabilities at least.

We have met Morozov and Larin, the Soviet tank designers who were giving NATO's tank designers so many headaches. But it is time to introduce somebody new, Manfred Held. Held holds a curious place in the design of modern tanks because the technology that he developed, and the physical concepts for which he is responsible, are quite revolutionary. Held designed something called explosive reactive armour (ERA), which is used by NATO, but is the primary form of protection for Russian and Chinese tanks, as well as those of their client states, which include India and the former states of the Soviet Union. Taken together, these users probably represent much more than two thirds of all tanks in the world. There are claims that the Soviets developed ERA independently of Manfred Held, but we will start with his journey, and work the Soviet assertions in. While looking into the armour from this era, I found the following account posted on a forum:

> I first met Manfred Held, the progenitor of ERA, at least in its initial fielded form, Blazer, at an AFV symposium run by SMi held in London in January 2004. He is not of course a Norwegian who once worked for Rafael, but a German academic specializing in ballistics.

> If I remember a conversation around a dinner table correctly, he came up with the idea for ERA when given permission to examine some of the hundreds of T-54s and T-55s the IDF had captured in 1967. He paid particular emphasis to those vehicles that had been damaged. To his surprise, he noted that in certain cases, where propellant for individual isolated shells had cooked off and hadn't caused a general catastrophic explosion, the force of the propellant had disrupted the efficacy of a penetrating shaped charge jet. Held then worked on methodologies for harnessing this phenomena [sic] and came up with the idea of ERA sandwiches and drive plates within steel boxes.[7]

Held's idea was to put a thin layer of explosive behind an 'additional wall layer made of a non-explosive, inert high-density material such as metal', all inside a box, according to a revision of his patent from 1980. The box would be arranged on the outside of a vehicle and when the shaped charge hit and detonated, it would pierce the box, triggering the explosives inside that would disrupt the formation of the jet.[8] According to some, Held had a difficult time gaining traction for his idea, but was welcomed by the Israelis. Perhaps the bruising experience of the 1973 war and Egypt's Saggers was still hanging over them. It appears that Held was able to demonstrate his idea in a test in 1974, during which prototype ERA was able to defeat both the Sagger's warhead and an RPG. In short order, a form of ERA known as Blazer was developed and fitted to Israeli tanks. This included the stalwart Centurion, which had become the Shot Cal by 1970, courtesy of a new engine that addressed most of the problems with the earlier designs. Shot Cal tanks had been used in Syria in the early 1970s and again during the 1973 Yom Kippur War. They were the scourge of Syrian T-55s and T-62s that had been supplied by the Soviets during the battle of the Valley of Tears, which took place on the border between Syria and Israel in 1973. However, many Israeli commanders had been lost to Saggers and RPGs. In one case, a Shot Cal gunner was decapitated by an RPG, causing understandable hysteria amongst the crew and forcing the tank's withdrawal. This type of loss was common enough that IDF tank commanders wore their dog tags around their ankles to aid identification, and tank crews took to cleaning the blood of their comrades away with diesel. It helped to mask the smell.[9] It is worth noting at this point that Israeli losses in the Sinai were primarily caused by the kinetic energy rounds fired by Egyptian T-55s, not the Sagger missiles that are often the focus of the war. CIA reporting after the war showed that of 119 damaged or destroyed Israeli tanks that were inspected, a maximum of 24.3% were destroyed by Sagger or RPGs. They note that many more were still in Egyptian territory at the time, but maintain that the Israelis adapted quickly to their use and losses caused by the missiles fell.

Nevertheless, Sagger and HEAT warheads had left their mark, so when Manfred Held came to inspect damaged tanks in 1974, the Israelis were open to hearing about it. By 1980, Blazer was fitted to Shot Cals, as well as the IDF's Magachs, upgraded versions of the M48 and M60. Fighting alongside them were 180 of the Merkava Mk 1, a new tank designed by a team led by Major General (Maj Gen) Israel Tal, who had fought in the 1967 war and developed Israeli tank doctrine. His team had studied the many battles fought by Israeli armour and the causes of tank losses, and they based the design of the Merkava on their findings. As it happens, the tank was primarily protected by what Ogorkiewicz described as 'special armour', which likely means something similar to Chobham.[10] So, we will not focus so much on the Merkava right now, but return to Blazer and the Shot Cal.

The first combat use for ERA can be traced to the streets of Lebanon in 1982. At the time, Israel's relations with Lebanon had worsened as the Palestinian Liberation Organization (PLO) used the country to launch attacks on Galilee in northern Israel. The PLO's presence in Lebanon had precipitated a civil war, drawing Syrian forces into the mix and complicating matters for the Israelis. The US, however, was keen to maintain peace in the region and had led on a ceasefire, which some claim was interpreted differently by the PLO and Israel. In particular, Israel believed the ceasefire applied to all PLO activities. So, when three men shot the Israeli ambassador to the UK in the head as he left the Dorchester hotel in London on 3 June 1982, this was the final straw for the Israeli government.[11] By 6 June, columns of Israeli tanks were advancing into Lebanon, destroying PLO forces and their weapons caches as they went. This war drew the IDF into urban battles to a much greater extent than the 1967 or 1973 war. If large open spaces with uninterrupted line of sight out to a few kilometres are the tank's home turf, where it is most effective and able to quickly shape a battle, then urban warfare is almost the exact opposite. Everything that makes a tank lethal and survivable across open countryside is reversed in a city. The long line of sight combined with a tank's optics and high power gun will typically mean that in the countryside the tank sees first and shoots first. It also means that tanks can manoeuvre, their crews putting them into more advantageous positions. Alternatively, they can be dug in, leaving just the turret proud of the ground. Generally, this means that a competent crew can always have its best, thickest armour facing the direction of attack. Of course, as the Syrian and Egyptian forces found out in 1973, this is far from a guarantee of survival. But, in theory, open space puts a tank in an advantageous position. A city, by contrast, reduces the line of sight to a few hundred metres. It tends to erode and eliminate the clear boundaries between forces, which means that in some cases all of a tank's armour might be exposed. The Soviets experienced this in Hungary in 1956, as did US Marines in Hue just 12 years later. And pretty much every military force before or since that has deployed tanks into a city has found that their advantages and strengths shift. They retain the firepower and protection that makes them formidable, but they become more vulnerable as a city presents an attacker with more opportunities to safely attack the weaker armour to the sides and rear, potentially out of sight of the main gun.

Lebanon is generally not suitable for the types of tank combat that the IDF had employed against Egypt or Syria in 1973. Full of ravines and orchards lining the roads, the country provided the ideal setting for PLO and Syrian anti-armour teams. The cities and towns became strongholds for the PLO, which is a common reaction of forces that are bombed from the air without respite or a suitable means to counter that airpower. Within weeks, Israel had secured the 40km buffer zone that its politicians said was the goal, but its forces continued on to Beirut as the government revealed its maximalist aims – to establish a sovereign Lebanese government, without Syrian or PLO influence.[12] The IDF used an offensive approach which included a bypass policy. This is quite common, and simply means that an armoured force will bypass areas of resistance if their defeat is not seen as essential to the mission's success. Then a follow-on force will take the time to clear enemy forces that have been left behind. However, the PLO was an urban force, and the IDF was ill-prepared for this, resorting to massed firepower to destroy urban areas rather than take them by force.

Even after largely destroying Lebanese towns and sending their armour in, they would encounter small anti-armour teams that proved effective at delaying and disrupting their armour formations. This led to the conclusion – one which was not unfamiliar to US Marines in Hue – that urban assaults should be led by infantry and backed by tanks, rather than led by tanks.[13] On the other side, the PLO had all the hallmarks of an insurgent organization. Although it numbered in the thousands, its units each had around 50 personnel, which tends to be the maximum that any one person can control and is a common cell size within a non-state force, which would also characterize the Islamic State some decades later. They were armed with AK-47 assault rifles, heavy machine guns, and the RPG-7, which a DTIC report describes as 'probably the most potent weapon fielded by the Palestinians'.[14] It certainly proved effective against the IDF's M113s, the lightly protected APCs, but most reports seem to conclude that the Merkava Mk 1 was relatively safe from most threats that it encountered. There is little evidence available on the movements and utility of Israel's M60s and M48s that carried Blazer. However, it is clear that Israeli forces were frequently engaged by Syrian forces with Malyutka (AT-3 Sagger) guided missiles and RPGs. What is clear is that later variants of the Merkava doubled down on the armouring methodology used in the Mk 1. This included the use of 'special armour' and modular armour suites that were designed to be upgraded. But ERA does not appear to have featured in later designs.

The Soviets, however, saw much more promise in ERA and are thought to have worked on their own version from the 1950s. It is often argued that the appearance of Blazer in 1982 led the Soviets to develop their own equivalent and field it shortly after. However, evidence gathered by Andrei Tarasenko, a historian of Soviet tank development, indicates that a report was approved by A.T. Larin, director of the Moscow Research Institute of Steel and Alloys in 1968, which established that the Soviets were in the seventh stage of a project for the 'Development of dynamic anti-cumulative protection for tanks'.[15] ERA is called dynamic protection in Russian parlance, and the papers described various efforts and tests of different models of dynamic armour to increase protection against shaped charges and HEAT warheads. The British were not alone in worrying about the ability of their tanks to defend against ATGMs, it seems. The Soviets had first worked with a form of dynamic protection that relied purely on explosive energy and would be built into the glacis of a tank. This was not considered effective enough for adoption, especially as the combined armour of the T-64 – which had also been adopted for the T-72 (much to Morozov's frustration) – provided enough protection against most major Western weapons. By the late 1970s this was changing and work resumed on dynamic protection, leading to tests of what is known as Kontakt-1. Tests started on Kontakt-1 in 1982 following a decision to conduct the tests that pre-dated the Lebanon War by four days, according to Tarasenko. If this is correct, then it is very reasonable to conclude that the Soviet development of ERA was entirely separate.

Kontakt-1 differed from the experimental KDZ-68 that preceded it in that it was (and is) made up of modules, or cassettes as they are commonly known, that can be mounted onto the exterior of an armoured vehicle. The cassette is a rectangular box that is installed on the glacis, the turret front as well as its roof and sides, and the sides of the hull. A fully-protected T-72 or T-64 will carry as many as 100 boxes of Kontakt-1, which provide reasonable but not complete coverage. There are four different types of cassette that are used for different locations on the tank, but each is provided with two 4S20 inserts – this is the ERA. 4S20 consists of a thin layer of plastic explosive weighing 260g that is sandwiched between two thin plates of armoured steel. The insert closest to the threat is positioned at an angle, while the second insert is flat. When an RPG or HEAT warhead strikes the armour, the jet is formed and passes through the thin flyer plate at the front of the first 4S20 insert, into the explosive in the middle. The energy of the jet triggers the explosive, which detonates, pushing the two steel plates towards the base of the jet and its tip simultaneously. The plates continuously push new material into the path of the jet, but more importantly introduce stress and uneven forces along its length, causing the jet to break up. The resultant fragments are too small to penetrate the armour behind the ERA (or at least that is the hope). Ideally, ERA needs to be hit at an optimal angle so that the inclination of the plates provides the greatest contact time against a jet. However, if the explosive is at least twice the diameter of the jet, then it can be effective against a strike at a normal incidence. Generally, ERA arrays will stack at least one set of flyer plates on top of each other, as the Soviet designs did, which provides more material to interact with the jet. Another consideration is that there should be space between the rear of the ERA and the vehicle hull, allowing the back flyer plate to travel further and interact with the jet for longer. Notice that, implicitly, a lot of the design of ERA relies on time.

For the Soviet tank designers, ERA was a valuable technology. If hit at an optimal angle, it could reduce HEAT round penetration by as much as 80%, providing the equivalent to hundreds of millimetres of steel armour at an overall weight gain of just over 1,400kg depending on the model of tank.[16] As a result, Kontakt-1 provided protection from most known anti-tank weapons using HEAT warheads in service with NATO at the time, from the frontal arc at least. This ERA was added to the turret front, roof, and glacis of the T-72, T-64, and T-80. In all three designs, the glacis also included a layer of steeply inclined steel with two thick layers of glass reinforced composite fibre, followed by one further layer of steel. This glass fibre material was made up of resin bonded glass fibres, which further increased protection against HEAT jets. The reason for this is that when glass is penetrated by a shaped charge jet, it has a spring-back effect, which can squeeze the jet out of the armour, limiting its penetration even more than a high-strength ceramic. The glacis armour on the T-72 was reported to have a mass effectiveness of 2.6 against shaped charges, which presumably means the T-64 had a similar capability.[17] Soviet tanks have a hard time because the propellant carried in the carousel located under the turret is prone to burn and detonate the ammunition when the hull is penetrated. This leads to the catastrophic destruction of the tanks and the tendency to throw the turret when this happens. All of the tanks that followed the T-62 have that issue. However, it is worth noting that Ukrainians praised the survivability of their T-64s following Russia's first invasion in 2014. T-64s would return from the frontline, completely stripped of their ERA, having taken multiple RPG strikes. This means that the armour did its job.

The first Soviet tanks fitted with ERA seem to have been noticed by NATO in 1984, but by that time the passive armour in the turrets of Soviet tanks was also improving, in particular the T-72B, which entered service in 1985. The T-72B included cavities either side of the main gun that were filled with a form of spaced multi-plate armour. Specifically, it consisted of a steel plate, around 21mm thick, that was backed by rubber and then another thin steel plate. Each of these created an array, and 19 or 20 arrays were found in each cavity, separated by 22mm spacers.

The thin edge of the array faced the likely direction of attack, rather than the flat face, which is similar to Chobham armour. This armour array was famously written about by Maj Jim Warford from the US Army in May 2002 for the *Journal of Military Ordnance.* Warford explained that the US Army had managed to acquire a T-72B and inspect the turret cavities, which he states:

> Confirmed that the Soviets had developed and unexpectedly fielded what is known generically as 'special armour'. Special armour is more advanced in design and application than the composite armour used to protect previous Soviet tanks. In fact, it was thought that special armour developments were still beyond the design constraints of Cold War-era Soviet tanks. This surprising confirmation was truly a revelation; the Soviets had perfected a type of special armour and successfully incorporated it into a tank turret; without making the leap to a large box-shaped design characteristic of U.S. and NATO special armoured MBTS.[18]

The T-72B was also fitted with Kontakt-1, significantly expanding its protection against HEAT rounds and missiles. Of course, Warford's surprise at the advanced state of Soviet armour in comparison to Western standards is likely a result of the post Cold War era and especially the 1991 Gulf War. A series of conflicts appeared to demonstrate that NATO equipment was significantly better than Soviet equivalents, which is accurate in some circumstances. However, as we have seen with Morozov, Kontakt-1, and the spaced armour of the T-72B, to say nothing of the 115mm smoothbore gun with its APFSDS, the Soviets were often ahead of the West in terms of their tank technology. It was, however, unlikely that many tank crews would have been aware of this at the time.

To make matters worse for the West, Kontakt-1 was rather quickly followed by Kontakt-5, a new ERA that is occasionally referred to as heavy ERA. This name most likely derives from the front flyer plate, which is thicker and much heavier than the plates in Kontakt-1. Kontakt-5 was approved for service in the mid-1980s and began protecting late-production T-72Bs from around 1988, as well as the T-80U. In contrast to Kontakt-1, it comes in much larger containers and is installed in arrow-shaped arrangements on the front of the turret. The glacis also receives a set and on some vehicles – primarily the T-80 during the Cold War – an array was fitted to either side of the hull.[19] Kontakt-5 provided protection against HEAT and APFSDS, whereas Kontakt-1 could only protect against HEAT. The reason for this is found in both the design of an APFSDS and the way that ERA works. APFSDS penetrators are much thicker and slower than HEAT jets, but they are also much harder. Overall, this means that it is more difficult to break an APFSDS penetrator into pieces. Kontakt-5 set out to achieve this through the use of a heavy 15mm-thick front flyer plate made of hardened steel. According to Paul Hazell, author of *Armour: Materials, Theory, and Design,* Kontakt-5 reduces APFSDS penetration through momentum transfer.[20] Put simply, this means that the energy from the flyer plate is transferred to the penetrator. As a result, the tip of the penetrator may be sheared off, which increases the surface area that the projectile's energy is applied to (because it's not pointy any more); the projectile may be broken into pieces, reducing the length-to-diameter ratio and kinetic energy of each segment, and the projectile might yaw – so that it has to penetrate the turret's armour at an angle. For any of this to happen, it is critical for the ERA to be at an angle, the greater the better. One study published in 2024 simulated an APFSDS strike against a turret carrying Kontakt-5 and showed that with the ERA flyer plates arranged at 0 degrees (vertically), the 730mm penetrator passed through the front wall of the simulated turret with 64mm of penetrator remaining. This would have been very bad for the crew: that 64mm of tungsten carbide would probably have enough energy to kill at least one crew member, damage equipment, and even hit ammunition. However, if the flyer plates were at an angle of 45 degrees, the same penetrator failed to make it through the turret, and at 65 degrees the penetration was even shallower.[21]

All of these developments were crucial for the modern tank, and one of the main reasons is confidence. As I have tried to establish, the main point of a tank is to take its big gun to a dangerous place and use it. Commanders need to have the confidence that their tanks will be able to make it to that place and survive long enough to make the mission successful. If they do not carry enough armour to withstand even the most basic of shoulder-fired weapons, then the commander must pick and choose when and where the tanks are deployed. The indications from Iran and elsewhere are that despite the introduction of the T-62, Chieftain, M60, and AMX-30, not much had changed from when Lt Nordstrom met T-34-85s in his M4 Sherman. Yes, the guns were bigger and the armour was thicker, but at typical combat ranges a Soviet tank could punch through a NATO tank and vice versa. The ATGMs deployed by either side were equally capable of penetrating the armour on both sides, although the behind-armour effects left a lot to be desired. The advanced complex armours introduced in this era gave commanders some confidence that their vehicles could survive long enough to achieve their mission.

Indeed, by some accounts, the Kontakt-5 fitted to the T-72B and T-80 greatly increased the protection of Soviet tanks. By how much is the subject of debate amongst the armour community. There are two well-known articles, both published by the *Jane's International Defence Review* in the 1990s, which basically claim that the vehicles were impenetrable by NATO weapons of the time. The authors were none other than Held himself and Ogorkiewicz, both citing NATO sources. In one case, a T-72 fitted with Kontakt-5 had been tested against the NATO weaponry of the 1980s; 'when fitted to the T-72A1 and B1 the "heavy" ERA made them immune to the DU (Depleted Uranium) penetrators of the M829A2 APFSDS', one source is reported to have said.[22] The available evidence indicates that neither author was misrepresenting what they had heard. Combined, Kontakt-5 and the T-72BM's turret would provide something like the equivalent of 1,300mm of rolled homogeneous armour against a HEAT projectile from the front.[23] At the time, the frontal aspect was what mattered to Soviet designers, even as their forces grappled with the Mujahideen in Afghanistan, and lost tanks to side-attacks and mines. It was always assumed that they would be advancing, attacking with their turrets forwards against NATO forces that had been softened with artillery, air strikes, and perhaps nuclear weapons. NATO was not sitting idle in this cat and mouse game of protection and firepower, although it had moved more slowly than some would have liked.

Chapter 13

Rheinmetall returns

By the start of this era, the L7 and its 105mm rifled barrel was the de facto NATO-calibre tank gun. The British clung on to their rifled 120mm and its APDS ammunition, maintaining that it remained effective and up to the job. You can judge for yourself how accurate their assessments were. Only one other new design tank has been built with a 120mm rifled gun – the Arjun, an Indian design built in low numbers – and while the British retained the core principle for Challenger 1 and 2, it has not been retained for Challenger 3. So, this is effectively where the UK drops out of the discussion on tank lethality. The US and Germany were set to shape the future of NATO tank firepower, if only because their two programmes, the XM1 and Leopard 2, would become the most-used tanks amongst NATO forces. As initially envisioned, both designs used the L7. After all, the Israelis had been very successful against T-62s and T-55s in the 1973 war. But interest was growing in an alternative, and it came from Rheinmetall, a German company that had manufactured the fearsome 75mm KwK 42 L/70 gun that armed many of the Wehrmacht's tanks during World War II. Rheinmetall's involvement altered the trajectory of the modern Western tank to the same extent as the 2A46 that armed the T-72. At the time of writing, derivatives of the German gun, which is known as Rh120, arms, or will arm, tanks developed and produced in the US, Germany, Turkey, UK, Japan, and South Korea. There is no escaping it. So, how did the Rh120 come about and why?

Rheinmetall's factories in Germany had been destroyed during World War II. Allied bombing had taken its toll, and after the war's end

Germany was prohibited from building new vehicles and weapons. Rheinmetall clung on after the war, launching an unsuccessful civil production programme until a company called the Röchling Group acquired a majority stake in what was then Rheinmetall-Borsig AG in 1956. Borsig AG was sold off and the remaining Rheinmetall Berlin AG started life under leadership of Otto Paul Caesar, who took the company back to its roots. Starting with general purpose machine guns, the company had also diversified into mechanical engineering by 1958. In 1959, it restarted gun barrel production with 20mm automatic cannon barrels and 155mm howitzer barrels. Development of 120mm barrels officially began in 1965, according to Rheinmetall's website.[1] The lead engineer on the development was Raimund Germershausen. Born in 1934, Raimund was fresh out of university when he began working with Rheinmetall in 1963, so he didn't carry the long experience of tank design of designers such as Morozov or Larin. However, he and his team were helped in no small amount by MBT-70, the disastrous US–German project to develop a new MBT. It's hard to point at any single point for the cause of the programme's failure. But it is notable that it aimed to use a 152mm gun/missile launcher. At the time, the US Army was convinced that it needed missiles as its primary anti-tank armament, a notion that you may remember the Soviet designers had abandoned in the 1950s. It was expected to reach targets at ranges of 3,000m with its missiles, but German news outlets noted this would be rare in Europe, making up around 16% of engagements. Developing the new gun, and its automatic loader, was an expensive endeavour. Overall the cost of the programme had reached $303 million by 1969. Using the US Consumer Price Index to adjust for inflation, this would equate to around $2.53 billion in 2023. For reference, this is not far off the price that Germany will pay for the 108 Leopard 2A8s ordered in 2024. It was enough for *Der Spiegel* to call MBT-70 'yet another catastrophe in the series of post-war German armaments disasters'.[2]

Before MBT-70 had officially been cancelled, the German Army had decided that it needed an upgrade for the Leopard 1 (which it did), as well as the MBT-70, and a third tank that it called Keiler, meaning boar in German. The Keiler was to carry a new 120mm gun, the gun that Germershausen and his team were working on, mounted on a hull developed by Kraus-Maffei, which had started work in 1968.

They planned to avoid the technically complex hydropneumatic suspension and autoloader of MBT-70, but take with them the electronics.[3] Most histories of the tank point simply to Russian and Soviet tank developments at the time, reasoning that the German response was driven by them. There is some truth to this – to which we will return shortly. But it is also important to bear in mind the conversations that were under way in Germany at the time. Since re-establishing its armed forces as the Bundeswehr in 1955 and joining NATO, West Germany had largely received its equipment from America. For a time, the way that equipment was provided can only be described as unfavourable to Germany. Old M47s could be supplied and the US Army would receive funding equal to the cost of a new M47 or M48. This meant that Germany received America's older kit and was generally resisted when it attempted to buy more modern platforms. In another example, the fledgling Bundeswehr had indicated its interest in the Centurion. The American embassy in London supported this in 1953, pointing out that Centurion offered commonality with Denmark, the Netherlands, and the UK. Centurion was also cheaper than the M47, which would have saved the Mutual Security Program that funded the procurements money.

The M47 was picked regardless, despite one German officer describing it as a 'travelling coffin'.[4] To be fair, some former German Wehrmacht officers also had reservations about the Centurion, noting that it was thought to be too heavy and slow, and that it should not be employed in the way that German planners were expecting.[5] The fledgling democracy experienced other shocks in buying abroad too; it had forced through the procurement of thousands of HS-30 APCs from Hispano-Suiza, a Spanish-Swiss company. However, the procurement had been based on pictures of the vehicles and a rushed review, which was revealed by German press in 1959. It would later transpire that members of the German government had also taken bribes to push the vehicles through.[6] So, with defence spending in West Germany set to soar following the country's entry into NATO, and foreign suppliers unreliable at worst and unsuitable for German doctrine at best, there was a desire – not all too unfamiliar to today's Europe – to keep that money inside Germany. It can therefore be safely said that at least part of the driver behind the development of the Rh120 was the German drive to re-establish and support its domestic defence industry.

Then, of course, there was the threat of Soviet armour. According to *Der Spiegel,* which maintains an extensive archive of its reporting at the time, the Bundeswehr was resting on the assumption that the Leopard 1 with the L7 was able to beat the T-62. However, when the Israelis loaned a captured T-62 to Germany for tests at some point in between 1974 and 1978 under Defence Minister Georg Leber, the Soviet tank was reportedly found to be 'significantly superior'. Exactly how it was superior is not made clear, but if it was supplied with APFSDS ammunition, then it would probably have demonstrated greater penetration than the Leopard 1.[7] This lone anecdote also fails to account for Israeli experience of the L7, which had proven its ability to destroy T-62s and T-55s. The gun would go on to perform well in the 1982 Lebanon War, albeit with a new APFSDS, suggesting that the reporting or tests may not have been as accurate as they could have been. Nevertheless, the T-72 and T-64 with their composite and spaced armours, and their large 125mm guns, were a problem. They challenged the notion that NATO would counter the USSR's numerical superiority with technologically advanced weapons, and indicated that NATO was both outnumbered and outgunned.

So, let's get back to the Rh120, the 120mm gun that Rheinmetall developed for Germany's requirements. At a very technical level, the 120mm smoothbore offers multiple advantages over the L7. It is a bigger gun, which means that larger projectiles can be fired. In the case of a high-explosive round, we can compare the M1010 105mm tank round, which is offered by KNDS, with the Insensitive Munition High Explosive-Tracer (IM HE-T) 120mm round from NAMMO, for example. The M1010 fires a 12.1kg projectile filled with 2kg of high explosive at up to 700m/s. The IM HE-T fires a 15.9kg projectile filled with 3.2kg of high explosive at up to 1,030m/s from an L44 barrel. So, the increase in calibre offers a more than 50% increase in explosive fill along with a larger projectile, which will create a more extensive lethal area. In the realms of kinetic energy, the 120mm/L44 M256 that armed the Abrams, which is based on the Rheinmetall Rh120, started to receive the notorious M829 APFSDS from 1984. The M829 had a depleted uranium penetrator weighing 3.94kg that was 616mm long including the fins with a diameter of 26.9mm. This provides a length-to-diameter ratio of 22.9:1. The round had a muzzle velocity of 1,760m/s and could penetrate between 525 and 540mm of steel at a range of 2,000m. By comparison, the M833 APFSDS round for the M68 105mm gun (the US version of the L7 105mm gun), which was type classified in 1983, had a 427mm depleted uranium penetrator with a diameter of 24mm providing an L:D ratio of 17.79:1. The M833 left the muzzle at around 1,500m/s, and could penetrate up to 420mm of armour at 2,000m. This means that the M829 offers a 25% increase in penetration at the same range.

The design and construction of the gun is important to these increased performance metrics. Let's look back at the M68, which was made through one of two processes. In one, a steel ingot was produced through a process called vacuum degassing. This is where the molten steel is poured into a cylindrical mould and then put into a low-pressure, high-vacuum environment. This forces the dissolved gases in the steel to escape, which helps reduce the impurities in the steel, a critical process to producing a high-quality blank for a gun barrel. The steel ingot was then open die forged, which means it would be held in place and hammered into shape with an operator manipulating the metal to get the correct shape. This process was critical to aligning the grains inside the steel and further reducing the impurities and potential cavities in the steel. Typically, the steel would be heated for the forging process and then trepanned. During trepanning, a ring of steel would be removed from the centre of the tube leaving a solid core in the middle that could then be recycled.[8] After that, the rifling would be cut into the inside of the tube and the whole thing heat treated, which is where it is brought up to a high temperature and then cooled to finally align the grains.

The second process used was rotary forging, where a solid ingot would be formed and forged to the length of two barrels before being cut into two. For rotary forging, an electroslag refined steel is used; this is a steel ingot that has been through a secondary refining process (electroslag refining) where the steel is melted through a slag, which is a complex mixture of fluorides and oxides that floats on top of the molten steel. As the steel is melted through the slag, impurities are removed, especially sulfur, which can make a steel brittle – not a good thing for a high-pressure gun barrel. Each barrel was then trepanned and rotary forged again using a mandrel. The American Watervliet Arsenal used an SXP 55 rotary forge from the Austrian company GFM (Gesellschaft für Fertigung und Maschinenbau), which it acquired in the 1970s. The SXP 55 was enormous, consisting of four hammers arranged in a circle. Steel was heated and passed through the middle of the hammers that each deliver thousands of kilos of force, with up to 1,000 blows per minute.

The steel would be rotated as it passed through the hammers to create a cylinder. Once the cylinders were formed, they would also be trepanned and then a mandrel, which is a highly hardened, long, cylindrical rod, would be inserted into the trepanned hole. The mandrel carried ridges that would create the rifling inside the barrel. As the tube was passed through the SXP 55, the hammers would beat the steel and compress it against the mandrel inside the barrel. The barrel could then be heat treated before the finishing touches, like the breech, bore evacuator, and thermal sleeve were added. This process sounds lengthy, but it could produce a complete 105mm barrel in a matter of hours, which would have been very important if a war with the Soviets had lasted more than a week. It is also interesting to note that the SXP 55, or very similar technology, was also sold to the USSR and used to make its 125mm 2A46 barrels for the T-72.[9]

The Rh120 uses similar processes but employs a cold drawn tube. This is where the steel tube is pulled through a die at room temperature or below. This is designed to induce strain or work hardening. Work hardening is a process whereby the dislocations (irregularities in the grain structure of the steel) within the metal are repeatedly moved into the path of other dislocations. This makes the overall product stronger as it is harder for the steel to deform because the dislocations cannot pass each other so easily. Strength is also increased through a process known as autofrettage. Autofrettage sets out to solve the problem of the steel of the barrel expanding, which is particularly challenging near the breech where the firing pressure is greatest. To get around it, a mandrel is introduced which is typically a little bit bigger than the bore diameter. It is pulled or pushed forcefully through the bore, compressing the interior steel, but leaving the exterior of the steel free. This essentially pre-stresses the inner steel, leaving it compressed by the outer wall of the barrel.[10] It may sound strange to cause mechanical stress to the steel of a barrel, but doing this means that it is harder for the firing of a round – which causes tensile stress – to deform the steel. The end result is that the Rh120 or M256 can accommodate higher pressures, enabling more propellant to be used and bigger rounds fired. The barrel is also chrome lined, an interesting process that leaves the interior of the bore plated in chrome to help extend the barrel life. When a round is fired, it creates enormous heat from the burning of the propellant, as well as friction inside the barrel, and it deposits chemicals inside the tube. All of this together would leave pits and damage in a naked steel barrel, which over time would rust or allow for the propagation of damage, shortening the barrel life. This can lead to a loss of accuracy or a catastrophic gun failure in a worst-case scenario. For comparison, a modern Rh120 gun can fire up to 1,500 rounds, depending on the nature. The L7 was not chrome lined until the M60A3 (1977 onwards) and original M1 Abrams entered service, and guns before that could only fire 200 rounds before they needed to be replaced unless additives were used in the propellant.[11]

In addition, the L44 had a large breech with a volume of 10.2 litres and a vertical sliding wedge breech block that together can withstand chamber pressures up to 96,000psi (660 MPa), which is the force generated by firing the M829A1 APFSDS.[12] To put that into perspective, 96,000lb is like taking eight fully grown male African elephants and stacking them on an area the size of your thumb. It is immense, and around 30% greater than the chamber pressure of the L7. This was enabled by the greater breech volume, as well as the improved strength of the barrel, but also by the lack of rifling. Rifling imparts stress and friction to the round as it is fired, so a lower velocity had to be used to prevent the round breaking up. Altogether, the move to a smoothbore gun, led by Rheinmetall, was a step-change for NATO, one the British would resist for another 40 years. But the gun was not alone: it came with the wider adoption of APFSDS ammunition, which was another development resisted by the British. The Soviets had taken an early lead on this nature of ammunition, with the T-62 entering widespread use in the early 1960s with its BM-4 APFSDS. Ogorkiewicz notes that he contributed to a US study in 1972, which concluded that APFSDS was the most effective anti-tank ammunition. He passed this recommendation on to the British, only to be told that the APDS would always be superior. Further trials in 1975 firmly established that APFSDS was more lethal, he states, which seems to have paved the way for the first NATO round – the M735 – to enter service before the end of the decade.[13] The M735 fired a sheathed penetrator, which means a dense tungsten carbide core surrounded by a steel jacket. The steel adds strength to the brittle tungsten, which can help it to penetrate a spaced and layered target.[14] Importantly, the M735 penetrator was allowed to rotate inside the sabot so that it would not pick up the rotation imparted to the round by the rifling. The round also included a titanium-dioxide liner inside the brass cartridge, which helped reduce the barrel wear.

So, close to two decades behind the Soviets, NATO finally had an APFSDS, which remains the most lethal nature of anti-tank ammunition providing that it penetrates the armour. But since starting the project that led to the M735, which had actually started in the 1960s, the US had been considering depleted uranium as an alternative penetrator material. However, it had proven difficult to manufacture the penetrators and fire them without them breaking up in the air. This all changed with the introduction of a depleted uranium alloy, which was combined with a small amount of titanium. The resultant round, the M829, had been in development for some time, with intense cooperation between Alliant, the Ballistic Research Laboratory, and the Army Research Laboratory from 1984 to 1988. Scientists from those organizations received $30 million in funding per year to develop the rounds, and relied extensively on simulation and modelling to reach the initial design. Something of a breakthrough was achieved in the mid-1980s when the Battelle Northwest Laboratory suggested that a process known as high-rate forming be used to produce the rod.[15] This addressed one of the primary problems with depleted uranium, which is that it is not very ductile or strong. A penetrator needs to be ductile so that it will not bend or simply shatter when it hits the enemy tank. High-rate forming involves rapidly applying force to the rod so that the larger crystals inside the depleted uranium are broken down, giving it a more uniform structure, which increases its strength – in much the same way that a finer grain structure in steel improves the strength of armour.

Some studies indicate that density – more than hardness or strength – is the primary determinant for the penetrator material of an APFSDS round.[16] This does not replace the velocity or L:D ratio, but does indicate that the density of the materials used is more important than its hardness. This is why tungsten and depleted uranium have been the materials of choice, with the exception of the earlier Soviet designs.[17] For comparison, tungsten carbide has a density of 15.6g per cubic centimetre, depleted uranium comes in at 19.1g, and steel at 7.8g. One way to visualize this would be to think of a tennis ball, which has an internal volume of around 150cm^3. If you filled that ball with water it would weigh 150g, about as much as an apple. If it were filled with steel, it would weigh just above 1kg, which is around the weight of a typical bottle of wine. Tungsten carbide and depleted uranium, however, would weigh 2.34kg and 2.87kg respectively – which is close to the weight of a small bowling ball, but in the area of a tennis ball. Notice also that depleted uranium is over 500g, or 22% heavier than tungsten for the same volume.

There are two other important differences between tungsten and depleted uranium. The first is how they behave when they strike a target, the second is cost. The impact behaviour is key to understanding the long infatuation with depleted uranium rounds. Tungsten erodes in much the same way as a steel penetrator, with a mushroom forming at the nose of the projectile that gradually reduces the material available to penetrate the target, while simultaneously increasing the surface area that it is trying to apply its energy to. The harder the tungsten, the worse this effect becomes, which means that increasing the hardness of a tungsten penetrator *can* reduce its performance, although I should emphasize that the physics behind this are very complex, so this is not always the case. Depleted uranium, by contrast, experiences something called adiabatic shear, which essentially means that the round self-sharpens as it passes through the armour, depositing small scrapes of depleted uranium on the armour as it goes. The word adiabatic means that heat is generated, but does not get transferred out of the small area that it applies to, the material being mushroomed from the head of the projectile in this case. The heat can't escape because the transition happens so quickly, and thin bands of the depleted uranium heat up very rapidly as a result and are continuously sheared off. The result is that the DU round loses its mushroom in a process that is sometimes called self-sharpening. The resultant armour penetration may have rough internal surfaces and be smaller in diameter than tungsten, but it does enable thicker armours to be defeated. And the harder the depleted uranium, the more this effect is noticed.[18]

Much of the cost difference between uranium and tungsten projectiles comes from the materials used and the production process. Depleted uranium comes from uranium tails, which are waste products produced during the enrichment process of uranium for nuclear power. Those are barely radioactive and contain the U-238 isotope, which is the most common natural form of uranium. Its half life – which reflects how radioactive the material is – is around 4.5 billion years. For that reason, U-238 is used to assess the age of the earth.[19] Once it has shed isotopes, it begins to form lead, and the remaining number of isotopes can be used to assess the age of a given rock. So, that is one of its uses, but this also helps to illustrate that it is not a concern in terms of the radiation it emits.

As a by-product of the nuclear energy production cycle, depleted uranium can be used for a variety of purposes, including medical shielding and as armour for a tank, but it is ultimately a relatively inexpensive material. A penetrator of depleted uranium is made by first melting it with a small amount of titanium and possibly molybdenum; it is then poured into a cylindrical mould lined with copper, which sticks to the outside of the ingot as it sets. Next it is heated and extruded, which is a process whereby the ingot is forced at high speed and pressure through a smaller die that is close to the diameter of the rods. This lengthens the ingot and rapidly reduces the diameter; it is also the high-rate forming suggested by the Battelle Northwest Laboratory. The rods are cut to length and the copper casing is removed; they are then very carefully heat treated, cooled, and normalized to produce rods with a tensile yield strength of 203 kilo-pounds per square inch (ksi).[20] That means it would take 203,000lb of pressure per square inch of a rod to permanently bend it, which is more than the maximum take-off weight of a Boeing 737. To shatter it could require as much as 267ksi, which is known as the ultimate tensile strength. Bear in mind that depleted uranium starts the process with a yield strength of between 67 and 102ksi, which is far too low for a penetrator material. Once the blank has been processed, the threads for the sabot and fins are cut into the body, and it is assembled into a full round of ammunition with its sabot petals and semi-combustible propellant case.

A tungsten carbide penetrator follows a radically different process. The raw material is a tungsten powder and materials like cobalt. Tungsten has an extremely high melting point, which means it cannot be melted and poured like other metals or depleted uranium. Instead, it is reacted at very high temperatures with carbon to produce tungsten carbide, which is then thoroughly mixed with a softer metal powder (cobalt), which will act as a form of binder. The resultant mix is poured into a mould, which is then compressed by an industrial press that might apply more than 100 tonnes of pressure per square inch of material. This sort of sets the powder, making it solid enough to move around. At this stage, the rod is machined to give it the shape and profile required of an APFSDS penetrator. This is an important element, because the next stage will essentially make the powder too hard to machine. That step is known as sintering, which is where the penetrators are loaded into large ovens known as autoclaves. Autoclaves are a type of vacuum

A Centurion hull on the production line in 1949. The message on the glacis reads 'Good will unto all men?' The thickness of the glacis plate is just visible from this angle. The firepower-protection cycle would lead to dramatic changes in the way a glacis was built within two decades of this image. (Getty Images)

Near Hill 854, the 76mm gun of a M4 Sherman tank from Company B, 72nd Tank Battalion, fires towards enemy bunkers on Napalm Ridge as they support the 8th ROK Division. (Getty Images)

US engineers carry a daisy chain of anti-tank mines in Korea. The mine is a constant and significant threat to the modern tank. Whilst the tank has evolved significantly since 1950 when this picture was taken, the anti-tank mine is essentially the same. (Getty Images)

North Korea's limited tank pool played a pivotal role in the country's early offensives, but actions like those of Lt Nordstrom's caused losses that were never replaced. (Getty Images)

Soldiers rest on a painted M46. The heavy armour of the tank was more than a match for the T-34s fielded by the North Korean forces. Mines and the terrain, however, were a challenge, as much as they are now for its successor, the M1 Abrams. (Getty Images)

A soldier prepares to fire a bazooka during the Korean War. Shoulder-fired weapons have always been a threat to the tank, driving many changes in situational awareness and protection. (Getty Images)

A Soviet T-55 fires on a target during the Hungarian Uprising. The modern Russian tank has evolved through several similar deployments. (Getty Images)

A Centurion provides fire support to British commandos during the 1956 Suez Crisis. Any hopes of a peaceful era following World War II had largely faded by this point, and the developments that would lead to the modern tank were underway. (Getty Images)

Tanks become more exposed in a city or town as everything is closer, allowing people to throw Molotov cocktails onto engine decks or lay explosives under turrets. This was as true for this T-34-85, destroyed on the streets of Budapest during the 1956 Hungarian Uprising, as it was for Merkava Mk 4s deployed to Gaza in 2023. (Getty Images)

Troops from the US 11th Airborne Division watch a nuclear explosion at close range in 1951. These exercises were quite common, and the modern tank evolved around the expectation that it would be used after nuclear weapons had been deployed. (Getty Images)

Two fighters stand guard over their Russian T-34-85 tank in Yemen in 1964. Despite newer designs being released and widely accepted into service, the T-34-85 has found a role in conflicts around the world. (Getty Images)

US Marines take shelter behind an M48 during the Battle for Hue City after a sniper had fired at them. The tanks provided vital firepower in the fight to retake the city, as is often the case in an urban battle, but they proved vulnerable to the RPG-2 rocket launchers. (Getty Images)

A female Vietcong soldier aims an RPG-2, which would evolve into the RPG-7 and the fearsome RPG-29. These weapons are one of the most common threats to the modern tank. (Getty Images)

It's easy to forget that tanks are there to protect people. This image shows a US tank driver in Vietnam, 1967. (Getty Images)

This unusual vehicle is the M50 Ontos, it carries six recoilless rifles and was used in close coordination with US tanks to retake Hue City. (Getty Images)

The tank in this image is an AMX-13. Lt Col Zeev Eitan and his battalion found that these tanks lacked the punch to defeat Egyptian T-55s until at very close range. Tanks are all about the guns, and if the gun isn't up to the job, neither is the tank. (Getty Images)

A column of Patton tanks in service with the IDF advances at the start of the Six Day War. The war saw massive tank battles, helping to firm up beliefs in the West that Soviet doctrine would involve a lot of tank-on-tank combat. (Getty Images)

A Mirage jet flies low over IDF Centurions during the Six Day War. Israel's successful strikes against the Egyptian air force and coordination with its ground forces showed what could be achieved when combined arms were properly coordinated. (Getty Images)

A Hezbollah fighter prepares a Sagger missile to fire in 1999. The missiles were used extensively during the 1973 Yom Kippur War. Despite multiple advances in armour and technology, they can still be effective against poorly prepared tanks. (Getty Images)

A front view of the XM1 Abrams, which carried the L7 rifled gun that would later be replaced by the M256. The M1 presented a significant departure in US tank design, with its welded turret (as opposed to cast) setting the mould for the modern Abrams we know today. (Getty Images)

One of the original Leopard 2s in 1981. The Leopard 2 has become the predominant tank in European NATO but the modern version is almost unrecognisable from this image. (Getty Images)

The hole surrounded by rust on this image was caused by some form of anti-armour round. Possibly one of the depleted uranium or tungsten APFSDS deployed by US and British forces during the Gulf War. (Getty Images)

An Iraqi Type 59 or T-55 lies abandoned in March 1991, after the fighting had come to an end. The T-54, which the Type 59 is based upon, had upset a lot of the West's planners when it first emerged. By 1991, however, it was hopelessly outmatched by tanks like Challenger 1 and the M1 Abrams. (Getty Images)

Soviet troops prepare their T-72s to leave East Germany in 1989. While NATO had caught rare glimpses of Soviet vehicles and did its best to build an understanding of them, the fall of the Berlin Wall allowed for unprecedented access. (Getty Images)

A 120mm barrel for an M256 is heated to nearly 2,000 degrees just prior to moving to the rotary forge at the Watervliet Arsenal. When this image was taken, the Arsenal was using the same Austrian forge it had acquired in the 1980s, which was the same forge used by the Soviets. (John Snyder/US DoW)

A Russian T-72 driving through a Chechen village in 1996. The heavy losses suffered by the Russians reflected poor doctrine and training, and threw some of the design flaws of Soviet armour into sharp relief. (Getty Images)

A Ukrainian soldier trained on the NLAW missile just before Russia's invasion. The NLAW was designed to target the weakest point of Soviet-style vehicles with auto-loaders. It has evolved from the concept that brought the Bazooka and RPG to life, and represents the sophistication of the current threats to modern tanks. (Getty Images)

It is not clear what knocked this Russian T-72 out, but this aerial view – most likely taken from a drone – is how much of the war has been experienced by the public. (Getty Images)

The Type 99A shown here is the mainstay of China's heavy combined arms brigades. Its design has its roots in Soviet tanks, although it has a distinct Chinese flare. (Getty Images)

A close up of the Leopard 2A8, showing the octagonal shaped radar panels for the Trophy APS on the cheeks of the turret, either side of the gun. (Getty Images)

The Challenger 3 will bring the UK's tank capabilities into the modern era, with an APS and a smoothbore 120mm gun from Rheinmetall. (Getty Images)

The T-14 Armata has been religiously displayed during Russian defence exhibitions and has reportedly been deployed to Ukraine and Syria, though there is little evidence to support those claims. (Getty Images)

The MGCS concept presented at Eurosatory in 2024 had an uncrewed turret and the ASCALON main gun, which can be a 120mm or 140mm calibre gun. (Getty Images)

furnace that can be temperature controlled. With a number of tungsten rods loaded into the autoclave, the temperature is carefully increased, sometimes as little as 30 degrees per hour, to the melting point of the cobalt or binder agent, which is generally around 1,500 degrees. This binds the tungsten carbide molecules together, and once set it becomes one of the hardest materials known to man. Any further grinding has to be done with specialist tools edged with diamonds. The powders, sintering process, and grinding requirements make tungsten carbide relatively expensive compared to depleted uranium: especially because tungsten is an in-demand material with hundreds of uses, whereas depleted uranium is a slight nuisance that many governments have to pay to dispose of.

So, as the US was considering the threat posed by Soviet tanks in the 1970s and 80s, it arrived at the conclusion that a bigger gun with better ammunition would help. Freed of the constraints imposed by the rifled gun that had dominated NATO designs for most of the Cold War, ammunition development in the US and Europe really took off after the introduction of the Rh120. The smoothbore design enabled longer and longer penetrators to be used, while the British remained limited by their rifled guns, an aspect they countered with the continued use of depleted uranium. The Soviets, however, were also constrained by design. The use of their autoloaders limited the length of ammunition that could be used and the armour penetration as a result. They also fielded depleted uranium rounds like the 3BM-29 Nadphil, and the 3BM-32 Vant, in 1982 and 1985 respectively. Both had relatively short L:D ratios, but the Soviets also developed the 3BM-42 Mango. Mango was a different beast; it employed a double rod configuration made of tungsten alloy. The penetrator, which became the primary APFSDS in Russian service after the USSR collapsed and remained in service through to the invasion of Ukraine, is combined with the 4Zh63 propellant charge to become the 3VBM17 round. Like the earlier BM-6 and BM-12 rounds, the penetrator and sabot are encased in a combustible cartridge case with loose pellets of propellant covering the rear ramp of the sabot, and straight propellant sticks filling the remainder of the space. The 4Zh63 is made entirely of propellant sticks and together the two charges give the BM-42 a muzzle velocity of 1,700m/s; this is equal to the M829 and should tell you something about the quality of Soviet metallurgy and gun design.

Mango was designed to overcome multi-layered targets and reflected a concerted move away from the steel penetrators that the Soviets had relied on for the T-62 and early T-64. Bear in mind that spaced armour like Chobham can have several effects on a projectile, including the introduction of yaw or extreme shearing forces on the length of the rod as it passes from a hard layer into one that is not compressed.

The designers of Mango worked to get through this by using two separated tungsten alloy rods arranged inside a steel jacket with a ballistic tip. The ballistic tip is an interesting addition; it is basically the pointy bit at the nose of the penetrator and it is designed to improve the aeroballistic profile of the round, rather than target penetration. The tungsten rods themselves have what is referred to in Western literature as a conic frustum nose. This simply means that the rod tip is flat with sloped shoulders; imagine simply cutting the tip off a spike, and that is what you would have. This is slightly counter-intuitive; it makes sense that a sharper object would penetrate a target better. And there is plenty of evidence to support that even a slightly rounded nose will be better when the round initially strikes a target. This is because the force of the rod is concentrated on a smaller area, which leads to reduced axial resistance (the resistance that the armour provides along the path of the projectile). However, experiments have shown that this effect is only temporary, and that once a penetrator has penetrated to a depth that is twice its diameter, the nose shape no longer matters as all rods will be equally deformed.[21] A sharp nose for an APFSDS also appears more important against a vertical target, but against spaced and sloped targets, that sharp point would almost act like a pivot, increasing the turning force on the projectile. A blunt nose, by contrast, has more surface area with which to grab the target armour, and that high axial resistance can also help to keep the rods flying straight rather than yawing as they pass through each successive layer.

But what about two rods? Well, some APFSDS rounds are a single long rod, which can be fine; however, it is easier to stress a long rod to breaking point. In fact, at an L:D ratio of around 30:1, which is where some of the more modern natures are, the rounds become too long for the tensile strength of the materials used and may even break upon firing, let alone when hitting the target. So, the idea of a segmented penetrator like the Mango is that the first segment creates a path through the armour, allowing the second segment to continue penetration through the holes created by the first. Technically, the kinetic energy of each segment is lower than if there were a single long rod, but that sacrifice is deemed acceptable if it guarantees target penetration. The steel jacket of the Mango is probably key to making this design work: it ensures that the two rods will travel in tandem, and that they can survive the first impact with the armour. Mango is another interesting example of Soviet advances in tank technology, if only because it effectively represented something that the West was apparently struggling to produce. It may be that Western engineers decided that the single piece round was sufficient for the time, although the widespread appearance of Kontakt-5 would eventually shift this, leading to new natures of APFSDS. But what is clear is that Soviet tankers would have entered battle in the late 1970s and 1980s with NATO in many tanks that were better armoured, and in some cases better armed, than their NATO adversaries.

To make matters worse for NATO, during this era the Soviets also introduced the gun-launched anti-tank guided missile (GLATGM): essentially an ATGM that could be carried in the vehicle's autoloader and fired from the main gun out to a range of 5km. It is close to the calibre of the gun in diameter and it is loaded into the breech in the same way as a regular round. The ATGM is propelled out of the barrel by a small charge and after a few tens of metres the rocket motor ignites and the missile winds its way towards the target, guided by the commander or gunner. The warhead uses the principles discovered by Munroe and his peers in the 1800s, which are the same principles used in the HEAT warheads of the RPG-7, Malyutka, and Western missiles you might have heard of like the Javelin.* However, as they are designed to be fired from the barrel of a tank gun, their ability to penetrate armour is limited by the diameter of the gun barrel (125mm). A rule of thumb for HEAT warheads is that they can penetrate around 10–12 times the diameter of their charge diameter. So, the greater the potential diameter, the greater the penetration potential. However, these missiles were a far cry from ground-launched versions, which had also been developed and improved at the time. The first GLATGM

*If you haven't heard of the FGM-148 Javelin, it is a shoulder and vehicle-fired anti-tank guided missile with a range up to 4,000 metres. It cannot be fired from a tank, but is specifically designed to counter Soviet armour.

to enter service was the Kobra, which had the Grau designation of 9K112-1 for the complete system consisting of the 9M112 missile, a control panel relay designated 9V387, and the 1A33 fire control system. Together, they enabled the crew to guide the semi-automatic command line-of-sight (SACLOS) missile onto its target at ranges up to a range of 4,000m. SACLOS is an evolution over the MCLOS command link of the Sagger/Malyutka. Whereas MCLOS requires the operator to track both the target and the missile, SACLOS requires the operator to track only the target. So, for the 17 seconds that it would take the 9M112 to reach its maximum range, the crew would have to keep the target firmly within their crosshairs.[22] A small box to the front of the commander's hatch automatically issued constant corrections via radio link to an antenna in the base of the missile, which would bring it back into the operator's line of sight. Once it hit, the original 9M112 could penetrate up to 600mm of armour, although later versions would increase this by as much as 40%.[23] The Kobra, or AT-8 Songster as NATO designated it, entered service in 1975 but only with the T-64B and T-80B because it could not be fired from the T-72's autoloader. This is also the era in which the Soviets maintained a two-tier tank system, with higher-quality tanks like the T-64 and T-80 reserved for specialist units and roles, while equipment that was technically less sophisticated – the T-72, T-62, and T-55 – would be used by regular line units. The Soviets clearly saw value in the GLATGM concept, which has never gained traction in the West, as variants would eventually be developed for every tank that they had in service, yes, even the T-55. The T-72 eventually received a GLATGM in the mid-1980s, which was called Svir, and operated in a similar fashion to the Kobra, albeit with a laser beam riding guidance system instead of the radio command link.

It is also worth noting that Soviet ground-launched ATGMs had come on during this period. The 9K111 Fagot started to complement the 9M14 Malyutka from 1970, and the 9M113 Konkurs entered the scene in 1974, improving the lethality of light vehicles like the BRDM and BMP-2. The 9M113 Konkurs ATGMs are particularly noteworthy within the very congested field of ATGMs. They were designed to be interchangeable with the 9K111 Fagot but offer increased lethality when fired from armoured fighting vehicles. However, it is the tripod-based, ground-launched version that is of the most interest to the modern tank. The reason for this is that, despite entering development in the

1960s and service in the 1970s, the Konkurs remains very common. This is because most users of the BMP-1 or 2 would have received the dismounted launchers and both the missiles and those vehicles were widely exported. The missiles were upgraded during the 1990s, improving their lethality to counter ERA and regular armour with a tandem HEAT warhead providing up to 800mm of penetration against RHA. These missiles, as well as the fearsome Kornet, which will make an appearance in the next era, are arguably the most common and lethal threat that the modern tank can face. This is because of how widely they have proliferated: the very lethal 9M113M has been observed in use with the Islamic State and with Hezbollah in Lebanon, as well as the Houthis in Yemen.[24] It has made its way into the hands of various Arab militias in the Middle East, and is still employed by a range of states as a secondary ATGM. It is wire guided, rather than using a radio or laser command link, and also employs SACLOS principles, although MCLOS is available as a fallback. At the time it entered service, it would probably have formed the leading edge of a Soviet anti-tank defence, concentrated in groups and supported by limited numbers of tanks and masses of artillery. In the modern day, it is used to hit tanks that have been isolated as well as infantry positions. Even a relatively modern tank that is well-protected with ERA may find itself vulnerable to the Konkurs. And this is why the ground-launched ATGM and its development is so relevant to the modern tank.

The relevance to Western tanks of the GLATGM is less clear. It was an interesting addition to the arsenal of Soviet tanks, and its development and use have continued under Russia. As a weapon, it extended the reach of some tanks, mostly the command variants in the earliest forms. The purpose for the upgrade appears to have been manyfold, although attention tends to focus on tank vs tank combat. In a NATO–USSR confrontation, however, the Kobra would have given tank crews the ability to engage NATO's own ATGM vehicles: platforms like the UK's FV438 Swingfire, which carried four, wire-guided Swingfire ATGMs that also had a range of 4,000m. In theory, the GLATGM also provided a rudimentary capability to counter NATO's growing arsenal of attack helicopters, things like the AH-1Q Cobra, which had been upgraded from 1974 to carry the TOW family of ATGMs.[25] The impact that those tanks could have on a battle became apparent in Ukraine. There, during Ukraine's 2023 offensive, Russian tanks sat on vantage points using their GLATGMs to engage Ukrainian mine clearance vehicles as they bravely tried to create passages through the Russian minefields.[26] They also used them to engage the combat vehicles following behind them, trapping Ukraine's limited armour in fire sacks for further artillery and loitering munition engagements. GLATGMs were also used to engage bunkers and stationary positions, their accuracy and large warhead proving lethal against lightly protected targets.

Overall, this era, from 1973 to 1991, was critical for shaping the lethality of the modern tank. The development of Rheinmetall's Rh120 helped shape the way that NATO thought about and used its armour. It led to the production of tanks and doctrine that were focused on their ability to move and fight rather than defending a piece of land. Without the lethality offered by the new 120mm gun, NATO planners could not have been confident that a meeting engagement with a Soviet tank army would end well. It was clear that the M60, the Leopard 1, and even the Chieftain – which was revered for its heavy armour at the time – would not fare well in an even fight with the T-62, let alone the T-64, T-72, and T-80 which were entering service in their thousands. So, the Rh120 levelled the playing field, and helped NATO build confidence in its armoured forces. The Soviets, as this chapter should show, maintained something of a technical edge throughout this era. At least theoretically. The tandem rod concept of the BM-42 Mango was a concept that US writers were referring to as complex as late as 2001, and yet the Soviets appear to have deployed it some 20 years earlier.[27] While the GLATGM concept is of debatable value, it is clear that Soviet ATGM technology, or at least its proliferation, was becoming a problem that would survive the Union itself by decades. At the same time, Soviet designers were forced to account for improvements in NATO lethality. From Kontakt-1 they had to move rapidly to Kontakt-5, which provided some ability to disrupt the APFSDS that was becoming the dominant anti-armour round by the mid-1980s. Of course, the purpose of a tank is to take a big gun somewhere dangerous and to use it. We have covered how designers were trying to keep those tanks alive at this time, as well as the way that the big guns themselves were developing. Let's now turn our attention to how the guns and armour would get there: the engines.

Chapter 14

On the subject of engines

As is often the case in NATO, the public discussion during this era was not so focused on the intricacies of Soviet anti-armour weapons. Instead, by 1976, the US and Germany were increasingly concerned about a term that is now common in NATO discussions: interoperability. The defence ministers of both countries were aware that in the event of a war, their spare parts supply would be threatened and their ability to maintain armoured vehicles put at risk. The Soviets and Warsaw Pact had no such problems, but Germany's defence minister, Georg Leber, and his American counterpart, Donald Rumsfeld, signed an agreement in 1976 to standardize key components.[1] Amongst them were assurances around the 120mm smoothbore gun developed by Rheinmetall and its ammunition. The Americans took this on and produced it at the Watervliet Arsenal with a modified breech as the M256. It was fitted to the M1A1 from 1985, and then as a licence-produced version to South Korea's K1A1s from 1997, replacing the venerable L7 once and for all. The Rh120 has been further developed, and we will come back to it in the next era. But by the mid-1980s with production of the Leopard 2 and M1A1 in full swing, NATO had finally caught up with the protection and lethality of its Soviet competitors. The 120mm smoothbore and its potent suite of ammunition meant that NATO tankers could engage the more capable Soviet tanks at 'typical combat ranges' and have a chance of success. However, there was one other element to that 1976 deal, and that is engines. Rumsfeld and Leber had agreed that while Germany would lead on standardization of the main gun, the US would lead on the engine. You may already know where this is going, but in this chapter we will look at the subject of tank engines.

Matching an engine, or as is more often the case, a power-pack, to a tank is a surprisingly difficult job. So much so that finding an engine and transmission for the Turkish Altay tank, after Germany refused to export them, has delayed the vehicle's entry into service by around four years.* This is because there are many complex engineering challenges that have to be overcome. As already touched upon, the engine should ideally maximize its power output – measured in hp – but minimize the volume inside the vehicle that it takes up. This helps reduce the area that must be armoured and helps fit within the overall design constraints imposed on tanks such as the maximum width, track-to-width ratio, and so on. There are a lot of 1,500hp engines in the world, but few of them can fit inside the small spaces required by tank designers, so this field becomes quite limited, and even more so if requirements for the engine to run on any fuel are taken seriously. The transmission, however, tends to be the more complex component to resource. This is because a tank transmission has to perform a number of heavy duty roles. Most prominently, it takes the high-speed low-torque power generated by the engine, and turns it into a high-torque power output through the drive sprocket. The transmission provides gear changes, allowing the tank to accelerate and overcome obstacles, but it is also the sole source of braking – no mean feat when you consider that some tanks have reached 70 tonnes in weight. Finally, the transmission has to turn the vehicle, which is typically achieved by creating a difference in speed between the inside and outside tracks while maintaining the power and torque to both as much as possible.

This is known as skid steering, and it is – or was – the almost universal method for steering tanks. Skid steering creates a significant engineering problem that can only be solved by the transmission, which contributes to the tanks' complexity. Consider a hypothetical 50-tonne vehicle that is moving forwards at 40km/h. If the driver needs to turn that vehicle,

*The production contract was awarded in 2019 with a planned entry into service around 24 months later. The first Altays did not enter service until 2025 (Samuel Cranny-Evans and Jon Hawkes, *Jane's Armoured Fighting Vehicles: Tracked, 2021/2022,* Janes Information Group, Coulsdon (2021), p.12).

it has a lot of forward momentum. The simplest transmissions complete a turn by releasing a clutch on the inside track and then applying a brake to that side. This allows more engine power to be transferred to the outer track, but the inner track continues to generate power as the vehicle is moving. That power must be absorbed and dealt with by the transmission and inner running gear.[2] A slightly improved version introduces two sets of gears to each side of the transmission, allowing the inner track to simply be run at a lower speed than the outer track. This helps mitigate the losses of speed and momentum caused by braking and disengaging the inner track: all very important considering the immense rolling resistance of a tank. These two designs are called clutch-and-brake steering and geared steering, although generally the geared steering method is combined with the clutch-and-brake, allowing both tight skid steering and larger turning circles with the geared method. The T-55 and T-62 followed this route, which makes changing gears quite difficult and makes general fine manoeuvring of the vehicle a challenge. I hope this provides some insight into the complexities of the transmission and its role in the power-pack of a tank.

All of the tanks introduced during this era brought new, much more complex transmissions, and more powerful engines. The technological trends that they set in place proved critical to the modern tank, and whilst the guns and armour have changed, the engines have stayed the same. We have three systems to look at: the T-72, the M1 Abrams, and the Leopard 2. I'm sorry to the fans of British tanks amongst you. The Challenger tanks have a dear spot in my heart, but beyond the suspension system, their mobility is unfortunately of little relevance to the modern tank. So, we will move on and come back to the Challenger family in later chapters.

To start with, there was a curious parallel between NATO and Soviet tank design in this era. On both sides of the Iron Curtain, there were competing schools of thought when it came to tank propulsion: On one hand, there were those favouring the conventional diesel engine, and on the other there were advocates for the gas turbine. The gas turbine ended up being selected for the T-80 and the M1 Abrams, the conventional diesel for the T-72 and Leopard 2.

The engine ultimately selected for the Leopard 2 was the MB 873 Ka-501 from MTU. It is a liquid-cooled 12-cylinder engine that provides a total of 1,479hp at 2,600rpm. It enabled the original Leopard 2s to move at speeds up to 69km/h, which is faster than the Leopard 1, despite a 15-tonne increase in weight. Importantly, the power-pack meant that the Leopard 2 could reverse at speeds up to 31km/h. With those speeds and weight came a considerable level of fuel consumption: around 300 litres per 100km of road travel, which is the smoothest and therefore most efficient driving a tank can conduct. This increases to an average of 500 litres per 100km off-road. The Leopard 2 has big fuel tanks to make this workable and avoid the shortfalls of the Centurion. It carries a total of 1,160 litres of fuel that are divided amongst five separate tanks. The engine is fed from the rear tank, and that tank in turn is fed by the four other tanks which can be found above the tracks and behind the turret. At the base of the power-pack is a 20kW generator, which provides power to two circuits. One circuit provides a lot of power to help run things like the turret drives and stabilizers, while the less powerful circuit is used for the tank's ballistic computer, sights, and other mission systems.[3]

Not long before, the Tagil designers had settled on the V-46 multi-fuel V-12 diesel engine to power the original T-72. It was relatively simple compared to the 5TDF engines produced for the T-64, but had proven itself to be quite reliable. In pre-production trials, a set of 15 T-72s reportedly travelled a total of 11,200km, marching up to 300km per day, with few technical breakdowns.[4] The original V-46 provided 780hp at 2,000rpm, but by the 1980s this engine had been replaced by the 840hp V-84M, giving the 44-tonne T-72B a power-to-weight ratio of 18.9hp/tonne. This was much less than the 27hp/tonne of the original Leopards, but was seen as sufficient for the T-72s of the time. The T-72 carried 1,250 litres of fuel, providing an operational range of around 500km, which is comparable to the Leopard 2, and it had a top speed of 60km/h. The reverse speed for all T-72s is woeful, however, at just 4km/h. This would come to plague T-72 crews in Ukraine, who struggled to reverse out of minefields or dangerous situations quickly enough. Importantly, the V-series engines were fitted with a mechanical supercharger, a technology that had been used in tanks since World War II. A supercharger works like a turbocharger on a car: it simply injects a lot of high-pressure, oxygen-dense air into the engine cylinders, allowing the engine to rapidly produce more energy. It includes an impeller, which is a little like a fan, except that instead of pushing air in a straight line, it sucks air into its centre and throws it out at much higher speeds. The impeller is mechanically connected to the engine and so needs some of the engine's energy to work. However, this means that it can provide an immediate and predictable boost to the vehicle's torque. A turbocharger, in contrast, is powered by the exhaust gases produced by an engine, which means that it needs the engine to reach a certain speed before it can act. This is no good for a stationary tank weighing 40+ tonnes. However, a supercharger is also connected to the engine's speed and revolutions per minute (rpm), so as the rpm of the engine drops, the supercharger's ability to push more air into the engine is also reduced. Overall, using a supercharger is a bit of a balancing act. It works on something called the gross brake mean effective pressure (BMEP), which is basically a term used to describe an engine's power density, and how hard it is working. A higher BMEP means that the engine is efficient but working hard, and may not last as long as a lower BMEP engine. Ultimately, the goal of the supercharger is to improve the BMEP without increasing the size of the engine: something that the T-72's engine does quite well.

Alongside its 780hp, the V-46 could produce 3,089 newton-metres (Nm) of torque, which increased to 3,335 Nm with the introduction of the V-84MS.[5] Torque really gets to the heart of a tank's mobility. The hp of the engine, which is a result of torque × rpm, defines how fast a tank will move and its ability to maintain momentum, but the torque and the amplification of the torque through the transmission define how well it will be able to navigate steep hills and obstacles, as well as in wet soil, or get going from a dead stop. This relates back to the tractive effort discussed in Chapter 3, because torque alone is fairly meaningless. You may remember that a tank's weight creates its own rolling resistance, which must be overcome. So a key factor in engine design is the torque-to-weight ratio and the tractive effort that a tank can produce. Tractive effort is the force that the tank applies to the road or mud it is travelling over and it is a result of the engine torque multiplied by the gear ratios of the transmission and final drives, which is spread over the radius of the drive sprocket. This means that if the tank gets heavier, it is possible to restore its mobility by increasing the gear ratio. In fact, the Leopard 2A7V developed for Germany in the 2020s had a new set of final drives introduced into its running gear. The tank weighed in at 64 tonnes, a significant increase over the Leopard 2A4 it was replacing, and the changed gear ratio enabled the design to maintain its acceleration whilst sacrificing its top speed of 69km/h.[6] For reference, the original Leopard 2 prototype was fitted with an MB 873 Ka-500 engine, which had a turbocharger and actually provided insufficient acceleration compared to the Leopard 1. As a result, MTU increased the bore and stroke of the engine, which brought the torque from 4,300 Nm at 1,950rpm to 4,600 Nm at 1,600rpm.[7] How does this work? Well, the bore is the diameter of the engine cylinders and the stroke is how far the pistons travel up and down with each cycle. Increasing the swept volume effectively added eight additional litres of fuel and oxygen to the engine for every cycle, which means more energy could be released to create more torque at the crankshaft.

One further element to factor in when considering torque is something known as the torque backup or torque rise. The torque backup is something you may have experienced in a car. When you drive a car up a hill, the gravity and the weight of the car will cause the rpm of the engine to drop, which leads to a loss of torque so that the car will begin to slow down. In a typical passenger car you will have to change down gears to increase the gear ratio and restore torque in order to keep climbing. Changing gears in a tank while it is climbing a hill is generally a nerve-wracking thing to do. There are accounts of Centurion drivers who dreaded the intensive process of changing a gear, especially uphill, as the loss of momentum and torque could cause the tank to stall or slip back down the hill. However, an engine that has a strong torque backup will generate a smooth torque profile at most of its rpm range, which means a lot of power is made available even when the engine is at a low speed. If the vehicle climbs a hill and the rpm begins to drop, an ideal torque backup will make *more torque* available as the engine speed drops. This enables the tank (or other armoured vehicle) to maintain momentum and speed as it climbs without the driver necessarily having to change gears. The examples of the T-72 and Leopard 2 help to illustrate how the raw horsepower of an engine can be misleading, and how efforts evolved during this era to help keep pace with the increased weight of the tanks. The focus, it seems, was on increasing torque, rather than hp, which is an effect observable in even the most modern tanks, few if any of which stray above 1,500hp. This selection also reflects the conventional and arguably well-founded wisdom that a diesel engine provides a tank with a preferable combination of torque, power, and fuel efficiency.

So why did the US and Soviet Union opt for something new and exciting in the gas turbines that were eventually picked for the M1 Abrams and the T-80 respectively?

What became the Abrams was designed by a team at the company Chrysler, which is now General Dynamics Land Systems. Chrysler had built the M60, which had made its defence division quite successful at the time. So, there was a lot of pressure on the XM1 team to win the contract. Dr Philip Lett led the team; he had been working on tanks at the company for more than 20 years when the XM1 programme started in 1973. Lett agonized over the design of the Chrysler entry, using Saturdays to make big decisions. One of these was for the engine: Lett had three options to power the tank, a German diesel engine, an American diesel engine, and the gas turbine which had been offered by Avco Lycoming. Avco had been working on a gas turbine for tanks since the 1960s under the MBT-70 programme, and offered it again for XM1. Development had been led by a man called Anselm Franz, who is described by Honeywell as 'a turbine pioneer'.[8] Technically, the US Army wanted an engine that could provide at least twice the power of previous generations. The M60 was powered by the Continental AVDS-1790-2 engine, which provided 750hp. At the time, the required level of power – 1,500hp – was quite significant for a diesel engine. The way that Germany attained the level of torque needed for its Leopard 2 has already been covered. It was essentially low risk from a technological perspective, while the other American diesel was not. It used a variable compression technology to alter the power output of the engine in line with what the vehicle needed.

For some reason, this was seen as a higher technological risk than the gas turbine. Perhaps it was something to do with institutional memory; Chrysler had proposed a concept tank called the TV-8 in the 1950s. The TV-8 was a hybrid electric tank, originally conceptualized with a 300hp V-8 engine providing charge for a generator. But the design road map also considered other engines like a gas turbine and even a nuclear-fuelled vapour cycle engine.[9] Imagine how different this book, and all the others that chart the history of tanks, would have been if the TV-8 had succeeded? Fortunately, it was abandoned, and a more sensible approach prevailed. At the same time, Chrysler's competitor, GM Defense, had also looked at the engines and selected the US diesel with few apparent thoughts for any of the others.[10] Lett, however, eventually picked the gas turbine, despite knowing it was less fuel efficient than the diesel. It is also worth noting that the gas turbine was expected to perform better, but an extensive set of trials based on a point scoring system ended up with both tanks being roughly equal. The GM Defense entry was also cheaper. However, the contract eventually went to Chrysler with the gas turbine. It appears to have been a decision that was at least partially influenced by politics rather than capability, which is a consistent theme in the story of the modern tank.[11] Regardless of why it was picked, the AGT 1500 was born, and it would go on to power more than 10,000 M1 Abrams in service with at least 12 users by mid-2026.

So, what makes the gas turbine so special? Well, in raw performance terms, it offers a consistent torque rise. A chart that compares the AGT 1500 with the MTU 883, a successor to the MB 873, shows that the turbine reaches peak torque of 5,000 Nm at less than 20% of its maximum rpm, which is 3,000. In fact, the faster the AGT 1500 is spinning the lower its torque, but even at its lowest, the torque is still equal to that of the MTU 883. That torque would be multiplied through the gears of the transmission and final drive to produce enough torque at the drive sprocket to drive the tank and overcome the rolling resistance. So what this means in simple terms is that the AGT 1500 should provide a more robust torque reserve that allows the driver to quickly increase torque to overcome an obstacle. But the differences are honestly quite small: both tanks can accelerate to around 32km/h in 7 seconds, and their top speeds are capped at less than 70km/h by the gear ratios in the final drives. The difference in fuel economy is dramatic, however, which we will come to after a short exploration of how the gas turbine works.

Gas turbines are used to power a lot of things. The application you are probably most familiar with is the jet engine. All jet engines are gas turbines, but not all gas turbines are jet engines. The differences lie in what the user does with the power, which is the final stage. The first stage is compression: the engine sucks air in and compresses it. The second stage is combustion, which is where the air is mixed with fuel and ignited. The third stage is where the gases created by that combustion are used to spin the blades of a turbine. After this, the energy can be used for a range of things. Direct the hot gases out the rear of the engine at high speeds and you generate thrust.

Per Newton's Third Law (every action has an equal reaction), pushing gas out the back of the engine drives the plane forwards. Alternatively, the turbine can be connected to a generator to create electricity. In a tank, however, the turbine is connected to a second turbine that captures the energy and turns it into rotation to spin a shaft that is connected to the transmission.

The first gas turbines for tanks had been explored during World War II by Germany, a mantle taken up and subsequently abandoned by British designers in the 1950s. It was pursued by the US from the 1960s leading to the contracts mentioned above in 1976. The engine that Avco Lycoming eventually produced has the following stages and elements:

- **Step 1:** Air is sucked into the low-pressure compressor through air intakes on the deck of the Abrams behind the turret. It passes through a two-stage air filter that is designed to remove particles before it is turned 90 degrees and fed into the low-pressure compressor. This compressor has a set of five fans arranged in a row that are attached to a shaft and driven by their own turbine connected to the engine. The low-pressure compressor reduces the volume taken up by the air before it is passed on to the high-pressure compressor.
- **Step 2:** The compressed air is passed into the high-pressure chamber where it is compressed even further by four additional fans arranged in a row. It then hits an impeller, which spins the hot, dense air at high speed, reaching a compression ratio of 14.5:1. This simply means that the air is now one fourteenth of its original volume. Compressing the air like this increases its temperature.
- **Step 3:** The hot air is then passed into the recuperator. The recuperator takes the hot air from the engine's exhaust and uses it to further heat the air from the high-pressure compressor. To keep the engine compact, the recuperator actually surrounds the output shaft of the engine. When the air enters the recuperator, it has already been heated to 454 degrees Celsius; as it leaves the recuperator and enters the combustion chamber, it will be 566 degrees Celsius.
- **Step 4:** The hot air is now passed into the combustion chamber where it is mixed with fuel and ignited, rapidly reaching

temperatures in excess of 1,000 degrees Celsius and creating a lot of very energetic, expanding gas that must escape the engine.

- **Step 5:** As it leaves the engine, the gas passes by three turbines: the low- and high-pressure turbines which power the pressure chambers, and the power turbine, which is connected to the output shaft. The power turbine is also fitted with variable angle stators, which are blades designed to alter the direction of flow of the air from the high-pressure combustion chamber before it reaches the power turbine. These are an important part of the AGT 1500, because without them the engine would make very inefficient use of its fuel at low and high ranges. The stators ensure that the air hits the power turbine in an optimal pattern in both cases so that it can provide the power needed on demand. That power is significant. The power turbine can reach an incredible 22,500rpm – that's 375 revolutions per second. So, the output shaft is connected to a reduction gear, which takes that 22,500rpm down to a more manageable 3,000rpm before joining the transmission.[12]

As the gases are finally expelled from the engine via the exhaust, they are extremely hot. Former US Marines have told me those gases can strip paint from a car, or give a nice crust to a steak, depending on how enterprising the marines are. But the design is quite compact and light compared to the MB 873 Ka-501. The AGT 1500 and MB 873 Ka-501 are compared in Table 2. Those figures, especially the total volume, help to demonstrate the trade-offs in engine selection. The gas turbine takes up much less space than the diesel engine, but both can provide similar overall performance.

TABLE 2 Comparison of AGT 1500 and MB 873 Ka-501

Specification	*AGT 1500*	*MB 873 Ka-501*
Length	1,629mm	1,801mm
Width	991mm	1,975mm
Height	807mm	1,030mm
Volume	1.3m^3	3.6m^3
Dry weight	1,134kg	2,220kg

Despite the deal between Rumsfeld and Leber in 1976, as well as the apparently similar performance, Germany appears to have refused to standardize around the AGT 1500. There are some very good reasons for that. Perhaps the most obvious is fuel consumption. While it is fun to imagine tanks constantly moving around the countryside, charging into battle with other tank formations and capturing towns, they actually spend most of their time waiting. If a tank formation is close to the enemy, or it needs the use of its sensors and radios, it will have to run its engines to power all of those things. Gas turbines need to maintain their very high speeds even when at idle, so fuel consumption can reach 50 litres per hour, in the case of the T-80. This proved challenging when the Russians deployed their T-80s to Chechnya in 1994, as the crews supposedly did not realize that their tanks would consume so much fuel without moving. Matters are made worse when the tanks advance, and the US experience during the 1991 Gulf War is often used as an example of this. The US Army's M1A1s spent 70% of their time idling and had to be refuelled every 3–5 hours.[13] Three brigades from the US 1st Division advanced so far, and so quickly, that they outstripped the ability of their supporting infrastructure to resupply them. The tanks needed to be refuelled three times per day, and each battalion had 12 Heavy Expanded Mobility Tactical Trucks (HEMTT), each carrying 2,500 gallons (9,464 litres) of fuel. Those trucks had to race hundreds of kilometres with their fuel, replenish their battalion and then make their way back to the rear echelons, find a logistics point, and refuel themselves before heading back to meet up with their battalion. As a result of this and the distances involved, it became increasingly difficult for the US armour to keep itself fuelled, and by 27 February, just four days after the offensive had started, all units in the 1st Armoured Division were reporting severe fuel shortages.[14] It is also worthwhile comparing the Abrams to its peer, the Leopard 2. Taking a US armoured division with 350 tanks as the base unit, an Abrams-equipped formation would require 667,450 litres of fuel to travel 426km, assuming that it could attain a constant speed on a road and did not spend any time idling. For 350 Leopard 2s to travel the exact same distance, they would need just 325,309 litres of fuel, and it is important to emphasize that in this hypothetical scenario, the Leopards would get there with 300 litres of fuel still available. The Abrams would be empty.

Despite these challenges, the US deployed 1,772 M1A1s and M1A1HAs (HA stands for heavy armour: they carried depleted uranium armour), and managed to attain a 90% readiness rate throughout the 100-day ground war. This is equally held forth as evidence of the AGT 1500's reliability. However, it is worth noting, as some US reports do, that many of those tanks were new-builds or with very low mileage. Spare parts from Europe were rushed to the theatre, enabling frequent maintenance and replacement of anything proving troublesome. Heavy equipment transports, which are just large trucks with enough power to carry a tank on a trailer, were borrowed from allies to carry the Abrams fleet and limit the wear and tear caused by the vehicles moving themselves.[15] Similarly, the British 1st Armoured Division managed to reach an average availability rate of 94% between 20 February and 4 March; however, that was achieved by cannibalizing most of the UK's European fleet, and through an immense effort from the Royal Electrical and Mechanical Engineers.[16] Finally, the inability of Iraqi forces to harass and pressure American units during their advance meant that the crews could regularly stop to refuel and clean the air filters. So, the readiness level was impressive, but it was also the result of a unique set of circumstances.

Fast forward to the 2000s, and the Iraqi Army had become a major user of the Abrams. It was reliant upon General Dynamics for the maintenance of its M1A1 Abrams fleet under a 2012 contract signed by the US Army. The tanks were vital during the fight against Islamic State of Iraq and Syria (ISIS), but nine vehicles had been given to militias or were captured by ISIS, leading General Dynamics to withdraw its maintenance support in December 2017.[17] Soon after, many of the Iraqi M1A1s were out of action because of breakdowns or battle damage. Even when the support was still operational, during the battle for the town of Hit in March 2016, two out of three M1s broke down before they could contribute to the offensive.[18] In fairness to the M1 Abrams family, tank maintenance is difficult and requires a lot of experience and preparation. The Iraqi forces eventually moved towards the T-90 as an alternative to their US tanks. But the incident helps illustrate that there is certainly a need for extensive support and maintenance for the M1 Abrams, and that in some scenarios only the US can meet those needs at any kind of scale. In the same vein, the immense fuel consumption and subsequent resupply challenges were also a result of the unique circumstances in the Gulf during 1991. It would be rare for tanks to advance so consistently over so many hundreds of kilometres, vastly outstripping their supply chains.

This does not mean that gas turbines do not require absurd amounts of fuel if they are not advancing, but it does mean that the friction introduced by logistics trucks having to drive 400km to conduct a single resupply may not be universal. Interestingly, the Soviet choice of the GTD 1000 is supposedly influenced by the assumption that they would be able advance relatively free of the need to await refuelling trucks in a war with NATO. It was assumed that the gas turbine's ability to run off any fuel would enable Soviet T-80s to race through Europe, scavenging fuel as they went, and preventing NATO from rolling back its advance.

The AGT 1500 and gas turbines in general have many downsides, but they also provide advantages compared to a diesel. One of these, which was particularly valuable to the Soviets, is the ability of a gas turbine to start in extreme cold. This led to the modernized T-80, the T-80BVM, being issued to Russia's Arctic warfare brigades. They also produce a lot of their torque at lower engine ranges, which makes their acceleration and movement around a battlefield quicker. This has value against things like an ATGM but also in repositioning forces during urban combat to take advantage of adversary weaknesses or to plug gaps. Gas turbines also tend to have a smaller volume than a diesel power-pack, which can help reduce the overall size of the vehicle. The Soviet designers certainly embraced this, and the T-80 came in at a similar weight to the T-72. The US, however, opted for a lot more armour and ammunition, but all of this increased weight also needed innovations in the transmissions, which take the power of the engine and turn it into rotational force at the drive sprocket.

Transmissions were also key and underwent some real improvements during the 1970s and 80s. This is an often underappreciated element of tank design. Guns are exciting, and the bigger the better. Armour is mysterious, it gives rise to intrigue and speculation that will never be satisfied. But transmissions are … complicated. The engineering behind them is extensive, the words used to describe that engineering are unfamiliar, and the role they perform is hard to appreciate if the engineering is made opaque through language. So, in this section, we will set out to make sense of tank transmissions, and there is an important reason for this. The weight of tanks has trended upwards, ever since 1945 and in spite of even the Soviet Union's best efforts. Table 3 provides in-service dates for Soviet and NATO tanks since the 1940s, reflecting the increase in weights of base models.

TABLE 3 Tank weights over time

Tank	*Weight*	*In service date*
Centurion	49 tonnes	1945
M48 Patton	45 tonnes	1952
T-55	36 tonnes	1958
Leopard 1	40 tonnes	1965
Chieftain	55 tonnes	1966
T-72	41 tonnes	1973
Leopard 2	55 tonnes	1979
M1 Abrams	54 tonnes	1980
Challenger 1	62 tonnes	1983

In percentage terms, the Soviets increased vehicle weight by around 14% between the T-55 and the T-72, not including the addition of ERA. The shift from the M48 to the M1 Abrams represented a 20% increase in weight, and the Leopard 1 to Leopard 2 marked a 37% increase. Increasing the weight of a tank places considerable additional strain on the transmission. This can include increased heat as the added weight increases friction between the components that make the transmission work. There is of course a serious increase in torque stress. Logically, the transmission has a lot more weight to move and greater rolling resistance to overcome, which it does by transferring more power to the drive sprocket. However, it is the gear teeth inside the transmission that must withstand that pressure. Turning adds further engineering complications because the transmission still has to manage the difference in speed between the interior and exterior tracks, but with much greater kinetic energy in the system. Take the Leopard 1 and Leopard 2 for comparison. At 40km/h, the Leopard 1 would have kinetic energy of around 2.47 MJ, whereas the Leopard 2 comes in at 3.4 MJ. This increase in energy is actually proportional to the weight increase of the vehicles, and it is an important number to understand because, in the case of the Leopard tanks, it means the transmission must be able to dissipate 37% more energy when braking or turning. That additional energy, which is close to 1 million joules, will be turned into heat. To give you some idea of what this means, one megajoule, or 1 million joules, is roughly enough energy to boil

3 litres of water in a kettle, or it would increase the temperature of 100kg of steel by 21 degrees Celsius. Note that this is only for the difference in energy between the two tanks: all of the kinetic energy of the Leopard 2 at 40km/h would be sufficient to heat that same steel to 73 degrees Celsius.

To understand why this happens, we can take a short (I promise it will be short) detour into the laws of thermodynamics. The first law of thermodynamics basically states that energy cannot be created or destroyed, only transformed. This leads to an energy chain for tanks (and other vehicles), that looks something like the following:

- Chemical energy is used in the burning of fuel, which also creates engine heat that must be taken away from the vehicle.
- That fuel is turned into kinetic energy – the movement of the tank – by the power-pack and running gear.
- The tracks, roadwheels, and transmission convert that energy into heat through friction.
- The tank's cooling system pushes that heat out of the tank.

In a nutshell, the diesel or jet fuel becomes heat through several mechanisms that must be taken away from the vehicle. The heavier the vehicle, the greater the energy that must be taken away. This all means that transmissions for larger vehicles needed to be more robust than their smaller predecessors. As has already been mentioned, it is quite easy to make a more powerful engine to cope with a vehicle's additional weight, but if the transmission can't keep up, there is no point adding a new engine.

But this is a problem. The tanks needed to be heavier, they needed more armour and a bigger gun to remain useful. So, transmissions had to evolve in order to accommodate this growth in weight. If they had not done this, then maybe tanks would have stuck at the low end of 40 tonnes, or would have been confined to relatively slow movements like the Centurion. The designers in Germany, the US, and the USSR took slightly different approaches to solving this problem. Let's start with the Leopard 2 and its Renk HSWL 354. The HSWL 354 entered development in the mid-1960s, specifically for the Leopard 2, according to Ogorkiewicz.[19] It was a 'double differential system with a split-path hydrostatic-cum-hydrodynamic steering drive, as well as a two-stage, two-phase torque converter with a lock-up clutch and epicyclic propulsion gears providing four forward and two reverse speeds'.[20] Makes perfect sense, right? Here, Ogorkiewicz is listing the key elements of the Leopard 2 transmission that enabled the tank to function. The double differential is the part of the transmission that enables turning. It simply means that the speed to both tracks can be controlled, and the power maintained. The split-path hydrostatic-cum-hydrodynamic steering drive, meanwhile, uses two different forms of fluid control. Hydrostatic basically means that power is transmitted using the static pressure of a confined fluid. It allows for very fine adjustments to track speed because the pressure applied to the oil in the system can be varied almost infinitely. This means it can give maximum torque straight away, and so it is good for fine adjustments at relatively low speeds. But tanks and tank crews don't want to drive slowly all of the time, and driving quickly creates a lot of shocks and forces that the transmission has to absorb. That is where the hydrodynamic system comes in: it acts as a part of the torque converter for moving, and the torque retarder for stopping. Unlike hydrostatic, the oil is allowed to move in a hydrodynamic system; that movement can be used either to increase the torque in the gear box by extracting additional energy from the engine, or to slow the tracks down by introducing drag.

Propulsion is provided by the two-phase torque converter with a lock-up clutch and epicyclic propulsion gears. In order, the torque converter uses fluid to multiply the torque generated by the engine, which helps the gears to smoothly accelerate the tank from a dead stop. The lock-up clutch comes into play once the tank has reached a cruising speed. When the tank starts, the crankshaft, which takes energy from the engine, is not physically connected to the transmission. Instead, the torque converter transmits the power of the rotation of the crankshaft to the gear box and final drives through the oil. There is an impeller, essentially a fan that spins the oil at the speed of the engine, attached to the crankshaft. As the impeller spins the oil, some of the oil is thrown into the turbine that is attached to the transmission's gears. This means that at low speeds, such as when the tank is starting or climbing a hill, there is no mechanical connection between the engine and the transmission. This is because of something called slip. Slip describes the difference in speed between the engine, which is measured in revolutions per minute (rpm), and the turbine. The oil is transmitted at incredible speeds, but the turbine will always lag, which means that if the engine is cycling at 2,000rpm, the turbine might only be operating at 1,500rpm. That difference is the slip, and it is useful because it means that the oil is hitting the turbine with more power, which allows for smoother acceleration. It also means that if there is a sudden stop, the kinetic energy is absorbed by the liquid, rather than mechanical components. However, coming back to the first law of thermodynamics, you may notice that there is an inefficiency here. No system can be 100% efficient in terms of energy transformations. So that must mean that some of the energy generated by the burning of fuel in the engine is transformed into heat. That all happens in the fluid in the torque converter, which must be taken away through the cooling system. And to come back to the lock-up clutch and its role in this system: this fluid transfer of power and slip is essential for getting the tank going in high load, low speed scenarios such as climbing an obstacle, or starting from a dead stop. Once it is up to speed, the lock-up clutch slams the turbine and impeller into each other, creating a mechanical connection between the engine and transmission. This mechanical connection is more efficient at converting the engine's energy into propulsion, with less energy lost to heat.

Still with me? I hope so, because we have one more component of the HSWL 354 to explore, and that is the planetary gears. Planetary gears get their name because they consist of three core components. The centre component is called the sun gear; the other components, the planet gears, orbit the sun gear; and then there is the ring gear, which surrounds them all with teeth on the inside. You may know how the gear box in a car works, but just in case, it very simply relies on you moving gears into and out of contact with the input shaft coming from the engine to create movement. The gear box will start with a larger gear, to generate the torque to get the vehicle moving, and gradually reduce the gear sizes as the speed increases. If you were to use the same type of system in a Leopard 2, it would be enormous and unworkable. So, planetary gears are used because they take up less space. Instead of moving gears into and out of contact with the input shaft, planetary gears change ratio and direction by holding different parts of the system still. For example, if the ring gear is held stationary, which is done through a clutch or similar, the sun gear and planet carrier are left moving, which provides the low gears and a lot of torque. This configuration has a number of benefits, including the compact space which allows the transmission to be built as a single block that spans the width of the tank at the rear. It also means that the power and weight of the tank are carried by multiple sets of teeth, as opposed to one set, which would be the case with a more conventional friction clutch. And finally, the teeth of a planetary gear are said to be in mesh, which just means that they are constantly engaged, eliminating the possibility of the driver grinding the gears into each other.

Once the engine's energy has reached the transmission, it is moving quite fast, but that speed needs to be turned into torque, which is the job of the final drives. The final drives are the last set of gears involved in the powertrain and they are attached to the transmission and the drive sprocket. Another set of planetary gears inside the final drives is used to slow the high-speed input from the transmission, which causes the torque to increase at the drive sprocket. If the transmission were connected directly to the drive sprockets, it would be able to spin very fast, but would lack the torque to drive the sprocket and tracks. In essence, the final drives increase the distance between the engine and the drive sprockets, which increases the torque. This also brings us to one final consideration in tank design, and that is the question of horsepower. We have already covered how much horsepower the Leopard 2's engine produces, but that number is a bit misleading. The output of the MB 873 Ka-501 engine is stated to be 1,500hp, but this actually refers to the engine's tested output when it is not connected to *anything*. But a truer measure of a tank's power is often referred to as the hp at the sprocket. In the case of the Leopard 2, the MB 873 has to power the cooling fans for the engine, the alternator to power the computers and stabilizers that enable the tank to fight, and also the transmission and its cooling. All of this before any of the engine's power is transferred to the ground by the drive sprocket and tracks. This means that a more efficient transmission can dramatically increase the power available at the sprocket, which in turn increases the torque available to the tank. So, measuring torque at the sprocket is thought to be a more accurate reflection of a tank's mobility. This does not mean that the power-to-weight ratio is useless, it still has purpose, but should be seen for the general sentiment that it is, rather than a cutting insight into the ability of a tank to navigate difficult terrain.

According to Ogorkiewicz, the HSWL 354 was one of the more complex transmissions to be fitted to a tank. And I think the description above supports that. However, he also points out that key elements of the design can be found in most tanks: 'With the exception of the transmissions of Soviet designed tanks, they all have two-phase torque converters with lock-up clutches, epicyclic trains of propulsion gears and double differential steering systems.'[21] So, that explains the key role that transmissions and new engines played in getting heavier tanks into service in the 1970s and 80s. Without those developments and the engineering that went into them, the Soviet and NATO fleets would have looked very different, as would the modern tank. It is also worth noting that the AGT 1500 continues to power the Abrams, despite several attempts to replace it with a diesel power-pack from MTU. And it is also noteworthy that despite MTU developing several power-packs that offer greater performance than the MB 873 Ka-501, this engine remains the powerhouse of German armour. With a surge in orders for newbuild Leopard 2s after 2022, KNDS Germany placed an order for 300 power-packs including the MB 873 with Rolls-Royce (the parent company of MTU) in December 2025.[22] This shows the extent to which the 1970s and 80s shaped the modern tank. A few contenders would appear in the 2000s with new designs and thoughts on mobility; we will return to them in the next era. But the core element was about ensuring requisite mobility with the right level of protection, which returns once more to the core role of a tank and mission success. By the 1970s and 80s, tanks needed a lot more armour to ensure that they could achieve their intended mission. A bigger gun was also necessary, for NATO at least, to improve the chances of success when that mission involved enemy armour. But all of this together increased vehicle size, leading to the need for new engines and transmissions to get them to where they needed to go.

Perhaps of equal importance during this era was the development of mission systems, where the introduction of thermal imaging took the lethality and utility of tanks to a new level as they could meaningfully fight in the dark. Of course, the collapse of the USSR from 1989 to 1991 precluded the possibility of the T-72 meeting an M1 Abrams across the imaginary Fulda Gap, but conflict in the Middle East saw to it that the two branches of tank evolution would meet sooner or later. They often met in the dark, through grainy first generation thermal imagers.

Chapter 15

The West takes the lead

As British soldiers deployed to Kuwait in 1990 ahead of Operation *Desert Storm*, they took with them the new Challenger 1, an evolution of the Chieftain main battle tank that had entered service in 1967. The tank had a mixed reputation; its lacklustre performance in the 1987 Canadian Army Tank Shoot had cast doubt on its ability to fight a war. But it did offer something that Chieftain did not – a thermal sight. The Thermal Observation and Gunnery System (TOGS) had been designed and integrated by a company called Barr and Stroud (now part of Thales) from 1983. The L11A5 rifled main gun was known to be relatively effective with its APFSDS-T and HESH rounds, out to 1,200m.

Capt Tim Purbrick commanded a troop of Challenger Main Battle Tanks during the 1991 Gulf War. On 26 February 1991, his troop had moved to Objective ZINC and spent the morning watching a Multiple Launch Rocket System (MLRS) barrage fall on Iraqi positions. They knew there were several battalions of tanks ahead of them, most likely T-55s or T-62s. The day before, the British 1st Armoured Division had mauled Iraq's 48th Infantry Division, capturing its commander, and the barrage that Capt Purbrick observed was probably elements of the largest British artillery bombardment since World War II. His crew settled down for some rest, and the second-in-command and his tank began digging scrapes for the troop's tanks. Purbrick took up position in his turret and started scanning:

> I took the first watch scanning the horizon, visually and thermally, flicking between the two systems. I used the commander's grip switch [a pistol grip used to rotate the turret], generally a 90 degree or wider

> arc in front of your tank. I had been scanning for 10 or 15 minutes ... When suddenly, in the distance I started picking up hot spots on the thermal sight. What the hell were they? They were moving from north to south and then, it appeared, away to the east. At the range they were and with the degraded sight picture, I couldn't tell what they were. But they were targets.[1]

Purbrick and his troops sprang into action, firing HESH and APFSDS rounds at the distant dots on their TOGS sights. That engagement had little success; the Iraqi vehicles were a long way away. But the next morning, they found more T-55s to their front, hidden behind sand berms. They set about engaging them, '"HESH tank, on" from me,' Purbrick shouted to his gunner, Gus, and loader, Pete. Purbrick gave the order to fire, which in a British tank gives the gunner permission to engage the target. Using a trigger on his control panel, the gunner first fired a laser range finder at the target, which adjusted the elevation of the immense L11A5 120mm rifled gun. The loaded round was a high-explosive squash head, which they fired at the berm protecting the Iraqi tank. 'Stop loading, load FIN,' Purbrick ordered, signalling that it was time to fire one of the recently adopted L23A1 tungsten carbide APFSDS rounds. It took three shots to observe an effect; they were shooting at a tank that was 3,600m away, which is a lot further than the Challenger 1 was designed to shoot.

Purbrick continued:

> The tank recoiled. Through the smoke and obscuration of the firing came a small lightning flash. 'Target' called Gus. The white flash indicated that the tungsten of the FIN round had struck the metal of the enemy tank. The flash was like a lightning strike. It shone through the smoke and explosion of the cloud of dust and explosives from our tank firing. This third round fired at the enemy tank had entered through its front glacis plate and exited vertically through the gear box at the rear of the vehicle, igniting the tank's bombload and removing its turret. 'Target Stop' called Gus.*

*When British tank crews have finished engaging a target, they will say a variation of 'Target stopped'. Captain Purbrick's gunner used 'Target stop', but other current serving crews state it is 'Target stopped'.

Versions of this story were repeated hundreds of times during the Gulf War. NATO's most advanced tanks were pitted against the earlier Soviet models that had essentially driven their development. As a result, tanks that could be defeated by a Centurion or M60 were being engaged by platforms that were two or three evolutions more advanced. From a pure armament and armour perspective, it was very one-sided. It is fair to say that if the Challenger 1s of 17th/21st Lancers had come close enough to an Iraqi T-62, they would have faced some risk, especially from the sides. But at the ranges Purbrick and his crews were firing from, there really was little hope for the Iraqi crews. Some who survived later told US personnel that they were confined to firing at muzzle flashes, which is not a recipe for success. Arguably, the dominance of the Coalition was a result of the mission systems that the tanks carried, including thermal imaging and laser range finders in particular. Together, the mission systems enabled the crew to fully exploit the range of their 120mm guns, a trend which has continued into the modern tank.

The introduction of thermal imaging is really where the West began to pull ahead of the Soviets. It was a lead that they would maintain and develop as the collapse of the Soviet Union put a significant damper on Russian tank development for some time. The T-90A, introduced in the early 1990s, did bring a thermal imager to the Russian Ground Forces, but its distribution was limited to that platform until the more widespread introduction of the T-72B3 from 2013. Thermal imaging was a big deal because it meant that at night a tank crew could see targets at range, even if they were somewhat camouflaged. It has since become an essential feature of every modern tank, whether Russian, Chinese, German, American, or Korean. Most sights now feature two channels: a very powerful day camera, and a thermal imaging channel that the commander can change between as required. However, the technology was not quite so refined as British and American troops advanced into Kuwait in 1991. Let's start with the Challenger 1.

The Challenger 1's Thermal Observation and Gunnery System (TOGS) had been designed and integrated by Barr and Stroud, which had supplied optics for the first British submarine. While most modern sights are built into the top of the turret roof, the TOGS was installed in a barbette (an armoured box) on the right-hand side of the turret; it accompanied the commander's sight that was located in his cupola on the right of the turret, and the gunner's laser range finder and sight, which were just ahead of the commander's cupola in a small recess in the turret. The Challenger turret was based on the Chieftain's and consisted of a steel core structure to which Chobham packs were added with an outer layer of cosmetic steel giving the turret its angular, blocky appearance.[2] The TOGS barbette added to this appearance. The commander's sight was called the No. 39; it provided a ×1 and ×10 view with a graticule pattern injected from the gunner's sight. This meant that the commander could only engage targets using his optical sights when his cupola was in a certain position. The TOGS used a system called the Thermal Imaging Sensor Head (TISH), which was the thermal imaging provider. TISH was connected to something called the Computerized Sighting System, which allowed both the commander and gunner to conduct engagements. They would, however, scan for targets using their optical sights set at a 1× magnification. This gave them the widest view of the area in front of them and the best chance of spotting a target. You can experience this for yourself using a smartphone if you have one. Open the camera and zoom in as much as possible on a car or object in the distance: it will feel as though you are looking at the world through a drinking straw; zoom out and you will be able to see much more, but in less detail. Once an object had been detected, the crew might switch to TOGS if they weren't already using it to carry out the engagement.

This is exactly what Captain Purbrick was doing on 26 February 1991. He had a pistol grip controller to operate the turret, which included the functionality to switch between thermal and optical imaging. However, he had to rotate the turret to scan the area in front of him; this would become an area of improvement for the generation of tanks that followed the Challenger 1 and M1A1. If the commander spotted a target, he would hand the engagement over to the gunner, who had control of the laser range finder, with an order like, 'FIN tank, on'. The gunner and loader would respond to all three words of this command. FIN means APFSDS, so the loader would insert an APFSDS followed by a bag charge into the breech of the gun before grabbing another round ready to go. The gunner would also toggle a switch on his grip to set the laser range finder to the main gun, rather than the coaxial machine gun. The word 'on' means that the commander has placed the aiming graticule somewhat close to the target and the gunner will complete a more precise laying in the next phase of the engagement. The gunner adjusts the aim until the aiming dot on the sight is over the centre of mass of the enemy tank; he will then press a button to fire the laser range finder at the target. He will also press a button for autolay, which will allow the ballistic computer and gun control equipment to automatically adjust the elevation of the gun and orientation of the turret to give the best chance of a hit. Once the gunner has found the target and the loader has loaded the gun, the commander gives the order 'FIRE'.[3] The gunner is then free to fire the gun declaring 'firing NOW', as he does so. If he has hit the target, he will report 'Target', and if the target was destroyed the commander will say 'Target Stopped – check MRS [muzzle reference system]'.[4]

This whole process could be completed in a matter of seconds, but the really key elements are the TOGS, which allowed the crew to find targets in low light conditions, the laser range finder, which provided a much more accurate indication of the range to the target, and the gun control equipment, which could automatically bring all of those inputs together to generate a firing solution. So, instead of the gunner having to manually adjust the elevation of the gun as was the case with previous tanks, the computer does it for him, taking into account things like the temperature of the ammunition, weather conditions, and data from the muzzle reference sensor at the end of the barrel. In effect, the gunner controls the sight and turret, the computer controls the gun. A similar engagement method had also been integrated into the M1A1. This made the Challenger 1 and Abrams more accurate and lethal, especially when firing on the move or in engagements with multiple targets simultaneously. The accuracy of the Challenger 1 with its aging L11 A5 rifled gun is perhaps best demonstrated through some of its successful engagements during the Gulf War. Captain Purbrick's gunner, Gus, is understood to have engaged a target, believed to be a fuel truck, at a range of 4,700m with an L23A1 tungsten APFSDS, as well as a T-55 at 3,600m – this was three times what was thought possible. The longer-range shot was the first round Gus fired at that target.[5] The M1 Abrams is believed to be capable of similarly accurate results using its fire control system. This is a really crucial element of this era. From the 1980s to 2025, the Rh120 has remained the primary main armament for the M1 Abrams and Leopard 2, which are together used by more than 30 nations, and so it represents the bulk of non-Soviet tank armament in the world. However, without an effective fire control system, all of these tanks would be far less effective than they are.

Let's start by looking at thermal imaging and the technology that made it possible. You may have heard that during the Cold War, it was the military that developed a lot of the new technologies that benefited the commercial world. The internet is the most prominent example, as is satellite aided navigation. The US military, in particular, was exceedingly well-funded during the Cold War, and able to invest vast sums into research and development. Thermal imaging is another technological development that came out of the US military and ended up in the commercial world. The technology had been through several revisions by the time that the Gulf War began, but most histories of thermal imaging start with the discovery of the infrared spectrum, which is commonly attributed to a man called Sir William Herschel. Herschel was a Royal Astronomer who worked for England's King George III; he had discovered the planet Uranus, and later set out to find a glass that could let him study the sun through a telescope by reducing the intensity of the light. In 1800, he found that some colours of glass on his telescope heated up a lot more than others, so he set out to find out why. Using a prism to separate the sun's light into its component colours, he found that the temperature increased as the colours approached red, but that the light's peak temperature was beyond the end of the visible light. So, he called this part of the electromagnetic spectrum the 'thermometrical spectrum', and referred to infrared as 'dark heat'.[6] This dark energy would later become known as infrared radiation, and it is part of the electromagnetic spectrum, which means it is another form of light.

The name includes the Latin word 'infra', which means below. That is because infrared radiation sits below or just next to the colour red. We cannot see infrared, but we can feel it in the form of heat. Literally everything emits infrared radiation, even the ice cubes in your freezer and your household radiators. However, the colder an object is, the longer its wavelengths are and the further it is from visible light. Conversely, as an object gets hotter, its wavelengths shorten. Heat an object up enough, and it will enter into the visible light part of the spectrum and glow a dull red. You may remember infrared from Chapter 8, in which we explored the use of infrared illumination combined with specialized goggles or sights to see at night in a limited fashion. Well, thermal imaging and infrared night vision are both in the same neighbourhood, but they might as well be worlds apart. Infrared night vision, such as that used on Centurions, Chieftains, T-55s, and pretty much every Cold War tank, relies on an infrared light to bounce off an object so that it can be seen. In that way, the night vision devices used prior to thermal imaging were essentially a very sensitive eye that depended on a source of light to detect and recognize an object. This had downsides; if the enemy were near and using their own night vision, they would see infrared lamps. Thermal imaging, however, detects the radiation that is emitted by an object, rather than that which is bouncing off it.

Fast forward to 1880 and the first bolometer was invented, by Samuel P. Langley, who worked at the Allegheny Observatory of the Western University of Pennsylvania. A bolometer was a microscopic thermometer designed to detect minute changes in temperature. As the material inside the bolometer heats up, its electrical resistance changes and that change is measured. It was supposedly used to detect the heat of a cow from 400m. This wasn't why Langley developed the bolometer, however; he wanted to measure the temperature of the sun and moon, but needed the cow to prove that his technology worked.[7] The next big step came from a Hungarian man named Kálmán Tihanyi (pronounced *Tee-hahn-yee*). You might know Tihanyi because he has also been recognized as one of the pivotal contributors to the development of early television. His inventions helped overcome the challenge of getting tens of thousands of pixels to load onto a screen in fractions of a second. One competing design took 12 minutes to transmit a 10,000-pixel image of a face, which is 0.03 seconds per pixel. Tihanyi's discovery, which became the basis for cathode ray tubes, could theoretically do the same in '1/400,000,000th of a second', he wrote in a 1925 article.[8] But that isn't why he has made it to this book; in 1929, Tihanyi was under contract to the UK's Air Ministry to develop an infrared camera for air defence and possibly to do some work on fire control systems for tanks. He is believed to have developed some form of active infrared imaging, which built upon the cathode ray tube technologies he had developed. As an aside, he also worked on a remotely operated aircraft at the same time.

A range of further developments occurred between the 1940s and 1980s, all building on Langley's discovery in the 1880s and Tihanyi's in the 1920s. By the 1940s, the US had developed a form of thermal imager that was built into the belly of a plane and used line scanning to create an image. These imagers used a detector made out of lead sulfide as a conductor. In a nutshell, a material painted with lead sulfide was wired into an electrical circuit with a lightbulb. Lead sulfide is bad at conducting electricity, but when thermal radiation hits it, its electrons loosen up and it suddenly conducts it more effectively. So, when placed within a circuit, it would respond to detected heat, giving the lightbulb the energy it needed to portray that heat onto a film. This film passed automatically past the bulb at a speed synchronized with that of the aircraft. The technique was incredibly slow, taking up to an hour to produce a single image, and the images had to be processed from a 70mm film in a similar fashion to traditional photos.[9] This meant that they were not available in real time. These early thermal imagers were known as map scanners, and seem to have been developed around 1947; they were critical to the development of tank-relevant thermal imaging. That importance comes from another drawback of lead sulfide, which is that it is only really effective at detecting short-wave infrared radiation. Think back to Herschel's original discovery and the definition of the infrared spectrum. The shorter the wavelength the hotter an object is, and an object emitting short-wave infrared radiation is very, *very* hot, around 600 degrees Celsius in fact. So, how could a lead sulfide detector see anything? Well, they had to be cooled, sometimes with liquid nitrogen or liquid helium, down to -200 degrees Celsius, which made them more sensitive to cooler objects. But the US military wanted to see people and things like missile launch sites. So, companies like Texas Instruments went to work on new detector materials that could detect mid- and long-wave infrared instead.

The US Army and others invested heavily in these developments, but as is often the case, it took a war to accelerate them. That came in the form of the Vietnam War, and Forward Looking Infrared (FLIR). You may have realized that the problem with early thermal imaging is that it was not instant; it was essentially thermal photography rather than a thermal camera, which is what the crew of an M60 tank would need to engage a T-62 on the plains of Europe. The US Army developed what is thought to be the first 'instant' FLIR device in 1960 through funding awarded to the Perkin-Elmer Corporation. This device used a small detector made of indium antimonide, which scanned the 5-degree field of view in a spiral. It was technically instantaneous – the users did not need to go and process any film – but it had a frame rate of 5 Hz.[10] This means that the detector would finish painting a complete picture of its field of view five times per second – which sounds like a lot, especially compared to the one picture per 12 minute framerate that Kálmán was working to address. But the problem is that the human eye and brain only start to see smooth motion at 15 Hz, and your computer monitor runs at 60 Hz, which creates a smooth and constant image. At 5 Hz the image would flicker quite significantly, with your brain and eye seeing each new image as it loaded on the screen. And here a cathode ray tube (CRT) came in. By painting the CRT with chemicals, it was able to store the charge of the captured light (phosphors), which meant that the illuminated parts of the screen would continue glowing until the next image was created 0.2 seconds later. This made the invention workable for humans, but it did not make it to Vietnam. In Vietnam, the US was facing the Viet Cong; these fighters had a penchant for operating at night, which reduced the US and South Vietnamese advantage in firepower, and they made good use of camouflage.

However, the first primary use for thermal imaging was in the line scanners, despite the huge lag between the capturing of the images and the striking of targets. The key developments in line scanners during the Vietnam War included better detector material and improved lamps to illuminate the film, as well as real time processing of the film on board. Doing this reduced the time from detection to targeting from 5–6 hours down to a few minutes. Yes, the US military and others have been focused on reducing the time between reconnaissance and strike for more than 60 years now. And yet, even this development could not provide real-time targeting: the pilots needed a thermal imager that could maintain contact with a target all the way through to an engagement, and this led to the first FLIR imager in 1964. It was an improvement over the line mappers because it looked, as the name suggests, forwards, rather than down. It was by no means suitable for a tank; it weighed 272kg and required 1,000 W of energy to work. But it provided a 50 Hz frame rate in long-wave infrared, the energy that humans emit. It enabled US pilots in a C-47 that had been converted to operate as a gunship in 1965 to engage concealed Viet Cong soldiers at night and through the forest canopy.[11] The success of thermal imaging during the Vietnam War led to further development, reducing the size and weight of the systems, as well as the resolution of the imagery that they produced. Resolution is a key element of thermal imager design, which we will return to later.

The US Army had noticed the Air Force's success and started its own programme in thermal imager development, initially focusing on a hand-held system and a seeker for the Dragon missile. These efforts, undertaken by the Army's Night Vision Laboratory (NVL), were not pursued much further. But the NVL and Texas Instruments worked together to develop a common module for FLIR imagers, which helped reduce the size of the imagers and their cost quite significantly by the 1970s. This meant that the TOW anti-tank missile launcher could be provided with a thermal sight and the M60A3 could too. By this stage, there were many companies in the West working on thermal imaging and detector materials, as well as how to cool the imagers and increase the sharpness of their imagery. The UK had its own line of development under an engineer called Tom Elliot at the Royal Radar Establishment in Malvern. And the French too began developing some very advanced thermal imaging systems. The history is long and complex with multiple simultaneous developments, and there are points where the efforts of different companies converged and diverged. If you would like to read further into it, I can recommend the DSIAC report by Teague and Schmieder, which is included in the footnotes. But, for the time being, it is enough to know that as the US and UK in particular went to war in 1990, their tanks and aircraft were carrying thermal imagers. Those imagers gave them a significant advantage over the image intensification and active infrared imagers available to the Iraqis. The technology rested on the shoulders of Herschel, Langley, and Tihanyi. Without their discoveries, thermal imaging would probably have taken much longer to emerge. But they showed, in order, that infrared radiation existed, that it could be measured at a distance using electrical circuits, and that storing the charge of photons could be used to overcome issues in frame-rates and sensitivity, which made early thermal imaging workable.

The Challenger 1 employed the Signal Processing In The Element (SPRITE) technology developed by Tom Elliot, and the M1 Abrams went to war with the first generation FLIR Common Modules. These two systems used slightly different technology. A US FLIR Common Module consisted of an infrared imager, which formed an image onto the detector array. The imager might include some form of magnification depending on the application. The detector had up to 180 photoconductive MCT detectors. What does this mean?

Well, more detector elements allows the imager to build an image much more quickly, as well as measure a wider range of light frequencies than a smaller number of detectors. The material, mercury cadmium telluride (HgCdTe), or MCT, is the detector material. MCT represented a significant advance on the earlier lead sulfide designs that had been used, as it could be tuned to be sensitive to different wavelengths of radiation depending on the ratio of mercury to cadmium. It is also a semiconductor, which simply means it is a material that only conducts electricity under certain conditions. Copper is a very effective conductor of electricity, while plastic is an insulator and unable to conduct electricity. Semiconductors are essential to the modern world; materials like silicon and gallium are used in the microchips that make your computer, your phone, and pretty much everything work. The lead sulfide used in the first line mappers was a semiconductor, and the MCT worked through a similar principle. When irradiated with thermal energy, the photons inside the MCT give the electrons enough energy to set them free, which enables electricity to flow through the material. And very simply, the more infrared that hits the detector, the stronger the electrical current. In the world of tanks, the hotter the object, the brighter it will show up on thermal imaging.

The way the thermal imager on the M1 and M1A1 worked is that a mechanical mirror inside the infrared imager scanned the scene and passed that infrared energy onto the 180 detectors, each getting a pass of the energy which would then be stitched together into a picture. This energy would then be passed to 180 matching light emitting diodes (LEDs), which would recreate the image for the user to see. The challenge for first-generation thermal imaging was that it was very sensitive to noise. As with any system that works on the electromagnetic spectrum, the FLIR Common Module would pick up almost any infrared radiation with a focus on the long-wave infrared (LWIR) end of the spectrum. This meant it could pick up the 'noise' of its own heat, which would create a much louder signal than the comparatively tiny radiation of a fuel truck at 4,700m. So, it had to be cooled to 75 degrees Kelvin. This might sound warm, but it is actually around -198 degrees Celsius, marginally colder than liquid nitrogen. Achieving that temperature on an aircraft was complex; the Americans used liquid helium in Vietnam, which boils at high altitudes. This meant that cooling was a core area of development for the first generation of thermal imagers, and something called a Stirling cryocooler was used to reach these crazy temperatures. It was a compressor fed by helium, which would compress the helium and heat it up in the process, before passing the hot gas into a chamber behind the detector array. Once in the chamber, the gas would rapidly expand, resulting in the temperature of the gas plummeting. This would suck the heat away from the detectors, allowing them to reach 75 degrees Kelvin. The detectors were also housed inside something called a Dewar, which is a bit like a Thermos flask, with two walls of glass or metal and a vacuum in between them, which stopped air from reaching the detectors. Still here? Ok, good. Let's take a look at SPRITE.

Whereas the US approach to thermal imaging used 180 detectors, which essentially means 180 little tiles of MCT, the UK's SPRITE used eight long strips of detector material. Like the FLIR Common Module, SPRITE used a mirror and an infrared imager to sweep the image across the detector array, but the material was designed so that the excited electrons would travel down the strip of MCT at the same speed as the mirror was scanning the image. This made the electrons even more excited, and they would gather together picking up more energy until they reached the end of the strip where that energy was turned into the image. However, because they had collected more energy, the image would be clearer and higher resolution than a 180-detector array. Now, to be clear, these references are made in respect to the standards at the time. Most tanks had a ×10 or similar optical sight for fighting by day. A thermal imager did not need to be very clear to make an improvement over this, and developing common standards for matching image resolution to clear targeting outcomes is actually seen as an important hurdle in the development of thermal imaging.[12] It meant that Capt Purbrick could see that there were sources of heat ahead of him on 26 February, but he still had to reach back to a higher level of command to confirm that they were enemies and not friendly targets. In current parlance, he could detect targets, but he could not identify them.

Like the FLIR Common Module, the Thermal Imaging Sensor Head of the Challenger 1, which used the SPRITE technology, was cooled by compressed air from a Joule-Thomson mini cooler. The coolers would take time to come online, potentially up to 10 minutes, and were reliant on maintenance and clean air to work. But they allowed for incredibly sensitive thermal imaging, allowing the detectors to pick up on differences in temperature in the order of a few fractions of a degree. Interestingly, this type of sensitivity would be relaxed in later generations of thermal imaging to allow imagers that did not need cooling. However, at the time it meant that US and British gunners could see through smoke, fog, and darkness to find Iraqi armour and engage it at ranges that Lt Nordstrom could only dream of. The fire control systems were key to this: they helped ensure a higher probability of a first-round hit. This is interesting because it reflects something that has been fairly constant for tank designs since tank-on-tank combat became common. See first, shoot first. That helps ensure survivability: it was true for Nordstrom, Lt Col Zeev Eitan when fighting the Egyptians in 1967, and Captain Batcheller as he and his men went to retake Hue in 1968, and it was also the case for the Israeli tank commander surveying lines of Egyptian Sagger operators in 1973. Until the 1980s, the ability to see first was largely equal on both sides of the Iron Curtain. Optical sights with magnification provided some form of parity and the image-intensifying night sights would have brought tanks from both sides to within a few hundred metres of each other – assuming illumination flares and shells were not used. All guns were stabilized and the introduction of APFSDS meant flat trajectories. The only weak link that could differentiate Soviet from NATO tank gunners was the gunner himself. He had to assess the range to the target, often using pre-set ranges or his own 'mark one eyeball' to assess the range, manually adjust the gun, and fire. As we have seen, the M1 Abrams and Challenger 1 introduced automated gun controls and ballistic computers that addressed much of this process. But there is one other element worth touching upon, and that is the laser range finder.

A ballistic computer takes in a lot of different data. For instance, the temperature of the ammunition propellant can impact its burn rate, which affects range. Wind is a major factor, as is to be expected, and so are other meteorological conditions. But if the range is wrong, none of that matters. The gun will be set to the wrong elevation and the round will either fall short or pass over the target. Range errors, when manually calculated, tend to increase the further you go. This means that you might be quite good at estimating short ranges, which most people can do by assessing how many football pitches (or rugby, American football, baseball, whatever your sport) could fit between you and your target. This is probably fine out to about three pitches, but Purbrick hit a target that was *47 standard European football pitches away.* This is likely beyond the abilities of accurate assessment, especially if you are being shot at. Gunners were provided with stadiametric range finders, which included lines on the sighting graticule that would be placed on the target and give an indication of range and elevation for the gun. But stadiametric range finders also relied on knowing the height of the target. Some tanks featured coincidence range finders, which provided two images of the tank that the gunner would have to line up, arriving at a range. And some tanks, like the Chieftain, included a ranging machine gun: a .50cal heavy machine gun that was approximately equal to the ballistic trajectory of an APDS round. This would be fired at the target and used to adjust the elevation of the gun. There are some obvious disadvantages to shooting at an enemy with a small gun before shooting at them with a big gun. To get around this, gunners and commanders would also be taught to recognize the approximate size of a tank or person at a given range, which could help shortcut the targeting process. Suffice to say, that it was difficult for gunners to achieve first-round shots for much of the Cold War. This was evidenced by Centurions in Korea and again in Israel when engaging Syrian armour on the Golan Heights.

So, how did the ballistic computer solve this problem? It's time to introduce the laser range finder. By now, it should not be too much of a surprise to learn that the Soviets were the first to deploy ballistic computers *and* laser range finders on their tanks. The T-64B was accepted for service in 1976, replacing the T-64A, which had entered service in 1968, in production. The T-64B carried a fire control system called the 1A33, which included the stabilized IG42 laser range finder and 1V517 ballistic computer. The computer took automatic inputs from the range finder to provide a ballistic solution and improve first-round hit probability.[13] Just how accurate that system was, we do not know. But the adoption of laser range finders spread throughout the Soviet forces, leading to additions to the T-55s and T-62s from 1978. The changes were not very sophisticated: a box with the laser range finder was simply installed above the gun mantle and the gunner entered its outputs into his targeting calculations. In that sense, the additions were broadly similar to the Chieftain Mk 3/3, introduced in 1970 with a laser range finder. But still, the Soviets were first to add ballistic computers *and* laser range finders to their MBTs. Once more, the Soviets were the first to introduce a core technology in the story of the modern tank.

NATO followed shortly after, however, and the Leopard 2, M1 Abrams, and Challenger 1 all entered service with ballistic computers and laser range finders. A laser range finder works by generating a high-energy pulse of invisible light that travels to the target and then bounces back to be picked up by a sensor. This is done by hitting a synthetic crystal or Neodymium-doped Yttrium Aluminum Garnet (Nd:YAG) with energy until it releases that short burst of invisible light. Some older designs, such as those fitted to the Chieftain Mk 3 and T-62, actually emitted a short burst of light, but the range finders deployed to the Gulf did not. Once the light has bounced back, the computer simply measures how long it took that light to travel there and back. This is quite a simple equation because we know the speed of light, 300,000km per second, and the time it took. The computer would multiply the speed of light by the time it took to reach the target and divide it by two – because it had to get there and back. On the M1, the gunner also had the option to gate the returns, which is where the computer would base its calculations off of the last object that the laser hits. This would be very helpful if there was a bush between the tank and the enemy, as the computer might base its calculations on the first return – the bush, rather than the enemy tank. By selecting the last return, the computer would use the last set of data provided by the laser to complete its calculations.

Iraq's tank gunners had no response to this combination of thermal imaging, ballistic computers, and laser range finders. If they had gotten close, their ammunition was unlikely to be up to scratch against the spaced multi-layer armour and ERA fitted to US and British tanks. The battles were therefore very one-sided and served to create a legacy and impression that NATO was technologically superior. While that may have been true in the air and the realms of precision munitions, we have seen how it was not really the case with tanks. It took NATO until the 1990s, the fourth era in our story of the modern tank, to reach a point where they matched or exceeded Soviet tanks in all areas of design. Nevertheless, the Gulf War served to illustrate that NATO's technology worked, and validated the importance of thermal imaging. Without thermal imaging, the battles would have looked quite different, with many more short-range engagements. But given the overwhelming disparity in firepower, the end result would likely have been the same, albeit with greater losses for the Coalition.

As 1991 came to an end, however, the future of the tank had been changed significantly. In part, this was because of technology, especially the growing power of microchips, but it was largely politics that started to shape the modern tank. Russia, now abandoned by its former Soviet states, stood alone. Its leaders focused on keeping the remaining republics of the Federation together. European NATO, and the US to some extent, set off reaping the 'Peace Dividend', which is a byword for a drastic reduction in defence spending as a percentage of gross domestic product. This cycle would be disturbed, barely, by counterinsurgency wars, which further shaped the modern tank, making most of them heavier. At the same time, other nations entered the field: China, South Korea, Japan, and Turkey all started to develop and produce their own tanks, introducing new technologies and new approaches. All would borrow, however, from the Cold War. The Cold War had produced tanks that had grown gradually in weight as the need for armour increased. There had been two major steps in firepower in both blocs from rifled to smoothbore, and the introduction of the APFSDS. Mobility had kept pace with these developments, meaning that tanks that weighed more than the Centurion could be much faster than their predecessors. Fire control systems and ballistic computers brought all of this together to the point where many of the major frailties of the tanks used by Nordstrom and his men were addressed. This era had, to all intents and purposes, set the framework and the foundations for the modern tanks.

PART 5

1992–2025: Conventional war and counterinsurgency – the tank adapts

By the time that the Soviet Union began to collapse, arguably beginning with the fall of the Berlin Wall in 1989, both sides were showing the strain of the Cold War. The International Monetary Fund noted that world economic activity in 1991 was expected to be the lowest that it had been since 1982. This was fuelled by recession in the US, UK, and Canada, as well as the collapse in output from the former Soviet republics.[1] The UK's economy had experienced regular instability since the end of World War II; it entered a recession in 1990 with inflation reaching 9.5% the same year, and unemployment sat at 9.9% by 1992.[2] An initial drive to slash the defence budget was upended by the Gulf War. Things were not going well in America either. The Savings and Loan Crisis of 1989 had cost the US taxpayer $132 billion, which was used to bail out failing banks that had taken too many risks in their lending.[3] In 1990, the US also entered a recession after an unparallelled period of growth. Although it only lasted into 1991, the recession left more than a million Americans out of work, primarily in manufacturing, and the wider economic uncertainty in Europe meant that exports were slow to rebound.

Given the economic straits that most states were facing, it is not surprising that politicians and academics were quick to proclaim a new era as the USSR continued to crumble. Francis Fukuyama published his famous 'end of history' article in 1989, declaring that, 'what we may be witnessing is not just the end of the Cold War, or the passing of a particular period of post-war history, but the end of history as such: that is, the end point of mankind's ideological evolution and the universalization of Western liberal democracy as the final form of human government.'[4] It is worth noting that not everyone agreed with Fukuyama, but international relations appeared to support his claims. NATO, the former Soviet Union, and the Warsaw Pact signed the Conventional Armed Forces in Europe Treaty in 1990: all signatories promised to reduce their conventional armed forces in Europe. The Conference on Security and Cooperation in Europe the same year declared that NATO and the Soviets were no longer adversaries.[5] The Gulf War even brought the US and Russia closer together, with US President George H.W. Bush stating the following in an address before Congress in September 1990:

> We stand today at a unique and extraordinary moment. The crisis in the Persian Gulf, as grave as it is, also offers a rare opportunity to move toward an historic period of cooperation. Out of these troubled times, our fifth objective – a new world order – can emerge: a new era – freer from the threat of terror, stronger in the pursuit of justice, and more secure in the quest for peace. An era in which the nations of the world, East and West, North and South, can prosper and live in harmony. A hundred generations have searched for this elusive path to peace, while a thousand wars raged across the span of human endeavor. Today that new world is struggling to be born, a world quite different from the one we've known. A world where the rule of law supplants the rule of the jungle.[6]

With all of this rhetoric circling, and Western economies shaking under the strain of defence spending and crises, which had averaged 5% of GDP for the UK and slightly less for the rest of Europe, politicians were eager to start slashing defence budgets. This marked the start of what is sometimes called the 'Peace Dividend'; money was redirected from defence to public services. Where the manufacturers of tanks, ships, and planes had profited, schools, hospitals, and infrastructure flourished instead. The cuts were deep. The Bush administration reduced US defence spending by 11% in 1992, compared to the spending for 1987, and had plans to continue at that pace. The US defence industry shed around 440,000 employees, and its military personnel declined by 300,000. They all joined a job market that was struggling from the economic instability mentioned above. Close to half of what was termed the 'defence build-down' in the US came from procurement budgets.[7] Most other nations, including Russia, followed suit. But the peace was short-lived. Russia would become an outwardly belligerent and aggressive nation towards the West by 2014. Islamic insurgents throughout the Middle East gained prominence and power to the point where they could challenge Western, and Russian, dominance in many countries.

As for the peace, NATO countries participated in no fewer than 11 conflicts between 1992 and 2025, and Russia fought ten, which includes its original invasion of Ukraine in 2014 and the larger invasion in 2022 as two separate events. Saudi Arabia and Yemen fought their own war in Yemen, seeing the deployment of the Leclerc into combat, alongside Saudi M1A2s.* Israel has fought around ten additional conflicts in this time, including the 2023 war in Gaza, while maintaining a constant presence on the northern border with Syria and Lebanon. This period was anything but peaceful. In fact, in 2025 the Peace Research Institute Oslo (PRIO) released data declaring that 2024 had seen the highest number of state-based armed conflicts since the end of World War II. The Institute's data recorded 61 conflicts for 2024, involving 36 countries. 'This is not just a spike – it's a structural shift. The world today is far more violent, and far more fragmented, than it was a decade ago,' warned Siri Aas Rustad, Research Director at PRIO.[8]

So this is the era that brings us to the modern tank. The tanks that define armed forces today have had to contend with insurgents, who are always very inventive, state-level armed conflict, advances in ATGMs with frightening levels of penetration, and shrinking defence budgets. Let's take a look at how they have fared, and what technologies emerged in spite of these conditions.

*The Leclerc is the French main battle tank, which is also used by the UAE and Jordan. It uses an autoloader and a unique engine configuration that makes it very fast.

Chapter 16

Active protection becomes essential

This chapter focuses exclusively on active protection systems. It will do that for two reasons. Firstly, there are certainly more advanced and modern armours in play on the most modern tanks. However, what they are and how they work is classified. In addition, it is probable that most of the armours fall somewhere between the complex multi-layered Chobham and Kontakt-5 ERA. There are non-explosive reactive armours and lots of different materials used in passive armours, but the projectile defeat mechanism is likely to be similar to those already discussed in early chapters. Secondly, active protection is critical for the modern tank. Without it, an insurgent in Syria that has received US aid, or raided a government warehouse, could destroy even the best armoured tanks in the world. The spread of ATGMs, especially things like Kornet and the Iranian equivalents, means that without active protection systems it would be difficult for the modern tank to survive on any battlefield. So, let's begin with a short trip to Russia, to explore the country's contributions to the survivability of the modern tank.

You may remember from Chapter 12 that there is some debate over who started developing explosive reactive armour first. The contenders are the Soviets and Israel. And it may surprise you to learn that these two countries were at the forefront of developing active protection systems. The consistent theme between the two technology trees is the driving force of counterinsurgency warfare. The Soviets developed Drozd from the 1960s in a bid to boost the protection of their tanks. It had a lengthy development process, which is understandable given the technologies and physics involved. The final version consisted of eight rocket launchers firing 107mm high-explosive fragmentation warheads added to the turret with a set of radar detectors. Drozd was designed to intercept RPGs and ATGMs; the first versions were mounted onto the old faithful T-55, which then became the T-55AD. The first systems are understood to have been delivered for state trials in 1982 and entered limited service the following year.[1] At some point after that, it was tested during the Soviet–Afghan War (1979–89), along with a number of other novel technologies including laser-guided 240mm mortars.

When assessing Drozd, we should keep in mind that there are a few characteristics that are important to an active protection system (APS), including the number of interceptors, reload times, reaction times, and the coverage that the system provides. Drozd was ok in terms of having interceptors with four rockets on each side of the turret, which is actually more than some modern systems like Iron Fist. But it could not provide 360-degree coverage, or intercept threats that came in on anything but a flat trajectory. However, it did use K-band radars for detection, which the Soviets are understood to have pioneered. K-band has a very short wavelength with just 10mm between the peak of each wave, which makes it good for tracking small objects moving quickly. However, this also means that the radar collects a lot of information, and can be disrupted by inclement weather.[2] Although it appears to have worked, one source claiming an 80% interception rate, Drozd was only taken into limited service with the Soviet armed forces.[3] This was partly because the end of the war in Afghanistan coincided with the end of the Soviet Union.

Generally speaking, Afghanistan was tough on the tank. The Mujahideen were effective and capable in the use of mines to block roads and ambush Soviet patrols, and draw them into fights in difficult terrain. The Soviet forces would deploy armoured vehicles at the front and rear of their patrols or vehicle columns, with soft-skinned vehicles in the middle. In one ambush, a logistics convoy was headed by three tanks, likely T-55s, and one brave Mujahideen fired at the second tank from the side of the road with an RPG-7. He had run to his position from breakfast, and his heavy breathing made aiming difficult so both the first and the second shot missed. Presumably, the crew of the second tank didn't realize that they had been fired upon. The fighter was able to run down to the road, exploiting the 100m that Soviet vehicles were required to keep between them, and fire directly into the third tank with his RPG. It burst into flames, bringing the convoy to a halt and initiating the rest of the ambush. There were hundreds of attacks like this, and the Soviet response varied. Sometimes, they would fly helicopter gunships ahead of the convoy, looking for the ambush sites. Occasionally, the tanks and infantry fighting vehicles in the convoy would return fire, and very occasionally they would dismount infantry to fight through the position.[4] The Mujahideen usually withdrew when helicopters appeared, but the T-55s generally fared poorly when faced with RPG-7 ambushes. Whatever was learned during this conflict about countering ambushes and fighting the Mujahideen would have to be relearned by the Russian armed forces in Chechnya a little over seven years later. And again by US and British troops who deployed to Afghanistan in 2001.

Perhaps because of the Soviet experience in Afghanistan, Drozd was further developed into Drozd-2, which was a modular system designed to distribute the effectors around the vehicle. However, the Russians did not stop there with APS. They developed another system for the T-90 called Shtora-1, which was a softkill system that entered service in 1993. Unlike Drozd, which destroyed threats with a rocket that exploded near them, Shtora-1 used infrared lasers to jam laser-guided missiles and deployed a multispectral smoke screen. This works, like most jamming, by reflecting a strong signal back at the guidance system to overwhelm it and stop signals from reaching the missile while it is in flight. This means it is only effective against certain types of missile and has very little impact on a wire-guided ATGM like the early TOW generations, or advanced weapons like the Javelin. However, the smoke screen could obscure the tank and interfere with certain types of seeker or sight. The system also provided an indication of the origins of the illumination, allowing the crew to slew the turret to face that direction. It had several shortcomings but the optical jamming elements of the system came to be a distinctive feature of Russia's T-90 fleet up until the T-90M took over as the main production version. However, elements of Shtora-1 are understood to equip the T-90M, including the laser warning receivers and aerosol smoke grenades.

So, Shtora-1 had some impact on the modern tank, but Russia's development of APS continued with another system called Arena, which is much closer to systems like Trophy in how it worked. The original version was also developed and tested in the 1970s and 80s. It included a pillar mounted on the roof of the tank, which deployed its interceptors down into the path of the incoming threat and used radar for detection. This version was refined, leading to Arena-M, or Arena-E for export customers, which includes modules located around the turret of the tank carrying a number of interceptors that can, according to the director of Rostec, intercept threats coming straight at the vehicle and over it.[5] If this is true, it would enable Arena-M to intercept things like the Next Generation Light Anti-tank Weapon (NLAW), which is designed specifically to destroy Soviet-style tanks by attacking the top of the armour with a shaped charge that targets the carousel loader. The designer of Arena-M, a company called KBM, filed a patent in 2025 that outlined changes made to the system so that it could intercept drones. The system faced the challenge that the radar return from a small drone would be too small and slow, which meant that the filter would simply let those objects through. Drones are often made of plastic and carbon fibre, with very few metallic components to reflect a radar's energy, and, as a result, the computer may simply decide they are a bird, or something else that is non-threatening. Instead, the update supposedly allowed the Arena system to base its assessments on the doppler returns of the drone's propellers. The adjustments allowed the radar to alternate between distance scanning for missiles and RPGs, and a more static, short-range scan for drones.[6] Arena-M's interceptors consist of a panel of explosives lined with square-shaped fragments. The panel is fired into the path of the incoming missile or RPG and detonated, showering the warhead in fragments that are designed to break it up and destroy the cone liner. Despite the extensive losses suffered by Russian forces in Ukraine, the system had not entered service at the time of writing. However, it has been integrated into the T-90M and a T-72B3M with Arena has been patented and photographed in what appeared to be Ukraine. Additionally, Russian news outlets carried stories in late December 2025 stating that work was under way to install the drone-capable system onto T-90M tanks, and that it was already included in the upgrade of T-72B3As.[7]

Unsurprisingly, the T-14 Armata carries a built-in APS called Afghanit. Afghanit combines soft and hard kill interception methodologies and an array of interceptors organized in vertical launch cells on the roof of the turret, as well as in canisters under the turret that are reminiscent of Drozd. It includes radar and electro-optical detectors, which should help it detect threats that are fired from close range by picking up the plume of heat and smoke. We know very little about Armata's APS and how effective it is because it has never been deployed, or at least it has never been documented on deployment. However, we can see from Russia's development of APS that it has concerns around NATO's preference for top-attack missiles and munitions against its tanks.

I'm keenly aware that although we have made it this far into the story of the modern tank, there has been very little focused discussion of the war in Ukraine and its impact on the modern tank. There are a few reasons for this, but I think one of them is that it has primarily influenced the development of the T-90M – more so than any of the Western equivalents. It has shaped, to some extent, the evolving concepts of operations of many NATO forces. The UK, for example, appears inclined to see the tank as a mothership for drones and hopes to destroy its enemies from a distance rather than getting up close and personal.[8] Germany, meanwhile, is re-evaluating the role of tanks in its reconnaissance battalions, and its procurement plans indicate the intent to double-down on heavy armour.[9] But its impact on the design of modern tanks is much less clear as most of them were developed before the war started. That said, the Ukraine War did prompt many European states to actually buy new tanks, primarily the Leopard 2A8, so it can be said to have shaped the modern tank in that way.

Of course, I would be remiss not to touch upon the impact of drones in the Ukraine War upon the modern tank. Up front, I will state that I think the impact of drones has been overstated. They suffer from the same syndrome as the Azeri use of the Bayraktar TB2 in Nagorno-Karabakh, which is that you will only see successful strikes. This gives drones something of a success bias, and in some cases it appears that they offer an incredibly effective counter to a heavily armoured tank. This is not to say that they are a useless invention, just that balance and perspective is important. So, let's take a brief detour through the first person view (FPV) drone, and how it does and does not impact the modern tank. The first thing to note is that most are armed with a modified version of the PG-7 family of warheads or a homemade high explosive, depending on the target or the specialism of the unit deploying them. This is an important factor because this family of warheads is a well-known threat to Western and Russian designers. The basic PG-7 can penetrate around 260mm of armour, and there are more advanced and capable warheads like the PG-7T with its tandem HEAT warhead that can penetrate up to 500mm after a single layer of ERA. These munitions have been used to attack tanks for decades, sometimes very successfully. Russia's 1994 war in Chechnya is one example of this, where small teams consisting of an RPG gunner and an RPG loader, as well as snipers and machine gunners, were able to cause considerable damage to Russian tanks including the T-72 and T-80. The Chechens benefited from poor Russian tactics and overly optimistic planning assumptions that allowed them to get to the rear and sides of Russian tanks when supporting infantry were unavailable.[10] However, it is worth noting that even the relatively thinly armoured Russian personnel carriers, and their tanks with their known ammunition vulnerability, required three to six RPG hits to be taken out of the fight, and all of the tanks that were lost, were lost to hits in areas without ERA.[11]

Western forces have routinely encountered high concentrations of RPGs and come out with relatively low armour losses. There are even accounts of British Warrior infantry fighting vehicles in Iraq returning to base having suffered multiple RPG strikes and survived. The point here is that the RPG is not a novel or new weapon, but the drone offers a novel delivery method. A Chechen armour hunting team had to be quite brave to engage a Russian column. They would probably have been tens of metres away when they fired their RPGs and reliant upon the machine gunner and sniper to pin any infantry down. They had nothing apart from the buildings of Grozny to defend them from Russia's artillery, air defence cannons, and airpower. Whether the adversary is insurgent forces fighting the Multinational Force-Iraq, or Hamas engaging IDF Merkavas, firing a shoulder-fired weapon at a tank starts an engagement that is quite likely to be one-sided and not in the attacker's favour. Drones change this equation. An FPV drone can be piloted from up to 60km away by a unit holed up in the cellar of a house. The attackers might even be far enough from the frontline to place them beyond the reach of long-range artillery. So that immediate threat to life is reduced, and the delivery mechanism also means that an FPV can be flown selectively into the weakest spots of a tank or armoured vehicle. In that case, there is nothing special about the PG-7, or any HEAT warhead for that matter. It has always been bad for a tank to take a hit on the engine deck or near the exhaust. The armour is thinner there by necessity. This control of the munition, which can also occur with loitering munitions like the Russian Lancet-3M, also means that other vulnerable areas of a tank can be targeted. For example, there is one video of a Lancet hitting the turret bustle of a moving Leopard 2A5, leading to significant damage.

However, there is a need for caution around what this means in general: in part because Ukraine is a unique battlefield. It is reasonable to state that it is an exceptionally dangerous place for vehicles of any kind. Observation of the frontline and the 30km behind it for both sides is persistent during daylight. Drones are used by every unit and they watch everything, allowing FPVs, artillery, and other munitions to be deployed against anything that moves.[12] But drones are not alone: Ukraine has been heavily mined by both sides, and those mines are a real threat to a tank. The reason for this is that it may take several successful strikes with an FPV to destroy a tank. Achieving those successful strikes will involve many failed strikes. The drones are often homemade and do not work when they get to the front. Or jamming adjusts to new frequencies, preventing them from taking off. If the pilots can get them into the sky, then they have to navigate to the target area without crashing, find the tank and successfully fly into it. Combined, these challenges meant that 60–80% of Ukrainian FPVs failed to reach their target in late 2024.[13] The fuzes are often rudimentary, which means that some FPVs will not detonate their warheads even if they do hit. Then, once a hit has been achieved, it is not guaranteed that one hit will be enough to destroy the tank, necessitating multiple strike missions. This is a problem for the FPV because pilots can only fly one mission at a time. Multiple pilots can of course increase the number of missions that can be flown simultaneously, but all of this is made much easier if the tank has been immobilized by a mine detonating under its track.

That is not all the tank faces in Ukraine. The Ukrainian artillery has access to BONUS, a guided anti-armour round that deploys two sensor-fuzed explosively formed projectiles (EFP). BONUS is a 155mm shell fired by a howitzer like the BAE Systems Archer, which dispenses the EFPs with their sensors to scan the ground below looking for a tank. Once one is identified, they detonate their EFPs, sending them through the roof of the tank. Russian forces have made extensive use of the Kornet ATGM, especially during Ukraine's counter-offensive, which can be devastating against even some of the best passive armours. The Ukrainians also put their Javelin and NLAW ATGMs to good use in the opening months of the war, as well as their domestic ATGMS that are at least as good as Russia's. Attack helicopters have been used to make decisive contributions during critical moments; the Russian Ka-52 in particular has demonstrated its ability to hold large formations at risk, despite heavy losses. And despite this, Ukraine still aims to maintain a tank presence at the frontline, concealing the tanks and using them to break up assault formations with their formidable and irreplaceable direct fire.[14]

All of this together with the persistent observation means that any manoeuvre has become exceptionally high risk and lethal. But it does not follow that *every* future war will look like Ukraine. For starters, Russia would have to seek air superiority, or at least temporal parity with NATO, in the event of a war. If one force had air superiority then the battlefield would look very different. To sum up, the threat of FPVs is one that the modern tank has to take seriously. However, active protection systems like Trophy have already been modified to address FPVs, and existing armour is likely sufficient to counter the warheads they carry in many scenarios. To that end, I would go so far as to suggest that the most dangerous threat a modern tank faces is the ATGM, especially Kornet and the Iranian equivalent Dehlavieh. These weapons have been widely exported, and there is a precedent for giving them to insurgent forces fighting against one's enemy, which means they are quite common on modern battlefields. Their penetration is challenging for modern tanks from the front (those without an APS), let alone the sides, and they can be used from beyond the engagement ranges of some modern designs, which reduces the opportunity to target the operator.

There is one other major contribution to the protection of the modern tank to have come out of Russia in this era, and that is the 'cope cage'. This unfortunate name is used to describe a grill-type structure that Russian forces started building over their T-72s around 2020. At the time, there was some debate within the analytical community about what these cages meant. Could it be a response to the US giving Javelins to Ukraine, some wondered. The line of reasoning seemed to be that the stand-off between the cage and the turret roof would reduce the penetration and save the crew. This is almost certainly not the reason for the development. It takes around 1m of stand-off to reduce the penetration of an RPG-7 to a negligible amount. An RPG can penetrate 300mm of rolled homogeneous armour, whereas a Javelin can penetrate more than a metre. So, the stand-off would do very little to save the crew of a T-72 from a Javelin. At the time, however, Ukraine was already proficient in the use of drones to drop small bombs onto the tanks deployed by the forces in the Donbass. It stands to reason that this threat was the driver behind the cope cage development. It would provide enough protection from a 30mm grenade or 60mm mortar dropped on a tank. The Russian adaptations, which often seemed to be ad hoc and thrown together at the unit level, were mocked extensively, leading to the cope cage nickname. I don't have an alternative name for them, but what we do know is that similar developments have been observed in China, Taiwan, Vietnam, India, South Korea, France, and even on the mighty Merkava in service with the IDF. So, with that, let's move to Israel, and something called Purple Thunder.

TROPHY: FROM LEBANON TO GAZA

In the 1990s a secret IDF unit known as the Nakhshol Company, part of the 188th Brigade, deployed to southern Lebanon. The IDF had remained in the country after the 1982 war, trying to enforce a safe zone across the border from Israel. However, the initial invasion had led to the growth of Hezbollah, and by the early 1990s, the terrorist group was equipped with a range of ATGMs including the Sagger and even some TOW missiles acquired from Iran. At the time, the primary threat to Israel's tanks was improvised explosive devices (IEDs), but three Merkavas were destroyed in late 1997 by ATGMs. It is not clear when the Nakhshol Company deployed to Lebanon, but its tanks were equipped with a system called 'Purple Thunder', an early type of active protection system. It seems probable that they were deployed in response to those missile strikes. 'There were situations where we knew about missile squads that were about to fire, so we were really exposed. We trusted the system. I, as a tank commander, knew that if a missile was fired at us, Purple Thunder would disrupt it,' one of the last commanders told an Israeli news outlet in 2020.[15] Purple Thunder was probably the predecessor to what we now know as Trophy, arguably the world's most successful active protection system.

However, it would take some time, and another war, for Israel to take its APS development further. Israel withdrew from Lebanon in 2000 after 18 years of occupation and constant counterinsurgency warfare dominated by IEDs. The occupation had fuelled the rise of

Hezbollah, which became the dominant militant faction in the country, overpowering several others. Hezbollah grew quickly, in part because of the credibility it gained from fighting the IDF. But the Israeli withdrawal did not end the tension or conflict. This should not be too much of a surprise, since Hezbollah's motto is 'Death to Israel' and destruction of Israel is enshrined in the group's founding documents.[16] However, with the IDF no longer patrolling Lebanon, Hezbollah had to go to Israel. There is a specific event that led to the war in 2006, namely the abduction of Israeli soldiers Ehud Goldwasser and Eldad Regev in the July of that year. But the background tension meant that the abduction was seen as a cardinal moment, leading Israel to declare war, rather than negotiate for their return as had happened in past cases. The war started, as most do, with extensive Israeli air strikes designed to damage Hezbollah's personnel and weapons. The terrorists responded by firing 122mm rockets into Israel, targeting towns and villages across the border. The IDF ground forces resisted pressure to call up the country's reserves and launch an invasion, eventually relenting and allowing limited incursions to start on 17 July. The IDF sent battalion- and brigade-sized formations with their usual blend of infantry, artillery, armour, and engineers. However, this was not the smooth and well-orchestrated operation of the past IDF. The forces were poorly prepared, many of them having spent most of their time on policing operations rather than preparing for large-scale combat.

Hezbollah, meanwhile, had received training from Iran, and its units followed the classical insurgent template of structuring their defence around anti-armour weapons and ambushes. Hezbollah had taken the time to prepare a tunnel network in major towns such as Maroun al-Ras and Bint Jbeil, some of which were over 8m deep with blast doors. The bulk of the Hezbollah force of 3,000 personnel was made up of local militiamen with a trained core of around 1,000 full-time fighters. They used the tunnel network to conduct an engagement and melt away if possible, denying the IDF the vision of victory and destruction of Hezbollah the Israeli government was looking for. They were also well versed in the use of ATGMs, and built up a stockpile that included the by now familiar Sagger, but also Kornet, one of the most capable ATGMs to come out of Russia. Kornet can penetrate more than 1,000mm of armour behind ERA in its export configuration. According to accounts of UAE troops who deployed to Yemen in 2015, Kornet's sights were better than those of a Javelin, allowing longer-range engagements, and the missiles are also relatively cheap at $26,000 per shot.[17] This meant that the Hezbollah forces could deploy them from a safe distance – up to 5km – from Israeli tanks and infantry. The training from Iran was not for nothing. In an earlier brush with a Merkava in 2005, Hezbollah had hit it no fewer than seven times, but failed to penetrate its armour. Iran sent its anti-armour specialists to Lebanon in response. They studied the video footage of the strikes and developed a set of tactics for attacking the tanks by targeting their more vulnerable areas.[18]

Many of Israel's casualties in 2006 came from ATGM strikes. They were used to strike infantry sheltering in buildings, as well as tanks and supply vehicles. The latter in particular limited Israel's willingness to push supplies into Lebanon. Hezbollah's resistance slowed the IDF's advance to a crawl, so that after three weeks its forces had advanced just a few kilometres. With the UN making moves to bring the war to an end, the IDF launched a last-minute advance with the goal of reaching the Litani, a river some 30km away from the current Israel–Lebanon border. As part of the plan, 24 tanks from the 401st Brigade headed into a wadi on their advance to the Litani River. Hezbollah was waiting for them, and detonated a massive IED under a Merkava, killing the entire crew.[19] This initiated a significant ambush, in which dozens of ATGMs and RPGs were fired at the IDF column. The tank crews failed to deploy smoke from their tanks, which could have reduced their losses. The engagement in Wadi Saluki ended up becoming the most intense of the war, and 11 Merkavas were hit during the battle, leading to the deaths of eight tank crew. The battle was a bitter and horrific exchange for the IDF soldiers involved, especially as most were aware that a ceasefire was due to come into effect a few days after it started. 'When we look at what happened there and what surprises were waiting for us, we just were fucked. We were caught unprepared,' one IDF soldier told an Israeli newspaper in the aftermath.[20]

In all, 48 Merkavas were hit during the war; 40 of them were damaged and 20 penetrated, leading to 23 casualties. However, some of the penetrations resulted in no casualties at all. A total of 30 Israeli tank crewmen died during the war, which is more than a quarter of Israel's losses. The ATGM losses are interesting because hundreds were fired at the Israeli tanks, and yet successful penetrations were relatively low. The two Merkavas that were catastrophically destroyed were lost to very large IEDs. The tank's protection certainly proved effective at minimizing the behind-armour effects of the ATGMs, and in saving crew lives. However, this conflict is what spurred the IDF to procure Trophy. The system was already available when the tanks rolled into Lebanon, but procurement had been deferred for reasons that are not entirely clear. It may have been a slightly unfounded belief in the concept of effects-based operations, which placed an emphasis on air strikes against Hezbollah's command and logistics, rather than a ground-based incursion. Regardless, the war marked a watershed moment in the IDF's armour development; it would not be found wanting again.

The Merkava Mk 4 had performed quite well in Lebanon in 2006, and served alongside the Mk 3 and 2s. Some state that the Mk 4s were targeted specifically by units with Kornet ATGMs, which is possible. However, as the main in-service tank with the IDF's professional cadre of forces, the Mk 4 was the first to be fitted with Trophy. The first batch of Mk 4s was equipped with Trophy in May 2009, close to three years after the Lebanon War. According to reports from Israeli news outlets, the decision to procure the system had been delayed before and after the war because of budgetary constraints. However, the damage suffered by the Merkava fleet forced the decision.[21] Some vehicles were retrofitted with the system, and those new-build Mk 4s coming off the production line had Trophy integrated into their turret at the factory. It was declared operational in 2010 and immediately went into service protecting the IDF's Merkavas. The complete system consists of four EL/M-2133 active electronically scanned array (AESA) radar panels that are called WindGuard, located around the turret to provide 360-degree coverage. AESA radars are electronically steered, unlike mechanical radars, which are rotated to face a target or detect it. This means that the radars can send beams of energy in all directions to detect incoming threats. Later iterations of Trophy brought a greater reliance on opto-electrical detection, as well as infrared detectors. The electro-optical sensors can be used to activate the radars for an interception, allowing them to be dormant rather than constantly emitting.[22] This is partly because there is some concern about the electronic signals that a radar emits, which could be used to monitor a formation from hundreds of kilometres away with the right equipment.

Once the radar has identified a threat, the system's computer conducts a calculation to determine if it is a threat to the host vehicle.

If the missile is expected to pass safely by, Trophy will likely leave it. If not, then a firing solution is sent to one of two pedestals that are built into the turret roof. The pedestal then rotates to face the threat and detonates its explosive charge, showering the threat with a tight cluster of shaped charges that break up the missile and its warhead. The pedestal then rotates and docks into the magazine behind it to reload another munition, in a process that takes less than a second. There are thought to be three reloads per pedestal, which means that the magazine depth for the system is finite, but it allows each tank to intercept a decent number of ATGMs and RPGs. And this is exactly what Trophy started doing from 2011 when it intercepted a missile fired at a Merkava Mk 4 from Gaza. It was tested again in 2014 during Operation *Protective Edge*, which was a relatively limited ground incursion into Gaza. But the real test came in 2023.

The events of 7 October 2023 shocked the world. The brazen and horrific attack launched by Hamas against Israel resulted in the deaths of at least 1,189 Israelis including 796 civilians.[23] The attack was coordinated with a massive rocket barrage of 4,300 rockets that were fired into Israel from Gaza. The attackers, many of them from Hamas's elite Nukhba forces (though many others were identified as not being aligned to Hamas), made their way back across the border with 252 hostages. The stage was set for a major war rather than the limited confrontations that had occurred in previous years. In most engagements, Israel had restricted its response to air strikes and limited actions by its special forces. But the attack was too egregious. On 13 October, Israel called up 1 million reservists. Social media outlets were filled with imagery of Israelis making their way home, and a defence exhibition being held at the time was left empty of Israeli companies. The ground forces began pulling their vehicles, the Merkava family of tanks, Namer APCs, and aging M113s, out of storage, filling them with fuel, ammunition, and the supplies they thought they would need.

The US urged restraint: 'justice must be done. But I caution this – while you feel that rage, don't be consumed by it. After 9/11, we were enraged in the United States. While we sought justice and got justice, we also made mistakes,' President Biden warned on 19 October 2023, as Israeli tanks lined up on the border with Gaza.[24] Meanwhile, he and his advisors shuttled between Middle Eastern states like Qatar, working to achieve the release of some of the hostages. He also questioned Israel's president, Netanyahu, about his plan for Gaza after the invasion. 'We will wipe this thing called Hamas, Isis-Gaza, off the face of the earth. It will cease to exist,' Netanyahu had said.[25] Before the invasion started, Israel had prepared for a pre-emptive strike against Hezbollah in Lebanon. Netanyahu sought support from Biden for the attack. Biden declined. He was concerned about the risks of the war turning into a regional conflict, which could draw US troops in the area in. Israel did not attack Hezbollah immediately, the ground invasion would not start until 27 October, but Israel was already bombing Gaza, leading to widespread condemnation. Biden and his team pressured Netanyahu to let aid into Gaza; the Israelis declined.

Ahead of the invasion, the IDF had gathered some 40,000 troops on the border with Gaza, organized into five divisions: the 36th Armoured Division, 162nd Division, 98th Paratroop and Commando Division, the 252nd Division, and the 99th Division, which included the elite Ghost Unit.[26] The Ghost Unit is the IDF's developmental formation designed to explore the future of warfare through multi domain integration. In theory. It has a combination of armoured units, artillery, and exotic capabilities like cyber-effects, as well as the ability to directly coordinate with air assets. While the Ghost Unit is very new, the 36th Armoured Division has a long history. Its Barak Brigade had fought in the 1967 war, held its ground in the Golan Heights during the 1973 Yom Kippur War, and led the advance up the coastal road to Beirut during the 1982 Lebanon War. It had maintained positions on the Golan Heights for 40 years until 2014, when it was rotated out of that deployment to become a wartime division that was designed to be sent to any front as required.[27] This brought the 36th Armoured Division to the borders of Gaza for Operation *Protective Edge* in 2014. In response to increasing tensions and violence, Israel had launched air strikes against Hamas rocket sites and then initiated a limited ground invasion to destroy the tunnels that Hamas had been building. Understanding these tunnels is key to the context behind the 2023 operation.

Generally speaking, whenever a force is subject to an intensive air bombardment, it will go inside or under ground. Hamas had experienced Israeli air strikes on many occasions under a policy that the IDF called 'mowing the grass', which was intended to limit the growth of the group's military capabilities. To help survive these strikes, and to support its smuggling operations which financed its military operations, Hamas had been building tunnels underneath Gaza for some time, and likely accelerated construction when it seized power over the region in 2007. The tunnels had been used to conduct raids across the border into Israel and to abduct IDF soldiers, and even formed part of a plan to launch a raid into Israel to murder as many civilians as possible. The plans for that attack were captured in 2014; it seems that Hamas rekindled them for 2023.[28] They had also extended their tunnel networks since 2014, deliberately building the entrances into densely populated areas. The word tunnel doesn't really do justice to what Hamas had built. Estimates in 2024 indicated that there could be up to 725km of tunnels under Gaza, with 5,700 shafts providing access. Some tunnels were rough and basic, as you might expect. But most were concrete-lined, and provided with electricity, cooling, and an air supply. Some led to workshops for the production of weapons and ammunition; some were protected by blast doors and reinforced concrete.[29] The network was estimated to have cost Hamas $1 billion, and it was used to protect the group's leadership and fighters from the Israeli bombardment as well as store weapons, and hide the hostages captured on 7 October.

Israel knew about the tunnel network and had targeted it in previous operations. There had been five operations since Operation *Cast Lead* in 2008, shortly after Hamas came to power. Of these, only two had included a ground component, and both had fairly limited aims, including targeting of the tunnel infrastructure. However, it takes a land army to defeat a land army. The IDF could not destroy the tunnels from the air, nor could it crush Hamas from the air. So, as the IDF and 36th Armoured Division prepared for the anticipated invasion in 2023, they knew they would be going further than ever before. There was no alternative to a ground invasion if Netanyahu was to keep his promise. The 36th was well placed for that operation. It included the highly decorated Golani Brigade, which had fought some of the hardest battles in Israel's history, including during *Protective Edge* in 2014. The 188th Armoured Brigade had received the new Merkava Mk 4 in 2020, bringing with it the Trophy APS built into the turret and a suite of advanced mission systems.[30] Hamas was estimated to have 24 battalions as the IDF geared up, numbering some 30,000 fighters, with the Palestinian Islamic Jihad thought to add up to 10,000 more.[31]

Those Hamas fighters were relatively well armed with ATGMs and shoulder-fired rockets, especially the Al-Yassin 105. The Al-Yassin 105 was reportedly developed by Hamas engineers building on experience gained with the Al-Yassin, which is modelled on the RPG-7 family of munitions. The 105 introduced a new larger warhead, which is thought to be 105mm in diameter, as the name suggests. This is useful because there are rules of thumb that can be used to assess warhead penetration. A well-built warhead with a precisely machined liner can penetrate armour ten times as thick as its diameter. So, a 105mm warhead could, in theory, penetrate the equivalent of 1,050mm of rolled homogeneous armour. However, the Al-Yassin 105 does resemble the PG-7R, which is a 105mm tandem-HEAT warhead capable of penetrating up to 660mm of armour behind ERA.[32] The previous Al-Yassin generation could deal with around 210mm of armour, which would not stand much of a chance against a Merkava from the front. So the Al-Yassin 105 was necessary to give the fighters any chance of getting through the armour arrays of the 36th Division's Merkavas. Hamas also had a number of ATGMs including the very potent Kornet and equivalents, but nothing like the numbers available to Hezbollah in the North. Hamas fighters knew they needed to get close to Israeli armour, preferably attack the back of the Merkavas and Namer APCs if they could, and ideally with simultaneous strikes to overwhelm Trophy. IEDs, obstacles, and the tunnels all had a role to play in the group's initial plans, which envisioned anti-armour ambushes against the IDF from pre-prepared positions. This would allow Hamas to deploy massive IEDs, which had successfully destroyed the heavily armoured Merkava in past wars. In many ways, the IED threat was the most lethal if they went undetected.

The IDF knew a lot of this as it went into Gaza. Its force approached the area from an unexpected axis, which negated a lot of the preparations Hamas had put in place for staged anti-armour ambushes. The IDF had formed ad hoc brigades, with a battalion each of armour, mechanized infantry, regular infantry, combat engineers, and artillery. Special forces were also attached to these brigade structures, which were also made up of professional soldiers, conscripts, and reservists.[33] On 27 October, the IDF committed forces to four lines of advance. Three formations moved into the north of Gaza, heading for Gaza City, and another cut straight across the strip below the city, heading for the sea. In the weeks before the ground elements of the operation started, the Israeli Air Force had pounded Gaza City with extensive strikes against buildings and infrastructure, killing thousands of Gazans and leaving many without power and, as a result, clean drinking water. Leaflets and information operations including thousands of phone calls encouraged the city's inhabitants to move south. The Israeli Air Force was active there too, and Hamas ordered the citizens to stay put, in the knowledge that a dense civilian presence would shape the way that the IDF fought. By 6 November, Gaza City was encircled and the IDF began clearing the urban terrain and pushing more civilians to the south of the strip.

The 188th Armoured Brigade formed one of these ad hoc brigade combat teams and appears to have been one of the formations that pushed across the centre of Gaza, reaching the Sheikh Ijlin neighbourhood on 11 November. There, it engaged the Sabra-Tel al-Hawa battalion, which was associated with the Tel Al-Hawa neighbourhood in Gaza City. The fighting was led by the Golani infantry brigade with the 53rd Battalion of the 188th Armoured Brigade in support.[34] The typical approach, although it varied by unit and circumstance, was for the IDF's D9 armoured bulldozers to lead each advance. The D9 is designed to clear obstacles, like the extensive rubble created by the air strikes, as well as IEDs, ahead of the armoured formations. A short distance behind the D9 would be a pair of Merkavas that would establish an overwatch position, allowing Namer APCs to move forwards with their infantry.[35] The overwatch position would give the Merkavas a good line of sight to the buildings or area that the Namers were expected to take. The purpose of the tanks was to provide fire support for the advancing infantry as they worked to clear the buildings. Light infantry worked behind the armour, clearing buildings and securing flank areas as best they could. Once the buildings were secured, the D9s would move ahead to the next area and the whole process would start again.

Hamas's original plan to resist the invasion had failed. Instead, they set about contesting the inner city. During this stage of the fighting, they would inhabit a particular building and attempt to draw IDF forces into combat from it. This approach proved costly. It is a bad idea to allow an enemy with superior firepower to concentrate against you, which is what Hamas fighters effectively did in some scenarios. So their tactics evolved again to include the much more extensive use of their tunnel network. Small teams of three or four, two of them armed with RPGs or the Al-Yassin 105, and often one of them with a camera, would use the tunnels to make their way behind Israeli armour and engage from close range. As mentioned, they hoped this would counteract the Trophy APS carried by most heavy IDF vehicles. In some cases it did, but the reasons are unclear. For instance, each Trophy launcher only carries so many reloads, and in some cases the system may have been deactivated to allow infantry to operate safely. Software updates, which also included the ability to intercept drones, and ensuring that heavy vehicles worked in pairs helped to ensure that Hamas rockets were intercepted. The point of Trophy is mission success. The Gaza operation is one of the clearest demonstrations of this principle in operation. The Merkava Mk 4 is well protected against most threats that it would face in Gaza. But some parts of the tank are less protected than others and shots would get through if the armour was all that the crews had. If a battalion loses four or five vehicles, then the entire mission could be jeopardized. However, Trophy gives a commander confidence. He knows that each vehicle can intercept a certain number of threats without having to rely on its passive armour.[36] In addition, there were hundreds of Trophy systems in use, and they reportedly operated with a very high level of success in intercepting both the short-range threats posed by Hamas, and the long-range missiles fired by Hezbollah.

Anyway, the IDF's mission was to destroy Hamas, and this meant getting to grips with the tunnel network and eliminating the group's commanders. Hamas had an array of tactical tunnels, which it used to move between buildings during an attack, and larger communications tunnels that connected different battalions and brigades. In the south of Gaza, the commander of the 98th Division began using the tunnels to his advantage. His special forces units were infiltrated into the tunnels and coordinated their movements with the above-ground manoeuvre of armour. The idea was that Hamas would not be alerted to their presence, and its fighters would run into the elite units as they attempted to use the tunnels to reposition themselves against the armour.[37] Overall, the IDF put a lot of pressure on Hamas. But it lost hundreds of soldiers killed and more than a thousand wounded in the process, including several high-ranking officers. Over time, Hamas adapted its tactics further, avoiding direct confrontation with groups of armour and focusing as much mass as possible against isolated units that were difficult for supporting forces to reach. At the time of writing, the fighting was not completely over. The IDF re-entered Gaza City with three divisions, including the 36th, in September 2025 to take another swing at Hamas. A ceasefire was announced on 10 October, 2025 which led to the release of the remaining hostages.

The 2023 war in Gaza is relevant to the story of the modern tank because it represents the only major deployment of what can realistically be called a truly modern tank. Yes, the T-90M has been used extensively in Ukraine, but the lack of an active protection system arguably means that it is not a fully modern design. The Merkava Mk 4, by contrast, has been able to operate in an environment that is full of shoulder-fired anti-tank weapons and ATGMs for 714 days. There have been losses, yes, but nothing like the number that would have occurred without Trophy. For comparison, the Oryx blog claims that Russia has lost 151 T-90Ms in Ukraine.[38] There is always some need for caution with these figures: tanks will often be recovered and repaired unless they are catastrophically destroyed. Nevertheless, Russia's tank losses have been extensive, and given Ukraine's widespread use of ATGMs and very potent Western anti-armour weapons like NLAW, which is designed to destroy Soviet tanks, it is not unreasonable to ask how different those losses would have been with an APS fitted. Returning to the IDF's experience in Gaza, it shows that an APS is a central requirement for the modern tank. The lethality of the Merkava, enabled by its advanced sights and mission systems, was sufficient for what the IDF encountered. But the whole operation would have involved much higher losses without the APS.

Whilst the Israelis were developing and getting ahead with the development of APS, Western forces were getting to grips with the tactics of insurgents in Iraq and Afghanistan. This led to extensive efforts to add mine protection to tanks, as well as something called statistical armour. You might know statistical armour as bar or slat armour. It refers to the metal cages built around the outside of Western vehicles deployed to Iraq and it is known as statistical armour because it offers a *statistical probability* of disrupting an RPG-7 type projectile. That probability may be around 60%, depending on the angle of the strike. It does not provide protection against anything that could hit it, like passive armour. In fact, bar armour is only effective against the PG family of warheads fired by the RPG-7 and its various copies. It works by damaging the fuze or the shaped charge liner inside the warhead, which has a very specific mechanism called a piezoelectric fuze.

It relies on the warhead being crushed, which crushes the piezoelectric crystal that then generates a small electric current. The current travels down a wire to the explosive and detonates it. Bar armour catches the warhead and crushes its outer skin, which either prevents the warhead from detonating or crushes the liner so that it collapses imperfectly and has reduced penetration. Alongside this, Western tanks went to war with a lot of additional armour; in Iraq, for example, the Challenger 2 weighed in at 75 tonnes with its full suite of Dorchester armour. There are famous instances of insurgents struggling to take these tanks out, and some cases where they succeeded. However, ATGMs like Kornet were relatively rare at the time, and so the pressure to procure an APS was reduced. But after Iraq and Afghanistan, the US, UK, and Germany have all placed orders for Trophy. The APS is now a standard part of the new-build Leopard 2A8 and the M1A2 Abrams SEP v.3, and Poland and Hyundai Rotem have signed an agreement to integrate it into the K2 Black Panther.

Trophy is not the only APS on the market. There are many others and it is likely that some competitors will be accepted into service soon. Rheinmetall has its StrikeShield system, which is a distributed APS, meaning that the interceptors and sensors are distributed around the vehicle. There are no moving parts, but the same module both detects and engages the target. Elbit's Iron Fist is a pedestal system that has been selected for the IDF's Eitan 8×8 infantry fighting vehicle as well as the Dutch CV90 upgrade. There are many others, but the core principle of the APS remains the same: to increase the chances of mission success. It is no longer effectively possible to fully protect the modern tank against the type of threats that a force like Hezbollah or ISIS can bring to bear. Not without producing an 80-tonne monster, at least. And so, an APS is a central element of the modern tank, and their performance will define future tank operations to a significant extent. But now, it is time to turn briefly to mobility, and how the modern tank evolved between 1992 and 2025 to cope with the weight added to it.

Chapter 17

Catch me if you can

The video starts with two uniformed personnel setting up a step ladder at the muzzle of a tank. They add two wine glasses to a platform connected to the side of the barrel that are then filled by an officer in dress uniform.[1] The tank then proceeds to bow, dipping its glacis low towards the ground, before returning to a neutral position again and lowering the rear of the tank to the ground. The gun is stabilized, so it stays balanced as the turret is rotated to the side, and the tank dips its right and then left side to the ground. Throughout this demonstration, the wine in the glasses stays more or less level. The demonstration was conducted by the Type 10 from Japan. We start this chapter with the Type 10 because at a time when the weight of Challenger 2, the M1A2, and the Leclerc was increasing significantly to address the threats of counterinsurgency, the Type 10 was built to be lighter and more mobile. When the Type 10 entered development in 2002, the country already had a relatively new MBT, the Type 90. That tank is similar in appearance to a Leopard but it has a crew of three and a weight of 55 tonnes. However, that weight meant that it could only navigate over 65% of Japan's bridges. Its size would also mean that it might struggle in an urban fight, although it is not as big as the Leopard 2. The Type 10 entered service in 2012 at a weight of 44 tonnes with room to grow, and the ability to navigate over 85% of Japan's bridges, according to a 2016 government report.[2]

There are three aspects of the Type 10's mobility that are worth examining, not so much for their relevance to the modern tank, but for what they might mean for the future tank. The first is its weight, and the relationship between weight and protection. The second is its hydropneumatic suspension, and the third is the continuously variable transmission it carries. Weight has become a decisive issue for the future tank mostly because the modern tank is so heavy. The worst offender is arguably the 75 tonne Challenger 2 with its Dorchester Level 2H armour during Operation *Telic*, the UK's name for its deployment to Iraq.[3] The M1A2 SEP v.3 comes in at 67 tonnes, but Trophy would add another two tonnes to that. The Leopard 2A8, which has Trophy integrated as standard, tips the scales at 64 tonnes, according to KNDS, and the Merkava Mk 4 Windbreaker is also around the 72-tonne mark.[4] All of these tanks are very well protected, but at these weights they pose serious challenges for the enablers that they need to get into battle. This extends from things like heavy equipment transporters, the big trucks used to transport tanks on long journeys, through to the armoured bridge layers that help tanks cross gaps in combat. If the bridges are not upgraded to account for the additional weight, they may collapse as the tanks cross them. In addition, Europe's own infrastructure might be unable to support the weight of these tanks, leading to damaged bridges and sewers, and reduced mobility. Moreover, off-road mobility generally trends downwards as the weight of a vehicle increases, and in turn, recovery of vehicles that are stuck becomes more difficult the heavier they are.

The Type 10 breaks this paradigm in its weight, but the obvious question is whether or not it provides the requisite level of protection. It does seem that prototypes were tested against 120mm APFSDS rounds during the development process, which would suggest that they are fairly well protected. The tank also carries laser warning receivers as standard, and has the ability to add different armour packs to the turret as dictated by the anticipated combat. The Japanese MoD also announced in 2024 that it was looking into Trophy, Iron Fist, and Rheinmetall's StrikeShield as potential active protection systems for the tank. Together, these protection solutions would probably increase the weight of the tank, but would provide a reasonable level of protection against most modern threats. So, it seems fair to say that the tank has, or will have, an effective level of protection for its weight that would make it sufficiently survivable, assuming that an APS is successfully fielded. But what does the Type 10 gain for that weight saving? Well, the available data gives it a top speed of 70km/h, both forwards and in reverse. This is a staggering reverse speed, especially when you consider that the Leopard 2 was fairly capable at 31km/h, and the T-72 can only break 4km/h, forcing the crew to pivot the vehicle – potentially under fire – to drive forwards and away from danger.

Table 4 summarizes the key mobility parameters of the modern tanks, helping to contrast them with the Type 10. Let's take a look at that continuously variable transmission. It is called the MT1200 HMT (Hydro-Mechanical Transmission) and it was designed by Mitsubishi Heavy Industries. Very little has been made public about the transmission, but we do understand something about hydro-mechanical transmissions and the benefits of being able to continuously variable the transmission output. First, think back to Chapter 14 and the role of the transmission in a tank. It has three main jobs: firstly, it must convert the power generated by the engine into torque, much more torque than the engine can produce alone. It must also steer the tank, handling huge forces as it does; and finally, it must provide the braking, which is no mean feat for a 50-tonne vehicle. With that in mind, the MT1200 HMT has two paths to transmit the power from

TABLE 4 Mobility of the modern tank

Specification	*Type 10*	*K2 Black Panther*	*Leopard 2A8*	*M1A2 SEP v.3*	*T-90M*
Weight	44 tonnes	56 tonnes	64 tonnes	>67 tonnes	>48 tonnes
Top speed	70km/h	70km/h	60km/h	60km/h	70km/h
Reverse speed	70km/h	30km/h (estimate)	31km/h	40km/h	14km/h (estimate)
Range	500km	450km	550km	400km	550km
Transmission	MT1200 HMT, automatic and continuously variable	EST15K automatic	Renk HSWL 354	X-1100-3B automatic	Automatic
Engine	Model 8VA34WTK 1,200hp	DV-27K, 1,500hp	MTU MB 873 Ka-501, 1,500hp	AGT 1500, 1,500hp	V-92S2F 1,130hp
Suspension	Hydro-pneumatic	Hydro-pneumatic	Torsion bar	Torsion bar	Torsion bar

the engine to the drive sprocket, a mechanical one with planetary gears and a hydraulic one; it uses them both at the same time by combining their outputs and transmitting that to the output shaft connected to the drive sprocket. The hydraulic element can add or subtract speed from the mechanical system to create the variable output. The planetary gears work like a regular transmission, with peaks and troughs in their torque generation, but the hydraulic component helps to fill in the gaps. A conventional transmission, such as that used in the Leopard 2, might have a hydraulic component to provide initial torque, but will then switch to mechanical planetary gears to take the shaft speed of the engine and turn it into torque. This means that the gears have to be decoupled and then reconnected to change the gear ratio, allowing the engine speed (rpm) to drop. In real terms this means that when a Leopard 2 accelerates, there will be noticeable moments where the gears change and it momentarily loses acceleration. The MT1200, by contrast, provides a smooth acceleration path, which means that it is able to generate much more of its torque at earlier stages of acceleration and continue providing power throughout the acceleratory phase.

Additionally, the transmission will essentially seek the optimal gear ratio for the given engine load. So, if the driver has to overcome a hill, which is quite common in Japan, the transmission will adapt its ratio to match the load on the engine and the rpm, allowing the driver to maintain acceleration without changing gears. Finally, the continuously variable aspect can also be applied to reversing. Whereas a Leopard 2 has two reverse gears and a T-72 just one, which limits the reverse speed, the Type 10 can have an unlimited number of reverse gears, which is what enables it to drive backwards as quickly as it does forwards. It does this by changing the angle of the swashplate inside the hydraulic component of the transmission. The swashplate is a non-rotating, tiltable metal disc that sits inside the hydraulic pump (the hydrostatic unit). A ring of pistons (arranged like bullets in a revolver) spins against the face of this plate. The angle of the swashplate determines exactly what the pistons do: if the plate is vertical, no oil is moved and nothing happens. But tilt the swashplate and the pistons start moving against the oil: the more the plate tilts, the more oil they act upon and the faster the tank moves. Tilt the swashplate in the opposite direction and the opposite motion is produced.

Table 4 helps to illustrate that on paper mobility characteristics for the modern tank are broadly similar, but the reverse speed of the Type 10 really sets it apart. Operationally, this would mean that the crew could quickly move the tank out of a firing position or away from an area if their laser warning receivers picked up the signal of a Chinese ATGM, for example. Combined with the suspension, which is hydropneumatic and fitted to all five roadwheels, this allows the tank to move quickly and smoothly, as well as change direction regularly. Its designers have also reported that the running gear enables it to fire accurately on the move while conducting aggressive manoeuvres. The suspension can be used to change the tank's ride height, or to lower the hull at the front or rear increasing the elevation and depression of the main gun. This is thought to be a deliberate design choice to help the crew make the most of Japan's hilly and rugged terrain. As ever, some caution is warranted. Manoeuvring aggressively can disrupt the aim of some ATGMs, especially older types like the Sagger, but a Type 10 is still a large target and a Kornet operator would only have to keep the tank within his sight to have a good chance of a hit. With the modern target trackers fitted to some tanks, it would also do little to cause an APFSDS to miss. That said, the Type 10 is interesting because it is undoubtedly a modern tank with networked capabilities, an APS potentially on the way, and good sensors. But it bucks the mobility trend and brings with it some unique features. The last era in this book looks to the future of the tank and the concerted effort to reduce the weight of these vehicles, for many of the same reasons as the Type 10. The MT1200 HMT and hydropneumatic suspension combination could be used to produce a lighter, compact, and yet powerful tank.

However, as Table 4 shows, it is very much the exception to the rule. Most modern tanks are heavy, much heavier than their initial designs, and that has had consequences. They are most obvious in the Leopard 2A7, the predecessor to the 2A8. The Leopard 2A7 is to all intents and purposes an upgraded Leopard 2A4. The Bundeswehr received 2,125 Leopard 2s between 1979 and 1992; the majority of them were in the A0–A3 standard, which meant analogue fire control systems. DigBal, the Leopard's first digital fire control system, was introduced in 1985, creating the Leopard 2A4, with 695 vehicles built at that standard. The remaining 1,430 were then retrofitted to make them 2A4s. And that was the fleet that Germany used to create the 2A5, 2A6, 2A6M, and 2A7.

It took the introduction of the Leopard 2A8 to prompt new production for the Bundeswehr. Why does this matter? Well, it has meant that almost every major upgrade has led to changes to the hull and the tank's centre of gravity. The Leopard 2A5 brought the distinctive arrow-head armour to the front of the turret as well as a number of modifications and additions to the turret. All of this added 4.5 tonnes to the weight of the Leopard 2A4, for a gross vehicle weight of 59.7 tonnes. Most of that weight went to the turret front, and the remainder to the hull. To compensate for the added weight, the torsion bar suspension had to be stiffened to maintain ground clearance. The Leopard 2A6 added the L55 gun to the mix, pushing the tank over the 60-tonne mark; again, much of that weight was towards the front of the vehicle. This led to the introduction of strakes, longitudinal rods welded to the bottom of the hull, to reinforce it.[5]

The 2A6 was followed by the 2A6M between 2006 and 2007, which added a heavy mine blast plate to the belly of the tank. It is worth pausing here to look at other tanks used in this era as this was a common modification. US M1 Abrams and British Challenger 2s deployed to Iraq had frequently encountered large IEDs and mines as Islamic forces began to increase their capabilities. One notable blast in October 2003 killed two of the crew in an Abrams.[6] Over time, the insurgents increased the amount of explosives used in their IEDs and adopted new techniques for operating them, including radio-frequency and infrared detonation. There are clever ways to degrade the performance of an APFSDS and HEAT warhead because they operate on such extreme physical principles. But protecting against blast is more difficult because an insurgent can always add more explosives to the next IED, which is what happened in Iraq. The only viable solution to that threat is to add a thick sheet of very hard and strong armour to the underside of the hull. The armour has to be strong because one of the main threats of blast is plate deformation, where armour can bulge by as much as 10 or 20cm under the blast impulse. Tanks are tight on space and that much movement in a very short space of time can lead to limbs being crushed. If the hull is flat, as is the case for most tanks except the Merkava, most of the mine or IED's energy will be directed into the bottom of the hull, which can overturn the vehicle and throw the crew. A V-shape hull is better at deflecting blast energy and preventing the vehicle from being thrown, but it also lowers the ground clearance, which can reduce mobility.

The blast IEDs were joined by one other threat courtesy of Iran, the explosively formed projectile (EFP). EFPs are similar to HEAT warheads, except that they use the Misznay-Schardin effect. Misznay and Schardin discovered that an explosive shaped as a flat or shallow disk, a little like a bowl, would expand in one direction once detonated. This is used to create an EFP by using a strong container and filling it with the explosive. A shallow dish-shaped copper liner is added to the open end. When the IED is detonated, the pressure wave hits the copper, inverting it and creating a large solid slug travelling at thousands of metres per second. It's not as fast as a HEAT warhead, but EFP slugs retain their considerable kinetic energy for some time, meaning that they could be set up at a distance from a road and still have an effect. A British Challenger 2 was penetrated by an EFP in 2007, severely wounding the driver, and they had soon proliferated around Iraq.[7] To help deal with the blast IED challenge, the US developed and deployed TUSK – the Tank Urban Survivability Kit. It added a whole range of new weapons and protective shields to the Abrams as well as ERA, a heavy mine protection belly plate and a new suspended seat for the driver. TUSK II was put into service in 2006, helping to increase protection somewhat, but adding an estimated 2 tonnes in weight to the Abrams, which was already carrying significant extra weight from the ERA added under TUSK I. The Challenger 2 went through a similar process: its additional belly protection, Dorchester armour blocks, and ERA brought the Theatre Entry Standard vehicles up to 75 tonnes. In these cases, these kits were removed after the Iraq War ended, but the US continued the weight growth of the M1A2 with the addition of Trophy. The point is that it is common to see the weight of a tank increase during war. As the users find out how well the armour fares against the enemy, they will usually ask for changes. This happened with the T-55 in Afghanistan, Leclerc in Yemen, T-72 in Syria, most tanks in Ukraine, and Western tanks in Iraq. This means that a drivetrain should ideally be able to accommodate additional weight without significant and lasting modifications.

The Leopard 2A7, which entered service in 2020, was not so lucky. As the tank evolved from the 55-tonne 2A4 to the 64-tonne 2A7V, the added armour placed extreme stress on the mobility system. Rather than redesigning the entire transmission, engineers adjusted the gear ratio of the final drives. By increasing the reduction ratio in the final drive, the 2A7V maintains the same 0–30km/h acceleration as the lighter 2A4. The trade-off is a lower top speed (reduced from roughly 70km/h to 60km/h), as the 'shorter' gears prioritize the massive torque needed to move the extra weight from a standstill. New tracks and torsion bars also had to be fitted to accommodate the extra weight.[8] Not all modern tanks exceed the 60-tonne mark, with the K2 Black Panther from Hyundai Rotem, Type 99 from Norinco, and T-90M from Uralvagonzavod all notable examples. However, their designers have tended to stay conventional in terms of the mobility design. Powerful diesel engines mated to automatic transmissions have become the norm, providing the tractive effort needed to make these immense machines move while reducing the burden on the driver. At the same time, aspirations for mobility remain modest, for the most part. The MBT is generally required to be capable of crossing difficult and muddy terrain, carrying enough armour and firepower to support infantry and other vehicles. No more, no less. Some, like the Type 10 and Leclerc, provide a blend of agility and mobility. However, there is one category of tank that is worth a mention at this stage, and that is the light tank.

One of the most photogenic light tanks in service at the moment is the Type 15 or ZTQ-15 from China. It is a light tank thought to weigh around 34 tonnes, rising to 36 tonnes when fitted with ERA. It carries a 105mm gun, probably a descendent of the L7, but fitted with an autoloader. It is built for use in China's more challenging terrain, especially the mountainous border that it shares with India. It has a 1,000hp engine, which provides a very respectable 27hp/tonne power to weight ratio. The armour is understandably light compared to the Type 99 MBT that equips China's heavy combined arms brigades, but it is probably sufficient for most of the threats that would be encountered in a mountainous area. Perhaps most importantly, two Type 15s can be carried by a Y-20 transport aircraft, which would allow the People's Liberation Army (PLA) to rapidly move forces into the border region with India, or anywhere for that matter. A similar approach shaped the US development of the now-cancelled M10 Booker light tank. The US Army intended to increase the lethality of its infantry formations and established a requirement for a mobile assault gun that could be delivered by a C-130. But it was also decided to make it tracked and somewhat survivable, so it ended up weighing more and the C-130 compatibility was lost.[9] But two other countries have invested in light tanks: Indonesia and the Philippines, with the Harimau and Sabrah light tanks respectively. The Harimau, built by Turkey's FNSS in partnership with PT Pindad from Indonesia, weighs in at 35 tonnes with a 700hp engine. It brings a high-pressure 105mm gun to the fight, and is well suited to navigating Indonesia's infrastructure and terrain. Similar considerations presumably shaped the Sabrah procurement for the Philippines, which comes in at 30 tonnes with a 720hp engine and similar 105mm main gun. Both can reach a top speed of 70km/h and are protected against heavy machine gun threats including the 14.5×114mm API. This might sound light for a tank, but the 14.5mm KPVT heavy machine gun is a fearsome weapon, and older rounds like the B-32 can penetrate up to 32mm of rolled homogeneous armour. They would not stand up well to RPGs or similar weapons, but should provide a good blend of protection and firepower for use in hard to reach areas.

So, we can see that mobility evolved in one direction between 1992 and 2025. Tanks got heavier, and drivetrains either adapted or they didn't, leading to lasting changes in vehicle performance. At the same time, some countries introduced light tanks to give them different capabilities in challenging places that are not suited to conventional MBTs. The Type 10 is one example of this, the Type 15 another. It reflects how, to some extent, modern tanks are shaped as much by the mobility requirements of some users as they are by the firepower and protection that dominated throughout the Cold War. Mobility and vehicle weight is a hot topic for the future tank, with most users signalling a desire to correct back towards the 50-tonne mark. However, there is one more aspect of the modern tank that needs to be addressed because it is, in my opinion, the most significant development of the modern tank since 1992. It's time to talk about mission systems; sights, networks, and radios.

Chapter 18

The sensors, not the shooters?

A well-known Russia analyst once told me that the Soviet Union did not collapse, but that it was still collapsing. What he meant by that is that the series of wars that have happened in the former Soviet Union since it was officially dissolved in December 1991 were all part of the break-up of the Union. For the most part, those wars have been the result of Russia trying to control the shape of that new world order referenced by Bush back in 1990. The subsequent wars in Chechnya, Georgia, Ukraine, and the 2022 intervention in Kazakhstan were all about controlling Russia's near abroad. The Nagorno-Karabakh Wars between Armenia and Azerbaijan from 1992 to 1994, and again in 2020, were a symptom of the break-up and the way the Soviet Union was ruled and organized. The relevance of this to the modern tank is that Russia, like the West, spent most of the 1990s and early 2000s fighting against what Western military thinkers would refer to as 'sub-peer' opponents. This rather unflattering phrase is used to refer to a variety of opponents from insurgent groups like ISIS or Al-Qaeda through to smaller states that may not be able to stand up to the same military standards. So, for Russia, Georgia is a sub-peer opponent, and Iraq's armed forces in 2003 were a sub-peer opponent for the Coalition. Despite Russia's focus on sub-peer opponents, the West still worked to build the lethality of its tanks; this was achieved through new types of ammunition such as the DM63 tungsten alloy APFSDS from Germany, which was designed to maximize the benefits and increased velocity of the longer L55 version of the Rh120 fitted to the Leopard 2A6. The DM63 was developed to provide stable performance in different climates, as firing its predecessor, the DM53, in a hot environment could lead to dangerous pressure spikes. Its muzzle velocity out of an L55 is 90m/s faster than with an L44.[1] This may not sound like much, but with a projectile weight of 8.5kg, possibly including the sabot, this results in a muzzle energy of 13 MJ out of an L55, compared to just 11.8 MJ out of the L44.

There were some other notable improvements for the Leopard 2 family when the DM12 multi-purpose round, which combined HEAT with HE-FRAG effects, was finally replaced by the DM11 programmable HE round. This change was implemented during the Bundeswehr's upgrade to the Leopard 2A7 standard, which was implemented on just 20 tanks from 2014, before the Leopard 2A7V entered service in 2021, which brought 104 vehicles up to this standard, including the 20 original A7s. The DM11 provided a programmable explosive, which means that the round is sent a signal when in the breech of the gun that tells it when to detonate. Options include a point detonating mode where the round would explode when it hit a wall, a time delay mode where the round would pass through the wall before detonating (assuming the wall was thin/weak enough), and an airburst mode where the round would detonate above the wall. Think back to the accounts of Lt Brown fighting in Korea and the poor fragmentation of the 20-pdr's HE round. That round had a relatively poor fragmentation pattern and would only detonate when it hit something. But the DM11 has an optimized fragmentation pattern and can be detonated in a way that maximizes those results. Infantry taking cover in a trench or behind a wall would be showered with up to 13kg of fragmentation, which makes it a better weapon for suppressing ATGM teams, according to the manufacturer.

The US introduced the M829A3 APFSDS which combined a heavy 10kg depleted uranium rod with a softer tip. It had a marginally lower muzzle velocity at 1,552m/s, but the rod was made thicker and produced with a total length of 730mm including the softer tip material. This was followed in 2014 by the M829A4, which maintained the depleted uranium rod and improved performance and reliability in different operation conditions. In all of these cases, the focus was on maintaining an edge over Russian tanks fitted with ERA. There was no driving need to introduce a new gun, at least until the T-14 Armata appeared in 2015, which rekindled some of the 1990s conversations around the need for a 140mm gun. But the point here is that lethality remained fairly stable for the modern tank between 1992 and 2025. The Leopard 2A8, Challenger 3, and M1A2 SEP v.3 all carry their respective versions of the Rh120. The British and German guns are, or will be, in the L55 configuration, while the US Army has held onto the L44. There are some good reasons for this, by the way. The US has fought a lot of urban battles with the M1 Abrams since 1992 and space is often constrained. The M1 is already big, but its gun barrel measures 5.3m in length, while the L55 comes in at 6.6m. This added length is valuable for increasing velocity, but means that from the muzzle to the bustle at the rear of the turret can be close to 10m. Now, bear in mind that a residential street in a well-planned town might only be 12m from curb-to-curb, and you can begin to imagine the challenges that an extra metre of barrel length introduces. The future will see the introduction of the DM73 for the British and German armed forces. Designed to be fired out of the high-pressure L55A1 gun, it increases the muzzle velocity, and presumably the size of the penetrator, by some margin over the DM63. However, the core technology and approach remains the same as it was in the 1980s. So, what has changed about the firepower of a modern tank? I think the answer is quite simple: the mission systems. But first, let's start with a short journey through a war that was fought between two peer adversaries in 2020.

In July 2020 Armenian and Azeri forces started fighting each other in low-level clashes along the Nagorno-Karabakh border. Already at that phase, drones and long-range missiles were playing an important role. Well, at the very least, that is how they were portrayed. Most of the video footage that made its way to social media outlets was recorded from a drone, which must have shaped perceptions of the fighting to some extent. The clashes led to losses and posturing on both sides, leading eventually to a joint Russian–Armenian counter-UAV (uncrewed aerial vehicle) exercise in September, and a Turkish–Azeri joint exercise as well. Tensions were running high, which wasn't necessarily unusual for the region. Analysts watched and waited, but there was a lot going on.

Then, in September, the frequency of the footage increased. Much of it was released by Azerbaijan's MoD, which had recently taken delivery of the Bayraktar TB2 strike drone from Turkey. The drone is quite large, with a wingspan of 12m, a maximum take-off weight of 700kg, and an endurance of up to 27 hours in newer versions. Its sensor suite includes a charged-couple device (CCD) camera and thermal imaging, which made it difficult for Armenian soldiers to hide, especially as it was used from above. The TB2 also comes with a handy feature that allows the user to download footage from the electro-optical suite in a widely acceptable format. This enabled the Azeris to release regular footage of strikes on Armenian positions. Those delivered to Azerbaijan could also carry four of the MAM-L and MAM-C laser-guided smart bombs, weighing 22kg and 6.5kg respectively. They are relatively small munitions, although the MAM-L carries a tandem HEAT warhead. Both are fired from above, at altitudes up to 5,000m, which meant they still made light work of Armenian armour. Many of the strikes during the opening phase were against Armenian air defence systems – platforms like the Tor-M2KM, which should have been able to detect and engage the drones as they carved their slow orbits through the sky.

It was apparent that the first wave of strikes was focused on the suppression and destruction of Armenian air defences. This was a key mission, but once the Azeris had reached a level of confidence that it had been achieved, the floodgates opened and the attacks increased to include command and control, logistics, tanks, and artillery systems. It was essentially a form of the air strikes that preceded *Desert Storm*, but the Bayraktar TB2 was seen as the leading edge, rather than advanced fixed-wing fighters and stealth bombers. As the Armenian frontline positions were weakened, Azeri special forces were infiltrated into areas behind the frontlines to support the targeting of reinforcements as they attempted to navigate the mountainous terrain. Azeri armour was committed only once conditions were assessed to be favourable, with Armenian positions suppressed or destroyed. The greatest risks they faced were not Armenian T-72s, but mines and ATGMs. Perhaps this was because of Armenia's heavy losses. The open-source tracking website, Oryx, used those TB2 videos to document and count the losses on both sides. The team behind that site assess that Armenia lost 146 tanks, many to TB2 strikes, with another 103 captured by Azeri forces.[2] Another 138 towed artillery pieces were similarly destroyed, with 102 guns captured, and 75 BM-21 Grad multiple rocket launchers were destroyed too. While the focus of this book is tanks, it is worth noting that Armenia's defensive doctrine was likely derived from Russia's, which places a focus on mines, ATGMs, and artillery to slow an offensive with tanks plugging gaps and adding fire support. The loss of so many artillery systems was probably a significant factor in the eventual collapse of Armenian forces. The same can be said of the 34 air defence systems that were destroyed. It has been reported that 3,822 Armenian personnel were also killed during the war.[3] Typical ratios of wounded to fatalities would suggest that another 9,000 or more may have been wounded.

It was not a bloodless campaign for the Azeris, however, which is an important caveat. This war in particular has suffered from the distorting lens of social media to give the impression that Azerbaijan steamrolled the Armenians. The Azeri MoD's own public tally lists 2,908 fallen soldiers, which would suggest a similar potential for wounded to the Armenians, depending on their ability to recover casualties and treat them.[4] Alongside this, 148 Azeri tanks were destroyed or damaged, including ten of the relatively modern T-90S. Another 57 infantry fighting vehicles, mostly the BMP-2 and BTR-82A, were destroyed or damaged as well.[5] Counting losses of vehicles and men is not always a helpful proxy for measuring success in war. To paraphrase von Clausewitz (somewhat reluctantly), war is an extension of politics, and is conducted to achieve political means. The Azeris lost nearly as many men and tanks as the Armenians, but achieved their political goal of pushing Armenian forces out of the Nagorno-Karabakh region.

Despite the heavy losses of armour on both sides, tanks did play a valuable role in the offensives that took place, especially during the battle for the towns of Hadrut and Susha, which happened in October and early November respectively. In both offensives, Azerbaijan task-organized several companies of special forces infantry together with a mechanized brigade that included T-72s. During the battle for Hadrut, Armenian forces made poor use of the urban terrain, enabling the Azeri special forces to clear most of the town without bringing their tanks into the town's limits.[6] Instead, they remained on the outskirts providing fire support into the town. The Bayraktar TB2 was used for much of the special forces' fire support needs. During the battle for Susha, Armenia also had T-72s, which proved problematic when the special forces ran out of ATGMs and poor weather grounded the TB2s.[7] Azerbaijan's advances were achieved through a mixture of special forces infiltration and the movement of conventional forces, mostly in the wake of drone and artillery strikes. ATGMs played an important role on both sides, attacking stationary positions, emplaced tanks, and tanks on the move at long ranges. The Spike system from Israel's Rafael Advanced

Defence Systems, which was used by the Azeris, proved quite potent, in part because it adopts a top-attack approach to a target, striking the turret roof of a tank.

Excluding the initial border skirmishes from July, the war lasted just 44 days from 27 September until 10 November. Various skirmishes and clashes continued long after the war ended, but not at the same intensity. The war had some impact on the modern tank because it helped cement the notion that drones were a major threat to tanks. The TB2 specifically had been used quite effectively by Turkey in Syria against somewhat disorganized forces, but Nagorno-Karabakh gave the impression that it could be a real threat to a conventional force. This is true to some extent. If a force is poorly protected by air defence, or an enemy is able to get the upper hand in suppressing that air defence, then drones like the TB2 will extract a painful price. But it is worth noting that Ukraine's TB2s, and Russia's Orion drones – which are similar – have played a limited role in Ukraine. They are relatively easy to detect and quickly shot down when used close to the frontline, which restricts their ability to shape a war and their impact on the modern tank. In effect, larger drones like the Bayraktar TB2 can be considered alongside conventional fixed-wing aircraft in terms of the threats that they pose to the modern tank. They are much cheaper than a jet, which means more forces can use them, but as a threat they can be addressed by the same systems and capabilities that protect a force from fast jets and helicopters. With that in mind, it is safe to argue that the 2020 war showed the value of tanks, but it also revealed something of their vulnerability, especially to ATGMs and mines. No major adjustments to the designs of modern tanks can be traced to lessons learned from this war; however, it did demonstrate the risk that can be posed to a force's rear echelons by different forms of strike assets. The Armenians were relatively effective in close combat against Azerbaijan's armoured formations, but that efficacy quickly declined as Armenia's rear echelons were degraded by successive strikes.[8]

However, the element of this war that is really relevant to the modern tank is the connectivity and synergy that the Azeri forces achieved between their combat arms. The TB2 stole the show, leading many to declare it the future of warfare, somehow ignoring the dozens of similar-sized drones that had crashed or been shot down in other conflicts around the world. When the TB2 was deployed by Ukraine against Russia, its numbers quickly dwindled and the operators were forced to fly the UAVs in complex, counter-productive flight patterns to complicate detection. This is not to say that strike drones like the TB2, MQ-9, and even the Russian Orion are useless, but that the armed forces using them need to set the conditions for their use. And this is where the modern tank and connectivity come in. The Azeri success was the result of an effective combined arms campaign with land and air assets coordinating their weapons and sensors in close to real-time against Armenian targets. This meant that data was collected and acted upon almost immediately by drones, artillery, helicopters, tanks, and fast jets. Combined arms collaboration is not new; it is effectively what happened during World War II in many battles. By the end of the Cold War, the US Army and Air Force had developed something that they called AirLand Battle. The idea was that instead of focusing on simply destroying the Soviet tanks in front of them, the Army and Air Force would coordinate to disrupt and destroy the second- and third-echelon forces and their logistics. The problem, as they saw it, was that the NATO forces with their M60s, Chieftains, Centurions, and Leopards were probably good enough to destroy the first echelon of Soviet forces. But a second echelon, as strong as the first, would follow in its place. If you were on the main line of effort, then there would likely be a third echelon too.

This is the concept that was tested in 1991 against the Iraqi forces, and it evolved into network-centric warfare, which held that networking all assets in a force together to share more data was the way forward. The full promise of network-centric warfare was hard to realize; however, it did have an impact on the modern tank. Most designs carry some form of battle management system, which enables commanders at different levels (typically squadron to brigade) to look at a map that shows the position of friendly and enemy forces as well as terrain elevation, and also acts as a simple bearer network for messaging and the passage of data. The US Army's system used in the M1 Abrams is called Force XXI Battle Command Brigade and Below (FBCB2). Meanwhile, the British Army deployed something known as P-BISA (Platform Battlefield Information System Application) for its Challenger 2s. Kongsberg from Norway developed the Integrated Combat Solution (IFS), which is built specifically for armoured vehicles and provides support for collaborative target engagements including cross-platform cueing. It is also able to integrate all of the sensors carried by a platform, which might include a driver's camera, situational awareness cameras, and the obvious sights for the commander and gunner, into a networked system for target engagements. The IFS is understood to equip Norwegian CV90s under a 2012 contract, and a range of other combat platforms including the K9 Thunder self-propelled howitzer. Another important battle management system, which is likely to become more important in the near future, is the suite of products developed by Danish company SitaWare. Its products also provide blue force tracking and the types of capability that are present in the FBCB2. However, a lot of work has gone into making the system open and accessible through different forms of communication. This allows it to act as a bridge between national units, which is something very difficult to do. So, with more and more nations procuring SitaWare, including Poland in 2023 for its newly acquired Abrams fleet, it could offer the connectivity between countries that FBCB2 offers between units.

The net result of network-centric warfare was that the US and NATO became heavily reliant on their networks. So, their adversaries developed systems and methods of fighting to target those networks. Then, in 2015, the US Deputy Secretary of Defense, Bob Work, told the US Army to get after AirLand Battle 2.0:

> We are going to have to think about fighting against enemies which have lots of guided rockets, artillery, mortars and missiles, and are using informationalized warfare to completely disrupt our heavily netted [networked] force. So what does AirLand Battle 2.0 look like? I don't know. The Army needs to figure this out.[9]

If you haven't heard it before and feel some mild discomfort at the word 'informationalized', it is a word that tends to mean the process of adding digital and networked capabilities across the force, which in turn leads to 'informatized' warfare – warfare that is led by information. These concepts are commonly used by the People's Liberation Army (PLA) of China to describe how they are trying to fight. They see information as being as important as fuel, ammunition, and personnel. At its greatest extent, it applies to knowing where US carrier strike groups are in the Indo-Pacific, so that the PLA Rocket Force can fire anti-ship ballistic missiles at them. But the PLA Ground Force also sees informatized warfare as key to the future of warfare, and is steadily digitizing its combined arms brigades so that they are better connected and able to share data between them. Anyway, Bob Work's speech led to the idea of the Multi-Domain Battle, which was a simple extension of AirLand Battle to include all domains, land, air, sea, space, and the electromagnetic spectrum. Working through some earlier concept studies, US commanders realized that they needed something called 'convergence' and 'integration'. Convergence refers to bringing the right capabilities from across domains together to achieve a given task in the same space and time. That task, for reference, is usually destroying an enemy's air defence and long-range strike assets in US parlance. Integration means the technical solutions required to get all of the platforms talking to each other so that the right data can be shared between them to do that task.

Multi-Domain Battle became Multi-Domain Operations in 2018 and it was shortly followed by the UK with its idea of Multi-Domain Integration, which is similar but different. The French armed forces, through their SCORPION programme, are also reaching for a future of highly networked warfare with seamless connectivity between platforms. The Italian army has a programme called Forza NEC (Network Enabled Capability), which similarly aims to connect all of its armoured units together in a combat cloud. The IDF is perhaps the most advanced, having launched an all-encompassing digitalization drive of its armed forces in the early 2000s. The Ghost Unit mentioned in Chapter 16 is the embodiment of the IDF's multi-domain efforts, designed to bring effects from all domains to bear against ground targets. Generally speaking, tying these concepts down can be quite difficult, in part because there seems to be some element of interpretation. But the relevance for the modern tank is that there is a perceived need to increase connectivity between platforms. In a nutshell, imagine how effective an Israeli armoured battlegroup in the 1973 war would have been if its tank commanders could simply have designated an Egyptian tank formation on their digital map in order to produce an air or artillery strike in a matter of minutes? This is the goal of greater connectivity, and to explore it, there are two key sets of technology: the software and radios that make it happen, and the sights.

We need to explore the sights because technology advanced significantly between 1992 and 2025. New types of thermal imager can bring levels of detail that allow a crew to see and identify targets at the limit of their gun's range. You may remember that Captain Purbrick from the British Army was able to identify hot patches to his front that were probably tanks, but could not see them in enough detail to *know* that they were Iraqi tanks. Modern thermal imagers are much better than this. They are accompanied by charged-couple device (CCD) cameras, which replace the old optical sights used in daylight. An optical sight is a bit like a telescope. It can magnify to the level of the lenses fitted to it. A CCD camera is like a phone camera. It can zoom in variably and uses a digital architecture that allows artificial intelligence and target trackers to be overlaid onto the sight picture. However, the software is critical. Computers are at the heart of the modern tank and the applications that run on them, like P-BISA, define a large part of what they are able to do in coordination with the force that they are a part of. This matters to the modern tank for two reasons: firstly, greater situational awareness including being able to automatically designate targets for engagement by another system is highly likely to be very beneficial in any war; and secondly, most armies, with a few notable exceptions, are shrinking in size.* This means that continuous frontlines are unlikely to feature in future wars. Instead, they will probably appear similar to that found in Ukraine, a series of fortified posts ideally within reach of each other to provide mutual fire support. As a result, tank units and infantry especially may have to get used to defending a large area with a relatively small force footprint, which in turn places a premium on knowing what is going on around them.

How the tanks will achieve this is not entirely decided, but some solutions have already emerged. One of them is a system known as Fireweaver, which is another Israeli invention. Fireweaver is effectively a fire control system that needs to be partnered with a battle management system. The IDF procured the system for its armoured brigades in 2020 and it is understood to have been used in the Gaza War.[10] It connects all sensors and shooters, including rifle sights if they are compatible, into a single control system that allows a battalion commander to

*The US Army had around 600,000 personnel in 1992, falling to approximately 440,000 in 2025. France went from 250,000 to 118,000 in the same time, although this was driven by the end of conscription. The UK went from 145,000 to 74,000, the smallest the British Army has been since the 1800s.

delegate targets to different combat units. This could mean that a tank identifies a soldier in a window, but the job of engaging him is given to a drone unit or ATGM team, for example. There are other efforts that are broadly analogous to Fireweaver, but try to achieve a similar result through different routes. Fireweaver is arguably a tactical system, meaning it is designed to be used at the battalion level where things can be quite messy. Other initiatives like the US Army's Tactical Intelligence Targeting Node, however, are likely to be held at a brigade level and fuse information from satellites, vehicles, drones, and ships. So, it is not really of that much relevance to the modern tank. The IDF, therefore, is arguably at the apex of network connectivity between armoured platforms insofar as getting systems into service is concerned.

But having systems that can run a programme is only one part of the story. The way that data is shared between tanks is also critical. Tactical radio sets supposedly played an important role during World War II, allowing tank crews to coordinate between themselves and with higher echelons as needed to call for fire and air support. The core technology for radio sets improved throughout the Cold War, but some very notable advances came in between 1992 and 2025. Advances in satellite communications (SATCOM) and navigation took on a new level of importance, providing links around the world and enabling navigation through GPS. The blue force tracking in FBCB2 is achieved through SATCOM and something known as the Enhanced Position Location Reporting System (EPLRS), which monitors the GPS coordinates of a tank and shares them over a secure network. GPS was also a critical enabler for Coalition forces fighting in the Gulf War in 1991. GPS has come to be really important for long-range precision strike and airborne navigation, which is why adversaries like Russia and China have developed so many systems to jam it. GPS also provides timing for things like radio networks, which will become important in a moment.

For most of the Cold War, radio networks were fairly limited in their capabilities. They allowed limited amounts of traffic in one direction, because radios had to be tuned to the same frequency. So if a person happened to talk on their radio for a long time, it would restrict the ability of everybody else to communicate. Until encryption became widespread, which was in the 1990s with the US Army's SINCGARS (Single Channel Ground and Airborne Radio System), anything said over a radio net could be intercepted and listened to by others in the area with systems that could pick up the same frequency. This effect was observed publicly during Russia's invasion of Ukraine when it became clear that its forces did not know how to, or chose not to, encrypt their radio traffic. SINCGARS also introduced frequency hopping, which is where the frequency used to send a signal changes hundreds of times per second, making it more difficult to listen in to. However, these radios still needed a line of sight to talk to each other. Remember that frequencies like VHF (30.000 to 87.975 MHz) are part of the electromagnetic spectrum and are essentially different parts of light. This means they can only travel in a straight line, and some don't deal with buildings or trees very well. For most of the tank's existence, radios have also used a push to talk system, which means only one person can speak on a channel at any one time. To do this, they have to press a button, and the military developed basic principles for talking over a radio, such as finishing a message with the word 'over', in order to let the other person know that it was their turn to talk. Duplex radios helped address this, allowing two-way communication in some examples, which is more like talking on a phone.

The distance a radio can communicate is in part decided by its power output, which is typically defined in watts. The elevation of the antenna is also key. This means that an infantryman with a handheld radio may have just 5 W of power and a short line of sight, leading to limited reach with his radio. It's not such a big deal for communication within a section of infantry: they shouldn't be more than a few hundred metres from each other. Vehicle radios, however, tend to go up in wattage compared to the infantry-carried versions. Some provide as much as 20 W of power, which enables them to send bigger messages or data packets over longer ranges. The vehicle has more power available and an antenna that will be 2 or 3m higher than that held by a typical soldier. However, even if a tank squadron is grouped together, its members will be spread out over quite a wide area and they need that power to communicate. On top of that, modern tanks are often sharing a much richer picture through their battle management and blue force tracking systems than their predecessors. All of this means they have more to send and receive, so they need an increased power budget. Overall, the radio is a core enabler for the modern tank. It ensures that units can gel together and fight effectively, but it certainly has its limits. There is one emerging technology, however, which may overhaul tank communications: the MANET.

A MANET (sometimes pronounced MAN-NAY or MAN-ET) stands for Mobile Ad-hoc NETwork. It simply means that all of the radios in a unit should form a network between themselves and share data as little packets of information. In theory, if one node of the network – a vehicle – moves out of range or is jammed or destroyed, the network should automatically find an alternative route for the traffic it is carrying. This is called self-healing, and it is also used to find the optimal route for the data with the least traffic and greatest bandwidth. In addition, because the nodes are likely to move constantly, a MANET will re-map itself in real-time. Modern radios being introduced into service like the AN/PRC-158 from L3Harris and AN/PRC-162 from Collins Aerospace, which are both used by the US, enable multi-channel comms and can, in theory, form a MANET. This also enables them to extend the communication range within a formation, and even out to other formations that would previously be difficult to reach, helping to address that challenge of smaller forces deployed over a wider area.[11] If MANETs enter service more widely, they should empower tank forces to cover a bigger battlespace and share more data between them than ever before.

Advances in radios were essential for the network-centric concepts that had led Western forces for the past four decades, but the changes to sights are just as important. One analysis of the Nagorno-Karabakh War went so far as to suggest that the sights on the TB2s and the general saturation of sensors on the battlefield were much more important than the weapons used. Indeed, the colour CCD camera and thermal imagers on the TB2 do allow for a very detailed view of the Armenian equipment, which shows how this type of technology has proliferated. It has also made its way onto tanks. The M1A2 brought the Commander's Independent Thermal Viewer (CITV) into service in 1992, adding a panoramic (meaning it can be rotated 360 degrees) sight to the left of the turret roof. This meant the commander could scan for his own targets independently without moving the turret or borrowing the gunner's sight. In theory, it fully enables a tactic called 'hunter-killer', which is where the commander independently scans for targets and, once one is identified, passes it off to the gunner to engage. While the gunner lases the target and fires the main gun, the commander scans the surroundings for another target and the process continues. Hunter-killer allows some parts of the tank gunnery process to be run simultaneously, rather than linearly, leading to a 45% increase in target acquisition speed and a 50% increase in the tank's offensive capability over the M1A1 as a result.[12] A System Enhancement Package (SEP) followed shortly after the M1A2 entered service, with the first version entering service in 1999. SEP v.1 brought with it a second-generation thermal imager.[13] What is a Gen 2 thermal imager, you ask?

Well, Gen 1 thermal imagers worked line by line with many detectors and a mechanical mirror that had to scan the scene to produce an image. This was ok, but the resultant image would be blurry and noisy because the detectors would pick up a lot of different signatures. Gen 2 makes the thermal imager digital and introduces the focal plane array, with a rectangular array of 480 detectors high and four rows of detectors wide. This move reduced the number of wires needed, as Gen 1 imagers required a wire for each detector, and the system also captured each point four times before digitally stacking them. This resulted in a much cleaner and sharper image, which in turn meant that the gunner and commander could fully exploit the range of their gun and also zoom in on identified targets. This new imager and sight provided a number of significant improvements over the Gen 1 systems. The idea was to increase the accuracy and clarity of the imagery, which in turn led to an increase in engagement range. You may notice that Table 5 shows a reduction in the field of view for the Gen 2 imagers. The field of view refers to how much of the scene the imager can see. For comparison, a modern iPhone will have a much wider horizontal field of view, close to 70 degrees depending on the model, but it will see very little at a range of 4,000m. The narrower field of view means that Gen 2 imagers provide a sharper image that is much better for target identification, but can lead to the gunner seeing a very narrow slice of the battlefield.

TABLE 5 Gen 1, Gen 2, and Gen 3 thermal imagers

Specification	*Gen 1*	*Gen 2*	*Gen 3*
Detectors	120 × 1	480 × 4	1,280 × 720
Resolution	320 × 240 approx	640 × 480	1,280 × 720
Wavelength	LWIR	LWIR	LWIR and MWIR
Wide field of view	7.5° × 15°	7.5° × 13.3°	2.8° to 22.2° continuous zoom
Narrow field of view	2.5° × 5°	2.0° × 3.6°	2.8° to 22.2° continuous zoom
Identification range	3,000m	4,000m	>5,000m

The most modern iteration of the Abrams, the M1A2 SEP v.3, was expected to introduce Improved FLIR. However, that capability is not listed on the General Dynamics website nor is it mentioned in the US Department of Defense documents covering the programme's progress. The capabilities it would have added included scanning in both MWIR and LWIR, as well as four fields of view which would extend identification and engagement ranges.[14] In December 2022, Leonardo DRS was awarded a contract for Gen 3 FLIR, which is understood to include the ability to sense in MWIR and LWIR.[15] So it stands to reason that the SEP v.3 does not include Gen 3 thermal imaging, but the M1E3 will. This technology will have several benefits to the modern tank once it comes into use. The two wavelengths are affected to differing extents by weather. The longer wavelengths of LWIR can bend around dust particles in the air, making them more effective in dry or smoky conditions. MWIR detectors are better in humid and maritime environments, as humidity can absorb LWIR radiation, reducing the clarity of the imagery. With access to both, the future tank crew will be able to switch between those modes to operate according to the weather conditions. Additionally, it may be possible to fuse the outputs from both into a single image. This would give the high-contrast capabilities of LWIR, bringing out the detail of vegetation and trees, and the sensitivity of MWIR, providing detailed images of the target for recognition and identification.

The Leopard 2A8, which is the first new-build Leopard 2 for the Bundeswehr since 1992, also carries a Gen 3 thermal imager. Both the commander and gunner are provided with the ATTICA imager from Hensoldt. ATTICA also works in MWIR and LWIR, providing a field of view that extends from 2.8 to 22.2 degrees. It has a very high resolution for the MWIR detector, which is 1280×720 heat sensing pixels.[16] This equates to more than 920,000 detectors, which is around three times the number of detectors in earlier generations of thermal imaging. This means that the resultant image will be many times more detailed, allowing for much better target identification and understanding even at extreme ranges. It should mean that even in a wide field of view the gunner and commander can see the target in quite good detail. The PERI RTWL that carries ATTICA also provides an aspect ratio of 16:9; this means that the sight gives the commander a rectangular view, as opposed to a square one. All of this imagery is relayed to the commander and gunner using a 3G-SDI video interface, which is a very high standard of digital interface that allows for 3 gigabytes of data to be smoothly shared from the sight to the user interface. If you think back to the introduction of thermal imaging in Chapter 15, you may remember that reducing lag in the time between capturing imagery and acting upon it was a key driver of development for the early systems. Well, the 3G-SDI provides that imagery with literally no latency. The high quality of the imagery means that it can be readily provided to a computer to run artificial intelligence or regular algorithms over the imagery for target and object recognition. Finally, it is worth noting that not all of the most modern tanks are pursuing Gen 3 thermal imaging. The Challenger 3 is moving to the Thales TrueHunter sight, which uses an MWIR focal plane array instead of the LWIR line scanner on the Challenger 2. It provides much greater clarity and crispness to imagery than the previous generation, but relies on artificial intelligence and augmentation for improved performance. This includes a full field-of-view assistance in target detection and tracking.[17]

The guns of the modern tanks are more lethal than what the Coalition took to war in 1991. That is undoubtedly true, although it is primarily a result of improved ammunition natures and only recently the increased chamber pressure allowed for by the L55A1 and newer Russian guns. However, adding lethality does not mean much if the crew is unable to identify targets, and that is why the modern tank is as much about the sensor as it is about the gun. Admittedly the accuracy of the sensors takes on a different importance in urban environments where ranges are reduced and it is clarity that matters, but the fact remains that the modern tank, best represented by the Leopard 2A8 and Merkava Mk 4 Barak, is made exceptionally lethal by its sights and ability to share that data with other platforms. It is this area that will see the most development in the tanks of the future. The issue of bigger guns is being discussed, but hangs in the balance with no clear consensus. Overall, the era between 1992 and 2025 saw the modern tank evolve and realize the benefits of modern computing to deploy with systems that automatically track friendly units, and sights that can identify enemy vehicles and ranges their forbears could only dream of. The impact of this new technology was felt in the Nagorno-Karabakh War, albeit from the air. It served to show what can happen to a force when the battlefield is saturated with sensors that are connected to effective and precise weaponry.

As we turn to the final era of the modern tank, it is time to look ahead to what the future holds. From this era we have learned that platform protection will have to change and that the available active protection systems do balance out platform survivability. Drones will continue to feature, both as a threat and as a capability for the future tank, but network connectivity is seen as a key enabler.

PART 6

2030–50: A brave new world

The modern tank has been through some tough times. The technology that makes tanks work has evolved constantly since Lieutenant Nordstrom went toe-to-toe with North Korean armour as the 27th Commonwealth Brigade raced to the Yalu River. As a result, the modern tank is a fearsome machine: one that an adversary will have to risk serious time, effort, and resources to defeat. However, as we look to the 2030s, which is when future tank concepts are expected to come into service, there is some notable divergence. For the first time since 1939, the defence and security goals of the US and Europe are not necessarily aligned. The result is that approaches to tank design are changing with the needs of their armed forces. At the same time, there are many new players adding their own technological experience and perspective to the scene. The future tank may look completely different from the modern tank, but how?

Chapter 19

The future of the modern tank

There are, I would argue, five tank designs that fit the bill of a next-generation tank. Are these designs truly next-generation designs? Well, we will see. Until now, there have been clear demarcations between tank designs that signify each new generation. At each stage of the tank's development, certain performance parameters were met by different forms of technology. This occurred at different times in each country; for example, we have seen how the Soviet Union was first to deploy tanks with an advanced ballistic computer in the form of the T-64B. Meanwhile, the US got a tank with thermal imaging into service shortly before anyone else. There are approximately four discernible generations of tanks, in my opinion at least, which are outlined in Table 6. Each generation came with a step-change in combat capability, enabling the tanks to do something fundamentally new over the previous generation. Each generation builds on the foundations of the one before, so a fourth-generation tank would have all of the capabilities of those that came before it, for example.

Where a tank fits into these generations is not clear cut. A tank may fall into Generation 3.5, for example, with a rotating sight head but no active protection system, or one that was added on as an upgrade. The M1A2 SEP v.2 is an example of this, whereas the M1A1 would fit neatly into Gen 3. This is my classification for tank generations, which clearly begins post-World War II and focuses on the technologies that had led to the modern tank. With this framework in mind, what do the current concepts for next-generation designs bring to the table? There are two things that stand out: the firepower of the new designs, and manned-unmanned teaming. The first is fairly clear cut: three of the

TABLE 6 Generations of the modern tank

Generation	*Capabilities*	*Technology*
First generation	Effectively limited to combat in daylight. Capable of defeating similar tanks and able to lead an offensive.	Basic main armament and ammunition combination that is effective against tanks of a similar generation but ineffective against anything more advanced. May have rudimentary stabilization. Heavy angled armour to the front.
Second generation	Able to see to a limited extent at night. Effective in combat against other tanks at greater ranges due to stabilization and able to lead an offensive.	Stabilized gun, passive infrared night vision, and a gun/ammunition combination that can defeat second-generation tanks at typical combat ranges. Protection primarily through RHA although may include some more advanced types.
Third generation	Fighting at night, firing on the move. Good protection against most battlefield threats. Effective situational awareness, but limited to commander and gunner.	Thermal imaging, high-quality stabilization combined with ballistic computers, and advanced armour that protects the tank without exceeding mobility characteristics needed for manoeuvre warfare. A gun/ammunition combination that can defeat third-generation tanks.
Fourth generation	Fighting connected, active protection against most significant ATGM threats, advanced situational awareness.	Gen 2 + thermal imaging along with CCD cameras in rotating electro-optical heads. Active protection systems built into the design, and a gun/ammunition combination that can defeat fourth-generation tanks. Situational awareness enhanced by connectivity with other units.

five designs have been displayed with bigger guns, one of them can be fitted with one, and the fifth is unclear. It seems fairly likely that if any of these designs make it into production the future modern tank will carry a much bigger gun than its predecessors. We will go into specifics shortly. The second aspect is more opaque than a bigger gun. The concept of manned-unmanned teaming (MUM-T) basically holds that a crewed vehicle, be it a tank, F-35, or frigate, will act as the control centre for similar vehicles that are not crewed. It is hoped that adding more combat mass through uncrewed platforms will help counteract the decline in manpower and force size that most militaries are going through. At the same time, MUM-T could support new concepts of operation. For example, one of the takeaways from fighting in Ukraine is that reconnaissance with crewed platforms or infantry can be fairly irresponsible. In one captured document from a Russian command post, a senior officer had recorded his complaints about artillery observers who were refusing to leave the safety of their bunkers to call in and correct indirect fires. The chances of them dying were so high, that they preferred to use drones and stay out of harm's reach. It is likely that any high-intensity war would see similar loss of life in the reconnaissance role, and so MUM-T offers opportunities for that very dangerous job to be delegated to an autonomous platform. Alternatively, as is the case for loyal wingmen in the air, they could genuinely increase combat mass. For example, Hanwha Systems is working on a leader-follower concept for its K9A3 self-propelled howitzer. This would mean one crewed howitzer that acts as the lead platform for two or three that are autonomous. If the concept can be successfully realized, it would deliver the same firepower as a traditional battery of guns, but with a much smaller frontline crew.

Theoretically, MUM-T is sound. It offers real and tangible benefits. But realizing it in the land domain is an immense challenge. When a UAV flies autonomously, which many do for portions of their flight, there is not much for the UAV to navigate unless it is flying in civilian airspace. There are some things that are difficult to adjust for without a pilot in the aircraft. For instance, if a UAV stalls and begins to lose altitude, loses its GPS signal, or is manoeuvred too enthusiastically, it can be lost without the pilot there to fix the error. But otherwise the navigation challenges are fairly simple. Similarly at sea there is a lot of space and the sea is relatively predictable. An enemy can't damage the sea. Put an uncrewed ground vehicle (UGV) in a city and then fight through it, and you can imagine the challenges. Buildings get crushed into rubble, craters appear in roads where the vehicle's map does not expect them to be. Equally in a field or more rural setting, the terrain will quickly be churned up and damaged, which requires a lot of skill to navigate. Things like holes filled with water can be very difficult for a UGV to interpret. Even crewed vehicles face difficulties interpreting terrain. Some IDF tank crews misinterpreted craters and rubble in Gaza, leading to the rolling of some vehicles and loss of life. The challenge may be addressed by the spread of expertise from the commercial world into defence. At the time of writing, companies like Applied Intuition were working on bringing that very thing to the UK and Europe. Applied had already integrated its autonomy stack onto light vehicles like the US Army's M1301 Infantry Squad Vehicle before bringing its offering to the UK.[1] Another company called Forterra has received a contract to build its autonomy solution into the US Marine Corps' Remotely Operated Ground Unit for Expeditionary Fires (ROGUE-Fires) platform. If successful, it would enable the ROGUE vehicles, which carry two anti-ship missiles, to navigate autonomously, without a soldier following them with a remote control.[2]

There is a whole world of challenges involved in the MUM-T paradigm beyond navigation. How can an uncrewed tank be taught to operate somewhat autonomously and responsively to the emerging battle, for instance. And here the future of the tank merges with that of the UAV. A UAV is often portrayed as a way to remove humans from the frontline, which is true – to some extent – but they do not necessarily result in a reduction in the number of humans needed to make them work. An MQ-9 Reaper, which is one of the most widely used medium-altitude long-endurance UAVs, requires a crew of up to two to fly it, and may be paired with an intelligence team to sift through its imagery in greater detail than the two operators. Then there is the ground crew responsible for maintenance, arming the aircraft, and launching it. The end result is a force footprint in personnel that may not be significantly lower than for a fast jet. Different capabilities are designed for different roles, but if an anticipated reduction in personnel is the driving force behind autonomous platforms, then the platform has to be autonomous enough to increase combat mass without adding personnel. What this means for MUM-T and the future tank is that the unmanned tanks *need to be autonomous.* Remote-controlled tanks would create the same situation as an MQ-9, with a relatively large crew still required, but sat some distance behind the frontline. In addition to navigation, this means that uncrewed UGVs, or robotic combat vehicles as some of the larger variants are known, need to be able to distinguish between friendly and enemy forces. In the latter case, they probably need to be empowered to make quick decisions about engaging them, likely with a human supervising or at least approving the process. The subject quickly crosses the bridge into the world of lethal autonomous weapon systems, which are politically charged. The politics of the autonomous tanks aren't the subject of this book, but the capabilities are.

The technology that would make autonomous navigation and target engagement possible is being developed. It relies on a few different capabilities within the world of artificial intelligence (AI). The first of note is machine vision, which is where a computer is taught to detect and recognize the objects that it is seeing. This is made possible and militarily useful by machine learning through neural networks. A neural network is essentially made up of millions of computing nodes. Ideally, tens of thousands of images and footage will be passed through the network to teach its algorithm to recognize a given set of things. It can be anything. One engineer trained a cat flap to recognize when his cat was bringing a dead animal into his house and refuse entry, for example. But in our context, and for a NATO state, it would likely be Russian tanks and armoured vehicles, both camouflaged and bare. The algorithm, or more accurately *algorithms*, would also be taught to recognize friendly vehicles. These outputs could then be condensed into their requisite metadata and passed to a command and control system for a human to act upon. Passing metadata is important for defence and often underappreciated. Metadata is essentially a very small packet of information that explains what a thing is and where it is. It could take up a few kilobits instead of the many megabytes that a full-motion video would require. These figures are critical because most militaries are operating with very high frequency (VHF) and ultra high frequency (UHF) radios, which have limited bandwidth. Choking that bandwidth with full motion video and imagery would help nobody. It follows that it would be very useful if an autonomous platform can sense its target and give a reasonable assessment of what it is before passing that to an operator as metadata. This could look like a string of text: [Target: T-72,

Coord: 123.456, Confidence: 94%] with a small thumbnail image to increase user confidence, for example. Elements of this have been trialled in the UK through a partnership between Helsing, which builds AI specifically for defence, and General Dynamics, albeit using the Ajax reconnaissance vehicle rather than a tank.[3]

The final piece of this puzzle is computing. Once the algorithms have been trained, which typically happens on the cloud (virtual computers that are just somewhere else), they can be loaded onto a small computer and installed into a vehicle. The most common computers used at the moment are the Nvidia Orin and Raspberry Pi, depending on how intensive the computing requirements are. They take up very little space and power and can fit easily inside a vehicle turret or drone. Most Raspberry Pi computers lack the CUDA cores for high-speed computer vision. What is a CUDA core, you might be asking? Well, it stands for Compute Unified Device Architecture, which doesn't help explain what they are. Instead, think of the processor you have inside your computer right now. Mine runs on an Intel EVO i7, which is able to run multiple complex tasks simultaneously. If I want to run a video in the background while I am researching with 30 different tabs open as well as a large manuscript, the 16–24 processors in my computer are built to handle that kind of workload. An Nvidia Orin, however, carries a processor as well as thousands of CUDA cores. Each CUDA core is designed to handle one mathematical operation at a time, which means an Nvidia Orin can handle thousands of operations in parallel. To understand why, think back to the simple explanation of neural networks above. They are essentially giant maths problems, with each layer assessing how likely a pixel is to be a thing. Each layer assigns a probability to the pixel it is looking at, as well as patches of pixels together, to arrive at an overall confidence score for the object in question. For a machine vision algorithm to detect an object in real time from a video feed, it needs to analyse every single pixel, comparing it to its neighbours, looking for edges, shapes, and colours, as well as patterns within patches of pixels. If this job were to be done by a standard processor, each processor core would look at the pixels in turn. It would still do this very quickly, but it would take time, seconds maybe, to arrive at a decision. Thousands of CUDA cores, however, can take a mathematical operation each and analyse them in parallel, arriving at a near instantaneous decision. Curiously, the CUDA core is working on the latency problem, which is a similar challenge to what had to be overcome at the start of thermal imaging.

Already there are efforts to integrate this type of technology into crewed vehicles. Companies like Thales UK offer a DigitalCrew, which provides AI augmented target detection and decision making for the TrueHunter sight on Challenger 3.[4] It is a relatively small step to take the same capabilities, combine them with autonomous navigation, and create a UGV that is quite straightforward for the crew inside a manned tank to command in combat. If this can be realized, there is a whole world of benefits awaiting the fifth-generation tanks, but they are definitely going to have to wait until one of the five tanks covered here comes into service. Even Germany, which stands to be one of the main beneficiaries and sponsors of the future Main Ground Combat System, is investing in new heavy reconnaissance battalions equipped with the Leopard 2A8, which signals its continued commitment to the tank, but also suggests that uncrewed UGVs in the reconnaissance role are in the distant future. It is also worth noting that some of the five designs appear to be content with integrating a form of UAV or loitering munition into the tank, rather than the more ambitious role as a 'wolf-pack leader'. With that, let's take a look at these designs and what they offer. They are all very nascent and for the most part are closer to technology demonstrators rather than prototypes. This simply means that the companies are telling their MoD customers, 'this is what we think you want, and what we think is possible'. Often things like integration of an APS are a much bigger deal than the demonstrators suggest, so there will be a lot of development ahead for these concepts.

MAIN GROUND COMBAT SYSTEM

The Main Ground Combat System (MGCS) is a combined Franco-German effort led by KNDS, which now includes the former Krauss Maffei Wegman of Leopard 2 fame, and Nexter, the design authority for the Leclerc. Other industry partners include Rheinmetall and Thales, and a single company – MGCS Project Company GMBH – has been formed in Germany to act as the contracting partner for governments. The programme started in 2017 with France and Germany announcing their intent to co-develop a tank. It is expected to go through a technology development phase between 2025 and 2029, which will lead to the integration of the developed technologies (gun, armour, etc.) into testbeds for trials. Production and delivery has been tentatively scheduled for the 2040s. The design ethos is for a system-of-systems, which puts the MGCS at the centre of a family of vehicles with the ability to command autonomous platforms in the air and on land. It introduces many novel features, which are reflected in its design; the autoloader for example, is as much a result of the monstrous ammunition the 140mm ASCALON could fire as it is about removing the crew from the turret.

It is certainly a promising and interesting concept. But it is worth remembering that the modern tank rests on the remains of failed cooperative projects. Most notably, the Europanzer from the 1950s failed, resulting in the Leopard 1 and AMX-30. Later, MBT-70 and MBT-80 led to the independent development of the M1 Abrams, Leopard 2, and Challenger family respectively. Arguably, Turkey's Altay, which was developed collaboratively with Hyundai Rotem, cannot yet be considered a success either. Doctrinal requirements have often disrupted these developments, but the French and German armed forces have at least agreed on a set of core requirements, including things like vehicle weight, which could negate some of those challenges. Industrially, the countries have delineated their responsibilities, with France responsible for the sensors for example, and Germany the mobility. That said, the development timeframe leaves a lot of room for change and political dispute.

Despite an ostensibly solid framework, major issues are yet to be resolved. The calibre of the gun is not set and KNDS France is positioning ASCALON in both 120mm and 140mm, with some tank concepts built to accept either calibre throughout their lifecycle. This is not the first time that 140mm has been explored as a tank calibre. NATO states had reached broad agreement in 1988 that the Alliance would shift to the much larger calibre in the future. The development included Rheinmetall, the Watervliet Arsenal, GIAT (now KNDS France), and representation from the UK. The monstrous gun was developed under a programme known as the Future Tank Main Armament as NATO feared the appearance of a Soviet 'Super Tank'. The initial versions produced 23 MJ of muzzle energy, and a similar Swedish development in 1999 penetrated 1,000mm of armour.[5] However, in 2022 a KNDS representative explained that the ASCALON was producing around 17–20 MJ of muzzle energy with its APFSDS including the sabot, which resulted in 7–8 MJ at the target. This was contrasted to the

120mm APFSDS, which has around 12 MJ at the muzzle and 6 MJ by the time it reaches a target. The representative explained that the gun was firing rods with a length-to-diameter ratio of 30 or 35:1 and that they were working on the aerodynamics of longer rods, which would help the gun deliver more energy onto a target.[6] Using the Mazda MX5 as a reference point, the upper end of the ASCALON's muzzle energy is the same as a Mazda MX5, which weighs around 1,000kg, travelling at 730km/h. By the time it reaches the target, although the range is not stated, the rod has energy equivalent to the same car travelling at 450km/h. Of course, this energy would be concentrated over a circle not much more than an inch in diameter. So, ASCALON brings plenty of punch and growth potential for future target sets, but not every country is convinced of the need to go for a bigger gun, and the US looks set on the 120 with its Abrams modernization.

M1E3 ABRAMS

The US has steadily upgraded the M1 Abrams family ever since they entered service. The move to the M1A1 brought the 120mm M256, which replaced the M68 105mm gun. There were a few upgrades to the M1A1 that enhanced situational awareness and the move to the M1A2 in the early 1990s introduced the Commander's Independent Thermal Viewer, a panoramic sight on the left-hand side of the turret. Not long after, a series of System Enhancement Packages (SEPs) were introduced to help the Abrams keep pace with the most prevalent threats at the time. There were three SEPs, giving the vehicles that were upgraded the designation M1A2 SEP v.1, 2, or 3 as they were applied. The US Army had also planned a fourth, which was initiated in 2017 to introduce Gen 3 thermal imaging, a multi-domain laser designator that would allow the commander to lase targets for a helicopter or jet, and a new type of programmable ammunition. 'This program began early enough to onboard any technology the Army deems critical to the future battlefield to include artificial intelligence, autonomy, APS, or advanced sensors', the US Army information page on the Abrams said in June 2022.[7]

A technology demonstrator called AbramsX was displayed by General Dynamics at the AUSA exhibition in 2022. It included a hybrid drivetrain from Cummins and the XM360 120mm main gun, which is lighter and has lower recoil than the M256. It was also fitted with a remote weapon station (RWS) carrying the 30×113mm calibre cannon, which the US Army uses for short-range air defence in a number of configurations. This was seen as a demonstration of the types of technology that could be included in a future tank.

Then, in 2023, the SEP v.4 programme was cancelled. 'The Abrams Tank can no longer grow its capabilities without adding weight, and we need to reduce its logistical footprint. The war in Ukraine has highlighted a critical need for integrated protections for soldiers, built from within instead of adding on,' the Program Executive Officer (PEO) for Ground Combat Systems at the time, Maj Gen Glenn Dean, said.[8] So, the US Army went back to the drawing board. They now want the APS integrated from the start, rather than simply bolted on as is the case with the Trophy integration for the Abrams fleet. Some of the efforts that were included in the SEP v.4 programme were rolled into the M1E3, which is scheduled to enter service from the 2040s. It is expected to keep the Abrams family as the 'apex predator on future battlefields'.[9] A lot of the technology that is indicated in the M1E3 is fairly standard for the emerging fifth-generation tanks. Hybrid electric drive has been mooted as an option, an APS integrated into the base design, and an increase in its sensor suite. But what is particularly interesting is the decision to stick with a 120mm gun. The Army's Chief Technology Officer, Dr Alex Miller, told a defence media outlet in 2025 that the 120mm gun worked well, adding that the US Army was more interested in the drivetrain and power generation.[10] So, it seems that many of the capabilities demonstrated by General Dynamics in 2022 are likely to find their way into the M1E3.

The US Army is also in a hurry, much more so than any of the other countries leading on the fifth-generation tank designs. The original programme schedule from when the M1E3 was launched expected the first vehicles to be delivered after at least five years, suggesting a delivery date of 2029 or 2030. However, this timeline was thrown out by Dr Miller and Army Chief of Staff General Randy George in April 2025, with the hope that new variants would be fielded within 24 to 30 months.[11] They planned to accelerate development and take risks with certain areas where the payoff was considered sufficient. It is interesting to note that development of the original Abrams followed a similar path, with the programme office at the time accepting some risk in the AGT 1500. A General Dynamics executive then said in October 2025 that a pre-prototype would be delivered to US troops in 2026 so they could get an initial feel for the vehicle while development work continued.[12] The US budget request for the same year also included $723.5 million for the production of four variants. Again, there is a parallel with the original Abrams, which was delivered to US trials long before Dr Philip Lett was happy for them to go. The trials threw up a lot of issues with the engine and other elements of his design that his team were hard-pressed to fix because they had no prototypes of their own to work from.[13] In any case, the development of the M1E3 looks set to proceed at a very fast pace. Perhaps the main competitor for the badge of the first fifth-generation tank into service will be the KF51 Panther from Rheinmetall?

KF51 PANTHER

The KF51 Panther began as a private venture by Rheinmetall, developed in secret starting around 2016 without a formal government requirement. It was designed to compete directly with the Franco-German MGCS by offering a 'ready-now' alternative. The tank was publicly unveiled at the Eurosatory defence exhibition in June 2022, including what Rheinmetall described as a fully functional turret with a 130mm gun and integration for the Hero 120 loitering munitions, effectively challenging the 140mm designs favoured by France.[14] The vehicle brought a range of capabilities, with the company claiming that it set new paradigms in all elements of tank design. However, it is worth noting that it retained the drivetrain of the Leopard 2 and at a weight of 59 tonnes it is difficult to see how the Panther could set new standards for mobility. Nevertheless, the design has added competition to the market, which in Europe would have otherwise been dominated by KNDS, with Hyundai Rotem and General Dynamics as runners up. And it has not been without its success.

A critical milestone was reached in December 2023, when the government of Hungary signed a €288 million contract with Rheinmetall to mature the Panther into a production vehicle. This moved the tank from a concept to a funded development programme, which was presumably necessary for Rheinmetall to get the vehicle production ready. The Hungarian variant (often called Panther EVO) focuses on integrating the new turret onto modified Leopard 2 hulls, with a plan to initially field them with 120mm guns before transitioning to the 130mm Future Gun System (FGS) once the ammunition supply chain is established. A new variant with an uncrewed turret was presented at the 2024 iteration of Eurosatory, and in late 2024 a joint venture was signed between Italy's Leonardo and Rheinmetall for over 1,000 armoured vehicles. The majority were to be Rheinmetall's KF41 Lynx, an infantry fighting vehicle, but the joint venture is also expected to produce 132 of the KF51, with another 140 support vehicles (bridging, engineering etc.) based on the same hull. The hulls will be manufactured in Germany and Italy, but the vehicles are also expected to retain the 120mm L55.[15]

So, despite the offer of the 130mm main gun, it seems that the two prospective users for the KF51 have opted for the familiar Rh120. This would technically make the KF51, as described for Italy and Hungary, more of a fourth-generation tank. The vehicle architecture and mission systems could still provide the scope for it to act as a command base for uncrewed platforms and it is designed to carry an active protection system. The K3 Next-Gen MBT as described by Hyundai Rotem, however, breaks the mould more extensively.

K3 NEXT-GEN MBT

The Next-Gen MBT (NG-MBT) is a concept study under way at Hyundai Rotem, the manufacturer of the K2 Black Panther. A scale model was presented at the 2022 Eurosatory showing some of the company's thinking, and a larger model at the ADEX exhibition in Korea in 2023. From those models and the company's materials, we know that it is expected to have a 130mm main gun in an uncrewed turret. An RWS is shown fitted to the roof and some reports indicate it will be fitted with a high-energy laser. Both concept models show a retractable pod for guided missiles installed on the left of the turret and an integrated APS. It is routinely said to carry radar absorbing materials and design features that will reduce its signature across the electromagnetic spectrum. However, again, it is important to remember that visual observation has been the primary mode of detection in recent wars. To that end, there is a compartment at the rear of the turret that provides space for a small drone. It is expected to have a crew of two, although that element is supposedly under debate, and a hybrid electric drive.[16] Hyundai has also stated the ambition of fitting the tank with a hydrogen fuel cell capability as part of the hybrid drive, which will eventually transition to a full hydrogen power-pack by 2040. Most of the above was retained in the patent filed by Hyundai Rotem in March 2024, and it also showed that a drone jammer would be included. The first prototypes are expected to be delivered in 2030 and the company has signed a cooperation agreement with the Polish Armaments Group to jointly develop a next-generation tank for Poland, which will presumably rest on the K3.

T-14 ARMATA

Few tanks have attracted as much criticism and public attention as the T-14 Armata. It was unveiled by Russia in 2015 during the Moscow Victory Day Parade. It is traditional for Russia to leak details of its new tanks during the Victory Day Parades; this is how NATO found out about the T-80, for example. The initial requirement was to create a 'Universal Combat Platform' that could serve as a tank, a heavy infantry fighting vehicle called the T-15, and an armoured recovery vehicle known as the T-16. When it was revealed, the Armata did mark a change in the world of tanks. At the time, only the Merkava Mk IV was built with an active protection system built in. It was also stated to carry a mysterious new ERA called Malakhit, touted as more effective than anything Russia had deployed before. The turret was uncrewed, carrying a new 125mm gun, but Russian media outlets emphasized its ability to carry a much more powerful 152mm gun. Within the armour, the crew of three are housed at the front of the hull and provided with a suite of touch screens to control the vehicle's operation. In 2020, Russian news outlets reported that an uncrewed version of the tank was undergoing tests.[17]

Various contracts have been signed for the Armata and deliveries reported, most commonly indicating that 132 vehicles have been ordered. There has not been any substantial evidence of delivery, which was common for other platforms like the T-72B and T-80BVM prior to 2022. However, the head of Rostec, the conglomerate that is the parent company for most of Russia's defence industry, said in 2024 that the vehicles were in service with Russia. He added, however, that they were too expensive to be deployed to Ukraine. The country would prefer to spend its funds on the T-90M modernization, which is much cheaper, he added. The tank is a very clear departure from previous Soviet designs; it has more roadwheels, a new engine that is much more powerful to drive its 55-tonne mass, and the uncrewed turret as already mentioned. If it does enter service in meaningful numbers, it will probably have to wait until the war in Ukraine is over, and will serve alongside the T-90M, rather than replacing it. The technical capabilities of these tanks and the equipment that they will carry is summarized in Table 7. This looks across all of the designs and aims to give an idea of what they are bringing to the table.

TABLE 7 Future tank characteristics

Characteristic	*MGCS*	*KF51*	*K3 NG-MBT*	*M1E3*	*T-14 Armata*
Manufacturer	KNDS	Rheinmetall	Hyundai Rotem	GDLS	UVZ
Main gun	120/140mm ASCALON or Rh130	130mm Rh130 or 120mm L55	130mm	120 XM360	125mm 2A82-1M or 152mm
Secondary armament	30mm ARX 30 remote weapon station and coaxial MGs	12.7mm coaxial MG	12.7mm or 30mm RWS	30mm chain gun in RWS and coaxial MG	12.7mm RWS and 7.62mm coaxial MG
Drone integration	Organic UAV Launchers	4 × loitering munitions in turret	Organic recce drones	Switchblade integration (conceptual)	'Pterodactyl' UAV tethered drone
Hull layout	Crew of 2 or 3 in hull	Conventional, but crew of 4 including specialist	Crew in hull	Unclear, could be conventional	Crew of 3 in hull
Protection	APS built in, passive armour and potential for jammers	StrikeShield APS built in with top-attack protection	Unclear	Built-in APS and new complex armours	Malakhit ERA + Afganit APS built in to design

Weight	Less than 50 tonnes	59 tonnes	Goal of 55 tonnes	Less than 60 tonnes	Approx 55 tonnes
Drivetrain	Hybrid-electric drive	Uses the Leopard 2 drivetrain	Hydrogen fuel cell / hybrid-electric drive	Hybrid-electric drive	12N360 diesel engine
Mission systems	Sensor fusion across vehicles	'Jump-in' stations (any crew can do any job) and 360-degree situational awareness	MUM-T central control hub and AI autonomous driving aid	AI-assisted target recognition	Automated target tracking

There are many novel technologies involved in these tank designs, but novel doesn't necessarily mean better. Indeed, the many different novel technologies involved in the MBT-70 project were a driver of that programme's failure. So, let's take a look at some of the new concepts and assess what they add to the future of the tank.

FIREPOWER

This is the area where the five new designs feel most familiar. Even so, there are questions to be asked. But first, all but the M1E3 have considered a bigger gun, which suggests that the current 120mm and 125mm are not up to scratch. The extent to which this is true depends on who you talk to. Some argue that there is untapped growth potential in the 120mm family, in terms of pressures, propellant design, and penetrator material. It may not be necessary to increase the calibre to address these threats, but that is unlikely to be something that becomes clear in the near term. What is clear is that there is at least a user demand signal for something bigger. The tank's core role is to take that big gun somewhere dangerous and use it. So, what are the downsides of a bigger gun? Larger-calibre guns mean much larger ammunition. ASCALON's telescoped ammunition, which tends to be more compact than regular ammunition, is 30cm longer than an equivalent 120mm round, with a total length of 1.3m. Rheinmetall's 130mm ammunition is thought to be similar, which makes it essentially unmanageable for a human, inside a turret at least, and necessitates the autoloader. This is not an inherently bad thing, but there is growing concern around the reduction in tank crews. This is because of a few things. One is the day-to-day maintenance. Regardless of how well built the tank is, it will need new tracks, and even if composite rubber tracks make it to 60-tonne vehicles, they will be heavy. Armour modules will always be heavy, and loading ammunition in and out of a turret will always be an intensive job. Tank crews of four allow this workload to be shared. It is not an unmanageable challenge: the Soviets and French have fought their tanks with crews of three for decades. But it is worth noting that a reduction in crew should not be seen as the future or an essentially good thing. It comes with pros and cons that need to be factored in.

Secondly, bigger ammunition means that there is less space for that ammunition, which results in less being carried. 'It's ok,' the manufacturers would likely say, 'this ammunition is more lethal, so they won't need to fire as many times.' This is probably true on a per-target basis. The 140mm APFSDS that ASCALON can fire could theoretically produce up to 18 MJ of muzzle energy. It would probably be unstoppable without a combination of advanced armour and an APS that can intercept an APFSDS. One hit would be likely to result in a catastrophic kill against most tanks. However, as we have documented, tanks are used for a lot of things, including urban warfare and to support infantry. In those roles it is staying power that matters. The longer a tank can sit and soak up damage, while dealing out its own damage, the more likely the mission is to succeed. This means that magazine depth is key. The move from the 20-pdr on the Centurion to the L7 eventually led to an *increase* in total carried rounds, rather than a decrease. This was seen as a good thing: it enabled the tanks to fight for longer without resupply. The IDF's experiences in its large tank battles showed that this enabled a tank commander to maintain an initiative and keep driving an offensive if it was going well.

Ammunition depth connects to another concept that has been proposed for the MGCS and Abrams X, which is the 30mm cannon. Israel explored adding a medium-calibre cannon to its tanks in the hope that tank crews would use it against soft targets instead of the main gun. In theory this works, but in reality, they found that in most situations crews will use the most lethal weapon at their disposal, the big gun, rather than a smaller one. These tanks are not the first to carry a medium-calibre weapon: the MBT-70 did, as did the original Centurion and AMX-30. But as always, space is a consideration and 30mm ammunition is much bigger than 7.62mm ammunition or 12.7mm ammunition for a general purpose or heavy machine gun. However, the one area where this addition makes sense is in drone defence. Advanced ammunition like the XM1211 proximity fuzed round from Northrop Grumman is designed to detonate when it senses the drone to be nearby. Conventional responses would use airbursting ammunition, which is programmed as it enters the breech of the gun. This means it cannot account for any changes in the drone's positioning once it has been fired. The differences may ultimately be marginal, but modern medium-calibre weapons do offer a range of benefits to the future tank that they may not have provided to their predecessors.

Finally, most include the ability to integrate a drone or loitering munition into the system architecture. This is an interesting feature, although the company John Cockerill Defense has been offering this feature for its 105mm gun turrets for some time. It is clear that a self-generated beyond-line-of-sight reconnaissance and strike capability is valuable. And there are also efforts to integrate missiles into the ASCALON for this very purpose. However, the question really comes back to crewing requirements. A tank crew is already lean, and all of these designs except for the KF51 would require the gunner or commander to take over operation of the drone and processing of its visual feeds. A lot of that work can be automated using the AI technologies mentioned above. However, it would have to be a seamless integration, one that the commander or gunner hardly registers as a task. This is because there is already a lot going on in a tank. The job of the crew tends to be all-consuming, and adding another alert to an already busy system saying 'there are enemies over there' might not be helpful. It does appear valuable if tanks are to be used as mother ships for loitering munitions and to conduct some of their fighting from camouflaged positions using long-range strikes, which is understood to be part of the MGCS concept of operations. But as it stands, it seems that only the KF51 would offer the bandwidth to fully exploit that additional capability. An alternative approach is the development of over the horizon munitions that can be fired from the tank's main gun, which is being pursued for the ASCALON. However, it is worth questioning whether or not the tank is the best platform for this type of engagement. The 155mm shell of a howitzer is arguably far better suited to long-range engagements than a tank's, in part because it can be made big enough to carry sensors and a warhead that is worth firing. The BONUS anti-tank round, for instance, carries two sensor-fuzed munitions that fire powerful EFPs through the roof of a tank. It is seen as a viable route to stopping massed armour advances, to which a tank or squadron of tanks firing relatively long-range missiles could only hope to be an accessory.

PROTECTION

As somewhat clean sheet designs, there is an opportunity for most of these tanks to break the protection paradigms of today. The modern tank is a product of both the Cold War and design constraints, which means that the majority of its most effective armour is concentrated at the front of the vehicle, in the glacis and the turret. This was based on analysis from World War II that showed most engagements came at the front of the vehicles. Tank armour, as we have covered, is also designed to counter different types of threat: kinetic energy defined by APFSDS and HEAT. This is a difficult challenge because the threats differ in terms of how they are best countered. Most of the tanks could take the approach of distributing more protection around the sides and rear of the hull to account for the increased likelihood of urban warfare and 360-degree threats. Tank design could also take the approach of delegating defence against HEAT warheads, which are mostly slow moving compared to an APFSDS, to the APS. This would allow the vehicle's passive armour to be designed specifically to deal with kinetic energy threats. Such an overall approach could provide a more effective suite of protection against kinetic energy and mine threats, allowing weight savings, and a statistically significant probability of intercepting HEAT threats.

One final thing to consider on the protection front is mobility. During one conference in 2025, Colonel (Col) Armin Dirks, head of operations in the MGCS joint project team, set out some of the defining assumptions behind the MGCS project. He included the statement, which is broadly accurate, that battlefields can be subject to persistent reconnaissance. This, he opined, means that friendly forces need to constantly move and engage enemy vehicles with 'rapid, precise fire'.[18] This is an interesting conclusion and one that is worth contrasting with previous efforts and observations from Ukraine. First of all, the idea that moving a lot confers protection was explored under the Leopard 1, AMX-30, and Swedish S-tank. Note that none of those concepts have survived, and even the very fast Leclerc has been up-armoured during its service life. Secondly, movement is something of a mixed bag in Ukraine. For an artillery system, relocating after a fire mission can be the thing that exposes the gun to a Russian strike. It is common for Russian forces to patrol an area for days on end if they know a tank or howitzer is present. It is the movement of the tank that they are looking for to initiate an engagement with a loitering munition like the Lancet-3. There is also the issue of operational boundaries. Armoured units will operate within set boundaries that are drawn on a map. Ideally, they should avoid crossing into a neighbouring unit's area without warning them as they could be fired upon. The IDF, which is technically very good at force tracking, struggled with this in Gaza City, and it was a challenge in the Gulf War, too. The fact of the matter is that armoured units are likely to have a relatively limited space to operate in, which will confine their ability to manoeuvre constantly as Col Dirks suggests. So, with that in mind, this is an aspect of the design to treat with some caution. Movement is often a condition of a battlefield; it can be set to some extent, but if the war has become static because neither side is able to bring enough force superiority to bear, then movement will be constrained. And, of course, if an APFSDS leaves the barrel of a T-90M at some 1,600m/s, travelling at 60 or even 80km/h offers very little in the way of protection, especially if a target tracker is fitted.

MOBILITY

Three of the tanks are exploring a hybrid electric engine. This often comes with manufacturer assurances about stealth, silent overwatch, and so on. They point out that hybrid engines are quieter than the diesel equivalents, which reduces the ability of an adversary to detect them. They add that the engine has a lower thermal signature, especially when at rest. All of this may be true, but these claims are worth examining.

Starting with the statement that the tanks would be quieter, this is a confusing claim for several reasons. First, if tanks are involved, both sides probably know they are at war and are likely to be looking for the enemy's tanks. It's not as if an armoured brigade will be able to sneak up on an opponent by being quiet. Additionally, as Col Dirks has observed, drones are everywhere. It is common to see most observations about the impact of drones on the modern battlefield leveraging Ukraine and the 2022 invasion. But Ukraine and Russia had been using drones for reconnaissance since 2014 to watch and bomb each other. Militants in Libya used them to correct artillery fire, and ISIS used them in its defence of Mosul in 2016. So, it is safe to assume that first contact will probably be through reconnaissance drones, rather than acoustic detection. Tanks will be seen, not heard. The silent overwatch is somewhat valid, although more from an energy use perspective. Russian T-80 crews in Chechnya struggled because of the immense fuel consumption of their gas turbines while at rest. It stands to reason that having a large bank of batteries to power a tank's systems without turning the engine on could be beneficial. While this could be achieved without a hybrid electric drive, through the addition of battery packs, those packs would be parasitic weight. In other words, they would add nothing to the mobility of the tank but weight, whereas a hybrid system's batteries are technically part of the drivetrain, so they contribute to mobility. The thermal detection piece is another mixed offering. When driving, tanks build up a lot of heat through their tracks, and would still produce hot exhaust gases from the engines that are used to run the hybrid systems.

Some other benefits could be realized from hybrid engines, depending on the type of hybrid arrangement that is used. For example, the use of electric motors to drive the sprockets could enable a smaller transmission to be used, which would free up space inside the hull. It could also improve torque, as electric motors generate 100% of their torque from the start, removing the need for the engine to reach a certain rpm to generate maximum torque. Not even the torque-efficient AGT 1500 can match that. Another driving factor might simply be the wider decisions of the commercial world. If all heavy good vehicles were made hybrid by the time that the MGCS came into service, for example, then the designers would have little choice but to make the vehicle hybrid. Anything else would risk having a vehicle with a supply chain that is obsolescent. This is a manageable risk for a gun, which has a specialized supply chain and its use can be limited. But it is unacceptable for an engine and transmission. However, there are still engineering challenges to overcome. Just because a tank has some electric assistance when driving, it does not mean that the laws of physics stop applying. When that tank turns, the energy sent to the inside track has to be dealt with and transferred to the outer track. This probably means that the motors, if used, would have to be rated to a far higher weight than the tank at rest. The inside motor would act as a brake and the outside motor as a booster. The inside motor would therefore *generate electricity*, potentially megawatts of it, which would have to be transferred to the batteries, meaning that some heavy-duty cabling would be required, as well as fairly advanced battery chemistries. Overall, the benefits of a hybrid-electric drive seem far from clear cut when it comes to tanks. Even fuel consumption is unclear. Tanks most often use their engines during combat, which means frequent starts and stops, sharp turns and changing duty cycles. A hybrid drive returns the best fuel efficiency compared to a standard engine when its engine is allowed to operate at a consistent and optimal speed. Tanks would only do that on long road marches when heavy equipment transports were the preferred method of transit. There are, of course, the fuel efficiency benefits to be gained from the tank being stationary, but as mentioned above, that could also be achieved through battery packs alone.

MISSION SYSTEMS

The mission systems of the future tanks are positioned as the critical enablers. It is hard to find a historical equivalent in the story of the modern tank. The impact that mission systems could have is probably in a similar world to the move to APFSDS as a primary anti-tank round. In the same way that APFSDS almost immediately increased the lethality of tanks against other tanks, the new missions system approach *could* unlock new ways of operating. As touched on above, a tank that is able to command several uncrewed robotic combat vehicles can increase the combat mass of its formation quite considerably. This requires operating systems that are able to manage and coordinate multiple processes and platforms simultaneously. For example, one British company called Arondite is working on a product called Cobalt that would enable a user to command and control several UGVs and UAVs, and coordinate them with crewed assets, from the same programme.[19] Consider the impact this could have had, if properly realized, on Ukraine's counter-offensive in 2023. Waves of UGVs and UAVs could have been coordinated with artillery to breach Russia's minefields and forward defences. Large UGVs like the Type X from Milrem, which is armed with a 30mm Bushmaster cannon, would have forced Russian defenders to respond with their ATGMs and other weapons, which Ukraine could then have suppressed. The first element of the offensive, which is always the most dangerous, could have been quite different with uncrewed platforms controlled from tanks some distance behind them. A range of companies are working on similar command and control solutions, all pitched at enabling an armed force to go from one uncrewed asset per operator, to many.

There are a range of other mission system capabilities on the horizon that could change the way tanks are employed. The multi-domain laser designator that has been pitched for the M1E3 could provide a tank commander with the ability to bring down very precise, heavy munitions from an F-16 patrolling the skies above, for example. Or even laser-guided mortar rounds that might be available within the tank's own battlegroup. This would shorten the targeting cycle, which would have benefits across almost every type of mission. Sights are evolving, bringing ever greater clarity and granularity at all ranges, which has always been valuable to the tank. But with AI-enabled recognition and detection, users can potentially make better sense of what they are seeing in a shorter space of time. However, there is always a balance. Manufacturers and MoDs alike worry about cognitive overload, where too much information is presented for the operator to process. This is as much auditory as it is visual; if you have children, you may be all too familiar with how difficult it is to drive a car through a city while two young humans talk/shout at you about two different things. A tank crew will be busy running multiple different processes, shouting at each other, and trying to digest the information on their screens, and somebody will probably be shooting back at them. So, it is a stressful environment to say the least. There are also some challenges around the use of AI, including the fact that users tend to place too much trust in AI when they first start using it. A large language model (LLM) like Google's Gemini or Chat GPT is a prime example. An LLM is trying to predict what the correct next word in a sentence is; it doesn't know.

This leads it to hallucinate or make things up because it is just trying to generate an answer that it thinks is what you want. Computer vision should not lead to the same types of mistakes, but at the same time it is just producing the results of a series of equations that were shaped by processes developed outside of a war, in all likelihood. This is not an insurmountable obstacle, and the whole point of AI is to retrain it quickly on new data and experiences so that it evolves to become the most useful version of itself. But it is a hurdle that armed forces will have to manage as these technologies are introduced.

The final aspect is connected, and that is around information sharing. A range of battle management systems like Fireweaver (Chapter 18) are already making their way into service. The point of them is that when one vehicle spots a target, it can be populated onto a shared map that all other vehicles and commanders in the same network can see. Theoretically, this allows a commander to select or designate a weapon system to engage that target. For example, if a tank spots infantry moving into a building, it might be best to use loitering munition or medium-calibre cannon, rather than blasting a massive hole in the building with a 120mm tank round. This type of connectivity has the supreme goal of connecting every sensor on the battlefield together into a single unified network. MoDs in the West call it 'any sensor, any shooter'. There is hot debate around this topic because if it is followed to its extremes, one might reasonably ask if an F-35 pilot really needs to know about the targets that a rifleman is seeing and vice versa. This tends to draw the response that 'any sensor any shooter' is for the corps- or divisional-level fight, rather than for brigade down. In any case, there are multiple healthy efforts to improve the connectivity and information sharing within armoured formations, which should lead to a future where commanders are better able to shape the battlefield in front of them from a more complete understanding of the enemy.

Two technologies worth watching in this regard are MIMO, and cognitive radio. Newer radios like the Silvus system have more than one antenna, which enables multiple input, multiple output (MIMO) communications. You have probably used a MIMO device at some point; it is a common approach to WiFi communications, for example. In a nutshell, a MIMO radio will take its information and break it into different parts before transmitting them over different channels, which can mean different wavelengths and frequencies within the electromagnetic spectrum. Those different signals sort of bounce around until they reach the receiving radio that pieces the message together. A standard VHF radio, by contrast, is a SISO – single input, single output – device. This might mean that a voice message or data arrives garbled or incomplete because there is only one route for that information to travel. This methodology provides more resistance to jamming as the user can transmit the same traffic on two different wavebands and different frequencies within that. The logic is that at least one of the signals will arrive, and the jammer has a lot more work to do to effectively degrade those signals. Imagine sending a message to a friend via text, post, and email with different pieces of information in each type of message. This would guarantee that all of your information reached your friend. However, the envisioned concepts for 'any sensor to any shooter' mentioned above are likely to require extreme levels of data to be shared over long distances. There are questions over how achievable that is, even with AI condensing key information into metadata. There is one final evolution of the radio that might find its way into the future tank, and that is cognitive radio. Modern radios are software defined, which means they have a computer running an application that tells them what waveform to use. This allows them to be changed with a software update, rather than a new handset and antenna. It also means that it may be possible to build sets of AI algorithms to run on the radios that would respond to their sense of the electromagnetic spectrum. Imagine that a Russian electronic warfare operator was effectively jamming most of the VHF band, for example. A cognitive radio would, in theory, be able to detect the unjammed section and transmit over that. A further extension of this, which is being looked at very seriously, is the use of tactical radios for signals intelligence. This could mean that the future tank automatically detects enemies based on their radio transmissions, and shares that information with others on the network as well as allowing its own crew to be able to act on it. In short, the future tank looks set to be a sensor and mission system powerhouse. The differences between such tanks are likely to be defined much more by what they can do in the electromagnetic spectrum than their guns. The gun will still be the point of the tank, but the way it is used will be shaped by what the tank can sense and see.

Final thoughts: A tank is like a ladder

There is a phrase that some people in the armour community use to describe a tank: 'a tank is like a dinner jacket, you don't always need one, but when you do, nothing else will do.' However, I feel that this doesn't really convey the purpose and crucial role of a tank, which I hope this book has. So, let me offer an adjusted version: *A tank is like a ladder*.

A ladder is often the safest way to do something that is quite risky. Say I need to reach a window on the first floor of my house to climb through it and unlock my front door. This is quite a dangerous thing to be doing anyway, but a ladder reduces the risk that I will fall. It doesn't have to be a ladder: I could stack boxes or chairs like some kind of whacky cartoon. I could ask a (very) strong friend to boost me up and through the window. Alternatively, I could try to climb the walls of my house, living my childhood fantasy of becoming a computer game character. In all cases – except the one that involves the ladder – the likelihood of failure is high, and the injury risk significant. If I were to use a ladder, that injury risk would not be reduced to zero, and neither would the chance of failure. My ladder might be too short, for instance, or I might have bought the cheapest one, reasoning that I would rarely use it anyway. And this is why I think a tank is like a ladder.

To see why a tank is like a ladder, let's return to the notion that it takes a land army to defeat a land army. This means that in the event of a war, an armed force will necessarily have to fight and defeat an enemy's forces on the ground. We can see that even during the 1991 Gulf War, when extensive damage was caused to the Iraqis from the air, a land invasion was still necessary to convince Saddam Hussein that the war was lost. In the Balkans, when NATO set about destroying Serbian armour from the air, the campaign quickly lost its efficacy, and a land force would have become essential if NATO had wanted to continue the operation. Even Israel in Gaza, with total air superiority and one of the most extensive intelligence operations in the world, and some of the most advanced technologies in terms of multi-domain operations, had no option but to plan around sending its forces in on the ground. So, it follows that in any scenario where a force has to get close to an enemy and fight through their positions, the risks are high, and so are the chances of failure.

It is possible to send infantry to do that job. The Chinese tried this during the Korean War, and the Vietnamese again during the Vietnam War; it was also a common tactic in the Iran–Iraq War. In all cases, those assaults generally ended badly, with thousands of casualties for very little gain. However, support those infantry with tanks and the chances of success increase, while the likelihood of failure falls. Tanks that are properly protected to a level that is commensurate with the threat environment will be able to take their big gun to a dangerous place and use it in support of mission success. They are the ladder that is designed to make the costs of war manageable to a certain extent. Indeed, in every conflict covered in this book, from Lt Nordstrom and his advance with the M4A3E8 Shermans against North Korean T-34/85s, through to Capt Purbrick's early morning engagement against Iraqi armour, or Azerbaijan's offensive to take Nagorno-Karabakh, the same results *could* have been achieved without tanks. However, the losses would have been dramatically higher, and with that the chances of failure. It is rare for the costs of not having tanks to be demonstrated, but China's massed human wave offensives in Korea (and Iran's again in the Iran–Iraq War) do suggest that armour and combined arms will generally prove a superior combat force over unsupported infantry.

That said, the tank is like many other capital platforms – things that tend to be big and expensive, like the aircraft carrier and strategic bomber – in that pundits and analysts are quick to write them off. Critics have been writing the tank off since 1916, and every new weapon that is introduced, especially the advent of HEAT warheads, has resurfaced those calls. Equally, extreme wars where everything seems to get destroyed, as is the case in Ukraine, and others where nothing gets destroyed, like the Gulf War, further distort the debate on the future of the tank. The fact is, war literally revolves around the act of killing enemy personnel, and damaging or destroying the vehicles that they use to fight. Ideally this should happen at a faster rate than the other side is able to achieve. Within this brutal and violent paradigm, nothing is safe. But the tank has evolved consistently to meet the new challenges brought to counter it. The most modern tanks like the M1A2C, Leopard 2A8, K2 Black Panther, Challenger 3, Merkava Mk IV, T-90M, and Type 99A are incredibly resilient and well protected. They are difficult to damage, and do a very good job of keeping their crews safe. Can they be destroyed? Of course. It's impossible to protect them from everything. But the point is that decades of engineering and evolution have forced weapons designers to evolve at the same pace, and tanks now stand at a point where the best of them, or those protected by an active protection system at least, can shrug off the majority of infantry-fired weapons. Drones present something of a challenge, but work is already under way to address them through active protection, and the warheads that the majority carry are, in any case, ineffective against advanced ERA and similar armours.

So, what would we be saying if this book were written in 50 years? Well, it's honestly difficult to assess. So much of what defines the success of a piece or type of equipment is based on how it is used. Russia's T-90M is technically very well protected. The Relikt ERA provides good levels of resistance to most battlefield threats. And yet, T-90Ms are very vulnerable if deployed in isolated packets, or as single tanks, without air defence, air power, or covering fire support. Despite this vulnerability, it is clear that the two nations that would arguably have the greatest reason to move away from the tank given recent experiences, are in fact doubling down on them. Russia is increasing production of all tanks that it has in service, as is Israel.[1] At the time of writing, ten European states had collectively ordered 1,090 MBTs since 2022, with potential for 1,000 more if Poland exercises all of its options for the K2. The tank is clearly on the up, regardless of how drones are shaping modern warfare. This is because it is hard to replicate the role that a tank fulfils. Warfare will always have some form of ground component; that is where humans live after all, and it takes a land force to defeat a land force. This means that tanks will be needed as long as we decide to continue settling differences through force.

As for the modern tank, the current prototypes indicate further evolution rather than any dramatic departure from existing norms.

Yes, there are attempts to make the turrets uncrewed, and ongoing debates around gun calibre. Even the fourth crewman's position is at risk of being removed or reallocated as a drone operator. But few are attempting to change the fundamental role of a tank. Looking back through the many wars covered within this book, it is clear that the tank has shaped battlefield outcomes wherever it has been used, but rarely in isolation. With that in mind, it seems safe to say that the core role remains unchanged: take a big gun somewhere very dangerous, and use it to complete a mission as part of a combined arms team. Many other things can be used to get the same end result, but none are as effective at holding ground as the tank. The most modern tanks, especially the Leopard 2A8, M1A2 SEP v.3, Challenger 3, and Merkava Mk IV can or will do this very well. At least technically speaking. But it has taken decades of continuous engineering and development to get them where they are. By now you have learned a little about their story. I hope you have enjoyed this journey and that it adds to your appreciation for the modern tank.

Glossary

AI	artificial intelligence
APFSDS	armour-piercing fin-stabilized discarding sabot
APDS	armour-piercing discarding sabot
APC	armoured personnel carrier
APS	active protection system
ATGM	anti-tank guided missile
BHN	Brinell hardness rating
CBRN	chemical, biological, radiological, and nuclear
CCD	charged-couple device
EFP	explosively formed projectile
ERA	explosive reactive armour
FLIR	Forward Looking Infrared
FBCB2	Force XXI Battle Command Brigade and Below
FPV	first person view
FVRDE	Fighting Vehicles Research and Development Establishment (UK)
GLATGM	gun-launched anti-tank guided missile
HE	high-explosive

HEAT	high-explosive anti-tank
HEMTT	Heavy Expanded Mobility Tactical Truck
HESH	high-explosive squash head
HVAP-T	Hyper Velocity Armour Piercing – Tracer
HZ	Hertz
IDF	Israel Defense Forces
IED	improvised explosive device
ISIS	Islamic State of Iraq and Syria
LWIR	long-wave infrared
MUM-T	manned-unmanned teaming
MWIR	mid-wave infrared
MBT	main battle tank
MCT	Mercury Cadmium Telluride (HgCdTe)
MCLOS	manual command to line-of-sight
MGCS	Main Ground Combat System
MOD	Ministry of Defence / Defense
NBC	nuclear, biological, and chemical
NLAW	Next-generation Anti-tank Weapon
NVA	North Vietnamese Army
PLO	Palestinian Liberation Organization
RHA	rolled homogeneous armour
RNZAC	Royal New Zealand Armoured Corps
RWS	remote weapon station
SACLOS	semi-automatic command line-of-sight
SEP	System Enhancement Package
SPRITE	Signal Processing In The Element

TOGS	Thermal Observation and Gunnery System
UAV	uncrewed aerial vehicle
UGV	uncrewed ground vehicle
UN	United Nations
VHF	very high frequency

Notes

PART I

1 'M4A3E8-76 Spec Sheet', the Sherman Tank. https://www.theshermantank.com/wp-content/uploads/M4A3E8-76-Spec-Sheet.pdf accessed 7 January 2026.
2 Steven Zaloga and Jim Kinnear, *The T-34-85 Medium Tank 1944–1994*, Osprey Publishing, Oxford (1996), p.19.
3 Russell A. Gugeler, *Combat Actions In Korea*, US Army Historical Office, Washington (1974), pp.39–44.

CHAPTER I

1 Richard Ogorkiewicz, *Tanks, 100 Years of Evolution*, Osprey Publishing, Oxford (2016), pp.290–93.
2 I.F.B. Tytler et al, *Vehicles and Bridging*, Brassey's Battlefield Weapons Systems and Technology Series, Vol. I, Brassey's Defence Publishers, London (1985), pp.42–43.
3 Christopher Chant, *World Encyclopedia of the Tank*, 2nd edn, Sutton Publishing, Stroud (2002), pp.207–15.
4 'M1A1, M1A1C, M1A2 Gun Page', The Sherman Tank Site. https://www.theshermantank.com/about/sherman-lee-and-variants-gun-data/m1m1a1m1a2-description-and-data-from-tm9-1308/ accessed 5 May 2026.
5 *TM9-1308 76 MM Guns M1A1C and M1A2 and Mounts for Combat Vehicles Technical Manual*, Department of the Army (1944), accessed via https://www.theshermantank.com/about/sherman-lee-and-variants-gun-data/m1m1a1m1a2-description-and-data-from-tm9-1308/ on 5 May 2026.

6 Jose Cosme, Jeff Ranu, and Shawn Spickert-Fulton, 'The 76-Mm Gun M1A1 and M1A2: An Analysis of U.S. Anti-Tank Capabilities During World War II', ARDEC Armaments, New Jersey (2018), p.9.
7 'Data for H.V.A.P. Ammunition for 76mm. and 3 inch Guns', War Department, Office of the Chief of Ordnance (May 1945).
8 Giovanni Di Benedetto, Paolo Matteis, and Giorgio Scavino, 'Impact Behavior and Ballistic Efficiency of Armor-piercing Projectiles with Tool Steel Cores', *International Journal of Impact Engineering*, Vol. 115 (May 2018), pp.10–18.
9 Cosme et al, 'The 76-Mm Gun M1A1 and M1A2'.
10 Steven Zaloga, *M4 (76 mm) Sherman Medium Tank, 1943–65*, Osprey Publishing, Oxford (2003), p.42.
11 Steven Zaloga, *T-34-85 Medium Tank, 1944–94*, Osprey Publishing, Oxford (1996).
12 H.W. MacDonald et al, *The Employment of Armor in Korea*, Vol. 1, Department of the Army, Washington (April 1951), pp.25–27.
13 Arthur Connor Jr, 'The Armor Debacle in Korea, 1950: Implications for Today', *Parameters* 22, No. 1 (1992), p.73.
14 'War: At the Bowling Alley', *Time* (4 September 1950), accessed via https://time.com/archive/6794116/war-at-the-bowling-alley/ on 24 September 2025.
15 Ibid.

CHAPTER 2

1 A. Hurlich, 'Review of Soviet Ordnance Metallurgy', Watertown Arsenal (1953), p.3.
2 Josua Siagian, I. Nengah Putra Apriyanto, and Kaharuddin Djenod, 'Development of Steel as Anti-Ballistic Combat Vehicle Material: Review', *International Journal of Education and Social Science Research (IJESSR)*, Vol. 5, Issue 1 (2022), pp.261–81.
3 'How to calculate Brinell hardness', Foundrax (18 August 2021). https://foundrax.co.uk/how-to-calculate-brinell-hardness/ accessed 14 September 2024.
4 Nicola J. Woolmore, 'The Failure of a Tungsten Carbide–Cobalt Cored Projectile Penetrating a Hard Target', The Defence College of Management and Technology Engineering Systems Department, Cranfield University (2005), p.60.
5 Paul Hazell, *Armour: Materials, Theory, and Design*, CRC Press (2016), pp.7–8.

6 Railway Regulation (Gauge) Act 1846, 9 & 10 Vict. c. 57, enacted 18 August 1846, Irish Statute Book. https://www.irishstatutebook.ie/eli/1846/act/57/enacted/en/print.html.
7 Tytler et al, *Vehicles and Bridging*, pp.41–42.
8 Simon Dunstan, *Centurion vs T-55: Yom Kippur War, 1973*, Osprey Publishing, Oxford (2009), p.16.

CHAPTER 3

1 W.J., Kingsley-Filshie, 'Trial by Fire: Centurion Tanks in the Korean War', *Journal of the Society for Army Historical Research*, 99(396) (2021), pp. 56–63. https://www.jstor.org/stable/27116250.
2 Lt J. Brown, 'Centurion Tanks in Korea', Report to the Chief of Staff (March 1952). Accessed via https://antipodeanarmour.blogspot.com/p/centurion-tanks-in-korea-report-by-lt-j.html on 25 September 2025.
3 Simon Dunstan, *Centurion Universal Tank 1943–2003*, Osprey Publishing, Oxford (2003).
4 Robert P. Hanger, 'The M26 Pershing: America's Forgotten Tank – Developmental and Combat History', Liberty University Department of History (2018), pp.103–104.
5 J.Y. Wong and Wei Huang, 'Wheels vs. Tracks – A Fundamental Evaluation from the Traction Perspective', *Journal of Terramechanics*, Vol. 43, Issue 1 (January 2006), pp.27–42.
6 J.Y. Wong, *Theory of Ground Vehicles*, 3rd edn, John Wiley and Sons Inc, New York (2001).
7 'Ukrainian MT-LB moving through mud. This is why these machines are so essential in Ukrainian conditions', Reddit [2022]. https://www.reddit.com/r/ukraine/comments/zlpop2/ accessed 26 September 2025.
8 Chant, *World Encyclopedia of the Tank*, p.216.
9 Tytler et al, *Vehicles and Bridging*, p.49.
10 Richard M. Ogorkiewicz, *Technology of Tanks I*, Janes Information Group, UK (1991), p.226.

CHAPTER 4

1 Selway, Jim. n.d., 'A Veteran Interview with Jim Selway'. Interview by Martin Bisiker. Legasee. https://www.legasee.org.uk/veteran/jim-selway/?t=2140 accessed 26 September 2025.
2 Ibid.
3 Lt J. Brown, 'Centurion Tanks in Korea'.
4 Ogorkiewicz, *Technology of Tanks I*, p.191.

5 Ibid, p.192.
6 Nicolas Moran, 'The Chieftain's Hatch: Centurion III Pt 3', World of Tanks (28 March 2015). https://worldoftanks.com/en/news/history/The_Chieftains_Hatch_Centurion_Pt3/ accessed 29 September 2025.
7 Ibid.

PART 2

1 Ogorkiewicz, *Tanks*, pp.177–78.
2 'History, Vehicles, T-34', Kharkov Morozov Design Bureau, Internet Archive (8 February 2008). https://web.archive.org/web/20080208095149/http://morozov.com.ua/eng/body/history4-6.php accessed 4 October 2025.
3 Ogorkiewicz, *Tanks*, p.176.
4 Steven Zaloga, *T-54 and T-55 Main Battle Tanks, 1944–2004*, Osprey Publishing, Oxford (2004), pp.6–9.
5 Ibid, p.10.
6 Nicholas Smith, 'The Beast of Budapest', History Net (19 July 2018). https://www.historynet.com/the-beast-of-budapest/ accessed 10 October 2025.
7 Ibid.
8 Zaloga, *T-54 and T-55 Main Battle Tanks*, p.40.
9 A.V. Longman, 'Tank Effectiveness: Conqueror, Conway and Charioteer', Memorandum No. E13, Army Operational Research Group (1954), p.6. https://archive.org/details/TankEffectivenessOfConquerorConwayAndCharioteer/page/n3/mode/2up accessed 5 October 2025.
10 Ogorkiewicz, *Tanks*, p.209.
11 Lawrence S. Kaplan, 'NATO and Adenauer's Germany: Uneasy Partnership.' *International Organization*, Vol. 15, No. 4 (1961), pp. 618–29. http://www.jstor.org/stable/2705555.
12 'Warsaw Pact', *Encyclopedia Britannica* (2 October 2025). https://www.britannica.com/event/Warsaw-Pact.
13 'Khrushchev and the Twentieth Congress of the Communist Party, 1956', Office of the Historian, US Department of State. https://history.state.gov/milestones/1953-1960/khrushchev-20th-congress, accessed 5 October 2025.
14 Samuel F. Wells, 'The Origins of Massive Retaliation', *Political Science Quarterly*, Vol. 96, Issue 1 (1981), pp. 31–52. https://doi.org/10.2307/2149675.

CHAPTER 5

1 Todd Avery Raffensperger, 'Freedom or Death: The Hungarian Uprising of 1956', Warfare History Network (February 2008). https://warfarehistorynetwork.com/article/freedom-or-death-the-hungarian-uprising-of-1956 accessed 5 October 2025.
2 Andrea Lauer Rice and Edith K. Lauer, *56 Stories: Personal Recollections of the 1956 Hungarian Revolution, A Hungarian American Perspective*, Kortárs Kiadó, Budapest (2006), p.106.
3 Ibid, p.21.
4 Bernadette Quémerais, 'Occupational Exposure to Atmospheric Emissions Produced During Live Gun Firing', Canadian Center of Science and Education (September 2013). http://dx.doi.org/10.5539/ep.v2n4p57
5 Capt Norton Nelson et al, 'Project No. 3 – Toxic Gases in Armored Vehicles. Final Report on Sub-Project No. 3-13', Armored Medical Research Laboratory, USA (1943), p.2.
6 Lt Col David Eshel, 'Soviet Tanks: An Israeli View', *Armor* (May–June 1988), pp.14–18.
7 Chant, *World Encyclopedia of the Tank*, p.286.
8 Armament Research Services (ARES), 'Soviet 3O8 240 mm Rocket-assisted Cargo Projectiles in Syria', accessed 7 October 2025. https://armamentresearch.com/soviet-308-240-mm-rocket-assisted-cargo-projectiles-in-syria/.
9 Ryan A. Then, 'T-54', Tankograd (10 January 2017). https://thesovietarmourblog.blogspot.com/2017/01/t-54.html accessed 7 October 2025.
10 Niko Kolkko, 'Mechanisms of Armour Penetration', Tampere University of Technology (March 2015), pp.4–5.
11 Then, 'T-54'.
12 Maj A.E. Hemesley QLR, 'Soviet Tank Company Tactics', Defence Intelligence Agency (May 1976).
13 Ogorkiewicz, *Technology of Tanks* I, p.70.
14 Richard Ogorkiewicz, *Observer of Cold War Tank Development*, The Tank Museum, England (2021), p.24.
15 Ogorkiewicz, *Technology of Tanks I*, p.79.
16 Ibid, p.79.
17 Then, 'T-54'.
18 Gen Donn A. Starry, *Mounted Combat in Vietnam*, Department of the Army, Washington (2002), p.209.

CHAPTER 6

1 Ja.E. Binowitsch et al, 'Tank Theory', translated by Foreign Technology Office, USA (1969), p.226.
2 Tytler et al, *Vehicles and Bridging*, pp.127–28.
3 Ogorkiewicz, *Technology of Tanks I*, p.338.
4 Ibid.
5 Bruce Maclaurin, *High Speed Off-Road Vehicles: Suspensions, Tracks, Wheels and Dynamics*, John Wiley & Sons Ltd, UK (2018), pp.1–6.
6 Ebisa Kejela Melka, 'Material Selection and Optimization of Torsion Bar Suspension for Military Vehicle in Case of Tank T-55', *Journal of Artificial Intelligence Machine Learning and Neural Network*, Vol. 4, No. 42 (22–23 February 2024), p.22.
7 Eshel, 'Soviet Tanks', p.15.
8 Lt Col Craig W. Collings, 'Operating in Contested Littorals: Israel, 1967 to 1973', US Army Command and General Staff College (2021), p.14.
9 Maclaurin, *High Speed Off-Road Vehicles*, p.7.

CHAPTER 7

1 J. Goetz, J. Klemm, and E. Ortlieb, 'Analysis Of Radiation Exposure For Observers And Maneuver Troops Exercise Desert Rock IV, Operation Tumbler-Snapper', Defense Nuclear Agency (1985), pp.12–13.
2 David Remnick, 'Soviets Exposed Troops to Nuclear Bomb Test', *Washington Post* (29 September 1989).
3 Goetz et al, 'Analysis of Radiation Exposure', pp.12–13.
4 'Honest John', US Army Aviation and Missile Life Cycle Management Command, n.d. https://history.redstone.army.mil/miss-honestjohn.html accessed 23 October 2025.
5 'Overpressure', Atomic Archive. https://www.atomicarchive.com/science/effects/overpressure.html accessed 23 October 2025.
6 Charles Grace, *Nuclear Weapons: Principles, Effects, and Survivability*, Brassey's Publishing, London (1994), p.33.
7 Samuel Cranny-Evans, 'In-Depth Briefing #90: Lessons from the Cold War', *British Army Review* (19 May 2025). https://chacr.org.uk/2025/05/19/in-depth-briefing-90-lessons-from-the-cold-war/ accessed 23 October 2025.
8 *FM 100-2-1, The Soviet Army: Operations and Tactics*, Department of the Army, Washington (1984), pp.4–7.
9 Then, 'T-54'.

10 'Individual Distribution CBRN, Filters and Systems', HDT Global (2019). https://www.hdtglobal.com/wp-content/uploads/2020/03/HDT_Individual-Distribution_15.pdf accessed 23 October 2025.
11 Dana A. Shea, 'Chemical Weapons: A Summary Report of Characteristics and Effects', Congressional Research Service (September 2013).
12 D. Vaughan, 'VX', *Encyclopedia Britannica* (17 September 2025). https://www.britannica.com/technology/VX, accessed 7 October 2025.
13 Sarah Marsh, 'Emergency Services Spent £900k Replacing Vehicles After Salisbury Attack', *The Guardian* (13 June 2019). https://www.theguardian.com/uk-news/2019/jun/13/emergency-services-scrap-900k-vehicles-after-salisbury-attack accessed 23 October 2025.
14 Grace, *Nuclear Weapons*, p.99.

CHAPTER 8

1 Dunstan, *Centurion Universal Tank, 1943–2003*, p.24.
2 'Anatomy of an infra-red scope from a tank!' Lottie The Tank Whisperer, YouTube (22 February 2024). https://www.youtube.com/watch?v=-7D2PwA9s3g accessed 23 October 2025.
3 Chant, *World Encyclopedia of the Tank*, p.286.
4 Ibid, p.277.
5 Dr Jack Watling, 'Emergent Approaches to Combined Arms Manoeuvre in Ukraine', RUSI (23 October 2025). https://www.rusi.org/explore-our-research/publications/insights-papers/emergent-approaches-combined-arms-manoeuvre-ukraine accessed 24 October 2025.

PART 3

1 Shabtai Teveth, *The Tanks of Tammuz*, Lume Books (2016), pp.274–76.
2 Kenneth Pollack, *Arabs at War: Military Effectiveness, 1948–1991*, University of Nebraska Press, Lincoln NE (2002), pp.67–69.
3 Teveth, *The Tanks of Tammuz*, pp.262–85.
4 Samuel Cranny-Evans and Jon Hawkes, *Jane's Armoured Fighting Vehicles: Tracked, 2021/2022*, Janes Information Group, Coulsdon (2021), p.251.
5 Cranny-Evans and Hawkes, *Jane's Armoured Fighting Vehicles*, p.4.
6 Dunstan, *Centurion vs T-55*, p.42.
7 Teveth, *The Tanks of Tammuz*.

CHAPTER 9

1 Steven Zaloga, *T-62 Main Battle Tank, 1965–2005*, Osprey Publishing, Oxford (2009), pp.5–10.
2 Donald E. Carlucci and Sidney S. Jacobson, *Ballistics: Theory and Design of Guns and Ammunition*, Taylor and Francis (2014), sections 4.7-4.9.
3 Zaloga, *T-62 Main Battle Tank*.
4 Carlucci and Jacobson, *Ballistics*, section 4.12.
5 William H. Drysdale et al, 'Sabot Design for a 105mm APFSDS Kinetic Energy Projectile', US Army Ballistics Research Laboratory (1978).
6 Zaloga, *T-62 Main Battle Tank*, p.12.
7 Andrei Tarasenko, 'Medium Tank T-62', BTVT. https://btvt.info/1inservice/t62/t62.htm accessed 26 October 2025.
8 Andrei Tarasenko, 'Ammo Set of Tanks T-62 and T-64, 115-mm Tank Guns U-5TS and D-68', BTVT. https://btvt.info/3attackdefensemobility/t62weapon.htm accessed 26 October 2025.
9 Ogorkiewicz, *Technology of Tanks I*, p.80.
10 William Walters, 'A Brief History of Shaped Charges', 24th International Symposium on Ballistics, 2008, Vol. 1, pp.3–10.
11 William Walters and Jonas Zukas, *Fundamentals of Shaped Charges*, Wiley-Interscience (1989), pp.309–11.
12 Yu. A. Gushchin, 'Selection Of Heat Projectiles For Testing Armor', *Armored Vehicle Bulletin* (1979), No. 3. Via https://btvt.info/5library/vbtt_1979_03_probivaemost.htm accessed 26 October 2025.
13 Todd A. Raffensperger, 'Prague Spring, 1968: "The Whole World is Watching"', *Military Heritage* (August 2011), p.24.
14 Michael S. Gerson, 'The Sino-Soviet Border Conflict: Deterrence, Escalation, and the Threat of Nuclear War in 1969', CNA (2010), p.26.

CHAPTER 10

1 Keith William Nolan, 'Battle at Hue City', *US Naval Institute Proceedings*, Vol. 108/4/950 (April 1982).
2 Jack Shulimson et al, *US Marines in Vietnam: The Defining Year, 1968*, US Marine Corps (1997), p.172.
3 Shulimson et al, *US Marines in Vietnam*, pp.180–87.
4 Maj William James, 'From Siege to Surgical: The Evolution of Urban Combat From World War II to the Present and its Effect on Current Doctrine', US Army Command and General Staff College (1998), p.9.
5 Ellsworth Adams, 'NATO Foreign Diesel Comparative Test Program: GM-MVO/MT883 Engine Evaluation', RD&E technical report (1991), p.14.

6 Chant, *World Encyclopedia of the Tank*, p.309.
7 '7.62 mm × 51 Armor Piercing 8 (M993)', Nammo. https://www.nammo.com/product/our-products/ammunition/small-caliber-ammunition/7-62mm-series/7-62-mm-x-51-armor-piercing-8-m993/ accessed 1 November 2025.
8 Ogorkiewicz, *Technology of Tanks I*, p.32.
9 Chant, *World Encyclopedia of the Tank*, p.314.
10 Ogorkiewicz, *Technology of Tanks I*, p.80.
11 Jim Storr, *Battlegroup! The Lessons of the Unfought Battles of the Cold War*, Helion and Company, UK (2021), pp.179–184.
12 Ibid, p.107
13 Ibid, p.181.

CHAPTER 11

1 Andrei Tarasenko, 'The History of Domestic Tank Building in the Post-war Period', BTVT. https://btvt.info/1inservice/history/_45_2006.htm accessed 2 November 2025.
2 Ryan Then, 'T-72: Part 1', The Soviet Armour Blog (May 2015). https://thesovietarmourblog.blogspot.com/2015/05/t-72-soviet-progeny.html accessed 2 November 2025.
3 Andrei Tarasenko, 'Main Battle Tank T-64A', BTVT. https://btvt.info/1inservice/t-64a/t-64a.htm accessed 2 November 2025.
4 Maj James Warford, 'The Threat of the Premium Tank: The Product and Process of the Soviet Experience', US Army (1992), p.41.
5 Andrei Tarasenko, 'History of Tank Building in the USSR: The Turning Point of 1973, Part 1', BTVT. https://btvt.info/4ourarticles/1973_%D0%A2-64_history.htm accessed 2 November 2025.
6 Lt Brown, 'Centurion Tanks in Korea'.
7 Yuri Kotsch, '125 mm Kanone D-81 (T-64A, T-72, T-80, T-90)', *Die Bordkanonen der T-Serie*. https://www.kotsch88.de/m_125_mm_d-81.htm accessed 3 November 2025.
8 'Range and Lethality of U.S. and Soviet Anti-armor Weapons', TRADOC Bulletin No. 1, September 1975, p.8.
9 Andrei Tarasenko, 'Protection of Second-generation Post-war Tanks: T-64 (T-64A), Chieftain Mk5R and M60', BTVT. https://btvt.info/3attackdefensemobility/432armor.htm accessed 22 November 2025.
10 Mark Cazalet, 'The Most Misunderstood Weapon in the World: Mythbusting HEAT Warheads and Their Countermeasures', *European Security & Defence* (20 June 2024). https://euro-sd.com/2024/06/

articles/38841/the-most-misunderstood-weapon-in-the-world-mythbusting-heat-warheads-and-their-countermeasures/ accessed 22 November 2025.

11 Ogorkiewicz, *Technology of Tanks I*, p. 371.

12 Vasily Chobitok, 'On January 22, 1973, the T-64A was Accepted into Service', LiveJournal (22 January 2025). https://andrei-bt.livejournal.com/2380400.html accessed 22 November 2025.

13 Andrey Tarasneko, 'Balls of Soviet Tanks', Tank Archives (25 April 2022). https://www.tankarchives.com/2022/04/balls-of-soviet-tanks.html accessed 22 November 2025.

14 Cranny-Evans and Hawkes, *Jane's Armoured Fighting Vehicles*, p.269.

15 V.L. Chernyshev, 'Tanks and People: Diary of the Chief Designer, Alexandra Alexandrovich Morozov, Internet Version, Part 2', BTVT. https://btvt.info/4ourarticles/morozov2/morozov2.htm, accessed 22 November 2025.

CHAPTER 12

1 M.G. Vigil, 'Explosive Shaped Charge Penetration Into Tuff Rock', Sandia National Laboratories, USA (1988), p.19.

2 R.M. Ogorkiewicz, 'Combat Vehicle Armour Progresses', *Jane's International Defence Review*, June (1995).

3 Kevin M. Woods et al, *Saddam's Generals: Perspectives of the Iran–Iraq War*, Institute for Defense Analyses (2011), p.133.

4 'Chieftain Battle Survivability', Loose Minute, BGS (Int) 16/13, pp.2–3.

5 Richard Ogorkiewicz, 'Tanks and Anti-tank Weapons', Adelphi Papers, 18:144 (1978), pp. 38–44, DOI: 10.1080/05679327808448524.

6 Cranny-Evans and Hawkes, *Jane's Armoured Fighting Vehicles*, p.174.

7 Marsh, comment on 'Explosive Reactive Armor,' *Sturgeon's House* (2 October 2015). https://sturgeonshouse.ipbhost.com/topic/574-explosive-reactive-armor/page/2/ accessed 15 April 2026.

8 Manfred Held, 'Protective Arrangement against Projectiles', US Patent 4,368,660A, filed 23 October 1980 and issued 18 January 1983.

9 Dunstan, *Centurion vs T-55*, pp.61–73.

10 Richard Ogorkiewicz, 'Israel's Merkava Mark 2 Battle Tank', *Armor* (November–December 1985), pp.39–42.

11 Ralph Mandel, 'Israel in 1982: The War in Lebanon', *American Jewish Year Book* (1984).

12 Ibid, p.12.

13 Doron Almog et al, 'The Lessons We Should Have Learned from the First Lebanon War', *The Jerusalem Strategic Tribune* (April 2023).

https://jstribune.com/almog-arieli-golan-lessons-from-first-lebanon-war/ accessed 6 December 2025.

14 Eric McMillin, 'The IDF, the PLO and Urban Warfare: Lebanon 1982', University of Chicago (1993), p.8.

15 Andrei Tarasenko, 'Dynamic Armor. The Israeli Shield was Forged in ... the USSR?' BTVT. https://btvt.info/4ourarticles/dz68.htm accessed 6 December 2025.

16 Ibid.

17 Ogorkiewicz, 'Combat Vehicle Armour Progresses', *International Defence Review*, June.(1995).

18 Jim Warford, 'The Soviet T-72B Main Battle Tank; The First Look at Soviet Special Armor', *Journal of Military Ordnance*, Vol. 12, No. 1 (May 2002), pp.4–7.

19 Andrei Tarasenko, 'Dynamic Protection of Tanks', BTVT. https://btvt.info/3attackdefensemobility/kontakt5_.htm accessed 6 December 2025.

20 Hazell, *Armour*, p.277.

21 Zhanping Ren et al, 'Analysis of the Effects of Explosive Reactive Armor during the Penetration Process of Kinetic Energy Projectile', *Journal of Physics* (2024): Conference Series. 2891, p.8.

22 Richard M. Ogorkiewicz, 'Impenetrable Russian Tank Armour Stands up to Examination', *Jane's International Defence Review* (July 1997), p.15.

23 Cranny-Evans and Hawkes, *Jane's Armoured Fighting Vehicles*, pp.274–76.

CHAPTER 13

1 Rheinmetall, '1956–1980', Historie. https://www.rheinmetall.com/de/unternehmen/historie/1956-1980 accessed 10 December 2025.

2 'Light From the Moon', *Der Spiegel*, 2 November 1969. https://www.spiegel.de/politik/licht-vom-mond-a-f5056456-0002-0001-0000-000045464941 accessed 10 December 2025.

3 Ibid.

4 Andre Birtle, 'Rearming the Phoenix: American Military Assistance to the Federal Republic of Germany, 1950–1960', Ohio State University (1985), p.391.

5 Mike Cubbin, 'A Standard European Tank? Procurement Politics, Technology Transfer and the Challenges of Collaborative MBT Projects in the NATO Alliance since 1945', Salford University (2019), p.104.

6 'The Zero Series', *Der Spiegel* (19 August 1958). https://www.spiegel.de/politik/die-null-serie-a-f49d215b-0002-0001-0000-000032216314 accessed 10 December 2025.

7 'Bonn's Wonder Tank: Only Conditionally Combat-ready', *Der Spiegel* (25 December 1977). https://www.spiegel.de/politik/bonns-wunderpanzer-nur-bedingt-kampfbereit-a-f8f405ae-0002-0001-0000-000040680175 accessed 10 December 2025.
8 H.J. Powis, 'Comparison of Mechanical Properties of 105 mm M68 Gun Tube Forgings', US Army Armament Research and Development Command (1980), p.2.
9 'Transfer of Austrian Gun-Barrel Forging Technology to the USSR', Intelligence Memorandum, US Directorate of Intelligence (1982), pp.1–5.
10 'What Is Swaging?', Thiot-Autofrettage. https://www.thiot-autofrettage.com/what-is-swaging/ accessed 13 December 2025.
11 Christopher F. Foss and Tony Cullen, *Jane's AFV Retrofit Systems 1993–94* (6th edn), Janes Information Group (1993), p.33.
12 'Army Ammunition Data Sheets: Artillery Ammunition, Guns, Howitzers, Mortars, Recoilless Rifles, Grenade Launchers, and Artillery Fuzes', TM 43-0001-28, US Army (1994), pp.2–112.
13 Richard Ogorkiewicz, *Observer of Cold War Tank Development*, The Tank Museum, England, 2021, p.26.
14 William S. de Rosset, 'An Overview of Novel Penetrator Technology', Army Research Laboratory (ARL) (February 2001), pp.17–19.
15 Richard Chait et al, 'Project Hindsight Revisited; Critical Technology Events in the Development of the Abrams Tank', National Defense University (December 2005), pp.16–19.
16 De Rosset, 'An Overview of Novel Penetrator Technology', p.17.
17 Ibid, p.19.
18 Ibid, p.19.
19 'Uranium and Depleted Uranium', World Nuclear Association. https://world-nuclear.org/information-library/Nuclear-Fuel-Cycle/Uranium-Resources/Uranium-and-Depleted-Uranium accessed 12 December 2025.
20 Michael F.G. Johnson, 'Armor-Piercing Ammunition', European Patent EP0536870A1, filed 7 October 1992, and issued 14 April 1993.
21 R.C. Batra, 'Studies in Penetration Mechanics: Final Report', Army Research Office (1989), p.24.
22 Cranny-Evans and Hawkes, *Jane's Armoured Fighting Vehicles*, p.262.
23 '9K112 Kobra (AT-8 Songster) Russian Anti-Tank Guided Missile (ATGM)', TRADOC Worldwide Equipment Guide. https://odin.tradoc.army.mil/WEG/Asset/9K112_Kobra_(AT-8_Songster)Russian_Anti-Tank_Guided_Missile(ATGM) accessed 16 December 2025.

24 Yuri Lyamin with Kenton Fulmer & N.R. Jenzen-Jones, 'Introduction to the 9M113 Konkurs ATGM', *The Hoplite* (28 July 2016). https://armamentresearch.com/introduction-to-the-9m113-konkurs-atgm/ accessed 16 December 2025.

25 Karl E. Cocke, *Department of the Army Historical Summary; Fiscal Year, 1974*, Center of Military History of the US Army (1978), p.135.

26 Dr Jack Watling et al, 'Preliminary Lessons from Ukraine's Offensive Operations, 2022–23', RUSI (July 2024), p.21.

27 De Rosset, 'An Overview of Novel Penetrator Technology', p.19.

CHAPTER 14

1 'Victorious Retreat', *Der Spiegel* (8 August 1976). https://www.spiegel.de/politik/siegreicher-rueckzug-a-afa ec461-0002-0001-0000-000041170560 accessed 10 December 2025.

2 Ogorkiewicz, *Technology of Tanks I*, p.280.

3 Cranny-Evans and Hawkes, *Jane's Armoured Fighting Vehicles*, p.86.

4 Ibid, p.305.

5 'V-84MS Battle Tank Engine', Argun Kazakhstan. https://argun-kazakhstan.com/products/v-84m-battle-tank-engine, accessed 17 December 2025.

6 Paolo Valpolini, 'Krauss-Maffei Wegmann: The Ever-lasting Leopard 2', *European Defence Review* (15 July 2021). https://www.edrmagazine.eu/krauss-maffei-wegmann-the-ever-lasting-leopard-2 accessed 17 December 2025.

7 Ogorkiewicz, *Technology of Tanks I*, p.254.

8 '15 Surprising Facts About Honeywell's 1,500 Horsepower Turbine Tank Engine', Honeywell Aerospace Technologies. https://aerospace.honeywell.com/us/en/about-us/blogs/15-surprising-facts-about-honeywell-1500-horsepower-turbine-tank-engine accessed 17 December, 2025.

9 R.P. Hunnicutt, *Abrams: A History of the American Main Battle Tank*, Presidio Press, California (1990), p.36.

10 Orr Kelly, *King of the Killing Zone*, W.W. Norton, Washington (1989), pp.144–57.

11 Ibid, pp. 158–159.

12 'Honeywell AGT1500 – Archived 3/2009', Forecast International, 2009. https://www.forecastinternational.com/archive/disp_pdf.cfm?DACH_RECNO=180 accessed 18 December 2025.

13 'Operation *Desert Storm*: Early Performance Assessment of Bradley and Abrams', US General Accounting Office (January 1992), p.25.

14 Stephen Bourque, *Jayhawk! The VII Corps in the Persian Gulf War*, Department of the Army, Washington (2002), p.352.
15 'Conduct of the Persian Gulf War: Appendix T, Performance of Selected Weapon Systems', Defense Technical Information Centre (April 1992), p. T-144.
16 Dick Taylor, *Challenger 1 Main Battle Tank, 1983–2001 (FV 4030/4 Model)*, Haynes Publishing, UK (2015), p.125.
17 David Axe, 'Made in America, But Lost in Iraq', Foreign Policy (2 March 2018). https://foreignpolicy.com/2018/03/02/u-s-made-tanks-that-fell-into-militia-hands-in-iraq-sparks-assistance-standoff/ accessed 17 December 2025.
18 Richard Sisk, 'The "Beast of Hit", Abrams Tank Plays Role in Iraqi Fight against ISIS.' Military.com (13 April 2016). https://www.military.com/daily-news/2016/04/13/the-beast-of-hit-abrams-tank-plays-role-iraqi-fight-against-isis.html accessed 17 December 2025.
19 Ogorkiewicz, *Technology of Tanks I*, p.292.
20 Ibid.
21 Ibid, p.292.
22 Rolls-Royce, 'Rolls-Royce Receives Major Order to Supply More Than 300 Leopard 2 Engines', MTU Solutions, last modified 8 December 2025. https://www.mtu-solutions.com/eu/en/pressreleases/2025/Rolls-Royce-receives-major-order-to-supply-more-than-300-Leopard-2-engines.html, accessed 18 December 2025.

CHAPTER 15

1 Capt Tim Purbrick, 'Desert Storm Part 22: Charge of the Heavy Brigade', British Army Blog (28 February 2016). https://britisharmy.wordpress.com/2016/02/28/desert-storm-part-22-charge-of-the-heavy-brigade/ accessed 16 December 2025.
2 Taylor, *Challenger 1 Main Battle Tank*, p.62.
3 Ibid, pp.77–78.
4 Ibid, p.78.
5 Capt Tim Purbrick, 'Desert Storm Part 24: Back to Germany', British Army Blog (11 March 2016). https://britisharmyblog.wordpress.com/2016/03/11/desert-storm-part-24-back-to-germany/ accessed 18 December 2025.
6 Nick Gromicko, 'The History of Infrared Thermography', International Association of Certified Home Inspectors, n.d. https://www.nachi.org/history-ir.htm accessed 19 December 2025.

7 'Samuel P. Langley (1834–1906)', High Altitude Observatory of the National Center for Atmospheric Research. https://www2.hao.ucar.edu/education/scientists/samuel-p-langley-1834-1906 accessed 26 December 2025.
8 Dr István Bartolits, 'Kálmán Tihanyi, Inventor of the Iconoscope and Pioneer of Cathode Ray Tube Television, was born 125 years ago', Hungarian Association of Telecommunications and Informatics (April 2022). https://www.hte.hu/fooldal/-/hir/125-eve-szuletett-tihanyi-kalman-az-ikonoszkop-feltalaloja-a-katodsugarcsoves-televizio-uttoroje accessed 26 December 2025.
9 Dr James 'Ralph' Teague and David Schmieder, 'The History of Forward Looking Infrared (FLIR)', DSIAC (October 2021), p.4–8.
10 Teague and Schmieder, 'The History of FLIR', p.5–1.
11 Ibid, p.5–3.
12 Ibid, pp.4–10 to 4–11.
13 Cranny-Evans and Hawkes, *Jane's Armoured Fighting Vehicles*, p.262.

PART 5

1 'World Economic Outlook, October 1991; A Survey by the Staff of the International Monetary Fund', International Monetary Fund (October 1991), pp.1–3.
2 Thomas Weston, 'The UK Economy in the 1990s', House of Lords Library (10 September 2024). https://lordslibrary.parliament.uk/the-uk-economy-in-the-1990s/ accessed 31 December 2025.
3 'The Savings and Loan Crisis (1989)', *International Banker* (29 September 2021). https://internationalbanker.com/history-of-financial-crises/the-savings-and-loan-crisis-1989/ accessed 31 December 2025.
4 Francis Fukuyama, 'The End of History?' *The National Interest*, No. 16 (Summer 1989), pp. 3–18, https://pages.ucsd.edu/~bslantchev/courses/pdf/Fukuyama%20-%20End%20of%20History.pdf accessed 31 December 2025.
5 Margaret Thatcher, 'Press Conference at Paris CSCE Summit', Margaret Thatcher Foundation, 21 November 1990. https://www.margaretthatcher.org/document/108249 accessed 31 December 2025.
6 George H.W. Bush, 'September 11, 1990: Address Before a Joint Session of Congress', Miller Center, 11 September 1990. https://millercenter.org/the-presidency/presidential-speeches/september-11-1990-address-joint-session-congress accessed 31 December 2025.
7 Ronnie Lowenstein and Richard Peach, 'The Impact of the Current Defense Build-down', *Quarterly Review, Federal Reserve Bank of New York*, Vol. 17 (Autumn), 1992, pp.59–68.

8 'New Data Shows Conflict at Historic High as U.S. Signals Retreat from World Stage', Peace Research Institute Oslo (9 June 2025). https://www.prio.org/news/3616 accessed 31 December 2025.

CHAPTER 16

1 Andrei Tarasenko, 'KAZ "Drozd" (1030 M)', BTVT. https://btvt.info/3attackdefensemobility/kaz_drozd.htm accessed 1 January 2026.
2 Dr Thomas Withington, 'Protection Racket', *European Security and Defence* (1 February 2023). https://euro-sd.com/2023/02/articles/29130/protection-racket/ accessed 1 January 2026.
3 Capt Tom J. Meyer, 'Active Protective Systems: Impregnable Armor or Simply Enhanced Survivability?' *Armor* (May–June 1998), p.8.
4 Ali Jalali and Lester W. Grau, *The Other Side of the Mountain: Mujahideen Tactics in the Soviet–Afghan War*, Good Press (2020), p.32.
5 Sam Cranny-Evans, 'Arena-M, Russia's Active Protection System Advances', *Calibre Defence* (31 March 2025). https://www.calibredefence.co.uk/arena-m-russias-active-protection-system-advances/ accessed 1 January 2026.
6 Andrei Tarasenko, 'KAZ vs. Drones?', BTVT (1 January 2026). https://andrei-bt.livejournal.com/2684597.html?es=1 accessed 2 January 2026.
7 'T-90M "Proryv" Tanks will Receive an Active Protection System', TASS (1 January 2026). https://tass.ru/armiya-i-opk/26067715 accessed 2 January 2026.
8 Sam Cranny-Evans, 'Project ASGARD; The British Army's Path to Doubling Lethality', *Calibre Defence* (21 July 2025). https://www.calibredefence.co.uk/project-asgard-the-british-armys-path-to-doubling-lethality/ accessed 5 January 2026.
9 Waldemar Geiger, 'The German Army is Apparently Planning to Establish Armored "Combat Reconnaissance Brigades"', *Hartpunkt* (19 September 2025). https://www.hartpunkt.de/deutsches-heer-plant-offenbar-die-aufstellung-von-panzerstarken-kampfaufklaerungsbrigaden/ accessed 5 January 2026.
10 Lester Grau, 'Russian Urban Tactics: Lessons from the Battle for Grozny', Institute for National Strategic Studies (1994).
11 Lester Grau, 'Russian-Manufactured Armored Vehicle Vulnerability in Urban Combat: The Chechnya Experience', *Red Thrust Star* (January 1997).
12 Sam Cranny-Evans, 'Calibre Interview: Kara Dag Technologies Unpacks the Drone War in Ukraine', *Calibre Defence* (22 May 2025). https://www.calibredefence.co.uk/calibre-interview-kara-dag-cto-unpacks-the-drone-war-in-ukraine/ accessed 5 January 2026.

13 Dr Jack Watling and Nick Reynolds, 'Tactical Developments During the Third Year of the Russo-Ukrainian War', RUSI (14 February 2025), p.10.
14 Ibid.
15 Assef Kamer, '"Purple Thunder": The IDF Experiment Conducted in Southern Lebanon has Been Revealed', YNet (17 October 2020). https://www.ynet.co.il/news/article/B100y9QDLv accessed 1 January 2026.
16 Wilson Center, 'The Doctrine of Hezbollah', Middle East Program. https://www.wilsoncenter.org/article/doctrine-hezbollah, accessed 2 January 2026.
17 Michael Knights, *25 Days to Aden: The Unknown Story of Arabian Elite Forces at War*, Profile Books (2023), pp.144–45.
18 Lt Col (Ret) David Eshel, 'Lebanon 2006: Did Merkava Challenge Its Match?' *Armor* (January–February 2007), p.12.
19 Capt Daniel Helmer, 'Not Quite Counterinsurgency: A Cautionary Tale for U.S. Forces Based on Israel's Operation Change of Direction', *Armor* (January–February 2007), pp.9–11.
20 Nava Tzuriel and Eitan Glickman, 'The Canyon of Death', *Yediot Aharonot* (16 August 2006). https://www.scoop.co.nz/stories/HL0608/S00204/translation-from-hebrew-the-canyon-of-death.htm accessed 2 January 2026.
21 Amos Harel, 'IDF Equips First Tank Division with Anti-tank Missile Protection', *Haaretz* (10 May 2009). https://www.haaretz.co.il/news/politics/2009-05-10/ty-article/0000017f-dbc9-d856-a37f-ffc9328c0000 accessed 3 January 2026.
22 Paolo Valpolini, 'Israel Starts Delivering the 5th Gen Merkava Barak Tank to its Armoured Units', *European Defence Review* (22 September 2023). https://www.edrmagazine.eu/israel-starts-delivering-the-5th-gen-merkava-barak-tank-to-its-armoured-units accessed 3 January 2026.
23 Agence France Presse, 'New Tally Puts Oct 7 Attack Death Toll In Israel At 1,189', Barron's (28 May 2024). https://www.barrons.com/news/new-tally-puts-oct-7-attack-death-toll-in-israel-at-1-189-3e038de6 accessed 28 December 2025.
24 Jason Burke, 'Joe Biden's Warning to Israel is a Nod to US Failures in the "War on Terror"', *The Guardian* (19 October 2023). https://tinyurl.com/3wk9yych accessed 28 December 2025.
25 Ibid.
26 Seth Frantzman, 'How Hamas Survived a Year of the Israel-Hamas War – Analysis', *The Jerusalem Post* (19 January 2025). https://www.jpost.com/middle-east/article-838227 accessed 28 December 2025.

27 Yaakov Lappin, 'Amid Raging Conflict in Syria, IDF Deploys New Division to Border', *The Jerusalem Post* (23 February 2014). https://www.jpost.com/defense/amid-raging-conflict-in-syria-idf-deploys-new-division-to-border-342314 accessed 28 December 2025.

28 'Operation Protective Edge: A Detailed Summary of Events', International Institute for Counter-Terrorism (ICT). https://ict.org.il/operation-protective-edge-a-detailed-summary-of-events-2/, accessed 28 December 2025.

29 John Spencer, 'Gaza's Underground: Hamas's Entire Politico-Military Strategy Rests on Its Tunnels', Modern War Institute (18 January 2024). https://mwi.westpoint.edu/gazas-underground-hamass-entire-politico-military-strategy-rests-on-its-tunnels/ accessed 28 December, 2025.

30 Einav Greenberg Cohen, 'The 188th Brigade Concludes its First Training Exercise with a Mark 4 Tank – Which Changes the Rules of the Game', IDF (8 September 2025). https://tinyurl.com/24438sdm accessed 28 December 2025.

31 Frantzman, 'How Hamas Survived a Year of War'.

32 'Ordnance & Munitions Forecast: RPG-7 and RPG-16', *Forecast International* (October 2023). https://www.forecastinternational.com/archive/disp_pdf.cfm?DACH_RECNO=1605 accessed 28 December 2025.

33 Dr Jack Watling and Nick Reynolds, 'Tactical Lessons from Israel Defense Forces Operations in Gaza, 2023', RUSI (3 July 2024), p.13.

34 Emanuel Fabian (@manniefabian), 'IDF says it has opened a second safe passage for Gazans to move south today, this time on the coastal road', X (11 November 2023). https://x.com/manniefabian/status/1723275630605738427.

35 Watling and Reynolds, 'Tactical Lessons from Israel Defense Forces Operations in Gaza, 2023'.

36 Sam Cranny-Evans, 'IAV 2025: Trophy Now Able to Intercept Drones', *Calibre Defence* (23 January 2024). http://calibredefence.co.uk/iav-2025-trophy-now-able-to-intercept-drones/ accessed 29 December 2025.

37 John Spencer, 'Israel's New Approach to Tunnels: A Paradigm Shift in Underground Warfare', Modern War Institute (2 December 2024). https://mwi.westpoint.edu/israels-new-approach-to-tunnels-a-paradigm-shift-in-underground-warfare/ accessed 29 December 2025.

38 Stijn Mitzer and Jakub Janovsky, 'Attack On Europe: Documenting Russian Equipment Losses During The Russian Invasion Of Ukraine', Oryx. https://www.oryxspioenkop.com/2022/02/attack-on-europe-documenting-equipment.html accessed 29 December 2025.

CHAPTER 17

1 'Wine Glass on Type 10 Main Battle Tank to Show Excellent Stability', Defence Blog, YouTube video (13 October 2015). https://www.youtube.com/watch?v=lGgS1j3c6sI.
2 Ministry of Defense (Japan), 'Defense Production and Technological Base', Technical report, Cabinet Secretariat (April 2010). Archived 4 March 2016. https://web.archive.org/web/20160304063832/http://www.kantei.go.jp/jp/singi/shin-ampoboueі2010/dai5/siryou1.pdf.
3 Cranny-Evans and Hawkes, *Jane's Armoured Fighting Vehicles*, p.42.
4 'How do you move a tank that weighs 80 tons???', Israel Defense Forces, YouTube video (26 August 2019). https://www.youtube.com/watch?v=L8CuRaqmXEU.
5 Cranny-Evans and Hawkes, *Jane's Armoured Fighting Vehicles*, pp.95–144.
6 'Two U.S. Soldiers Killed in Iraq as Tank Destroyed', *CBC News* (16 September, 2005). https://www.cbc.ca/news/world/two-u-s-soldiers-killed-in-iraq-as-tank-destroyed-1.388627 accessed 6 January, 2026.
7 Ian Bruce, 'Insurgent Bomb Pierced Armor of British Tank in Iraq', *The Guardian* (24 April 2007). https://www.theguardian.com/uk/2007/apr/24/iraq.world, accessed 6 January 2026.
8 Paolo Valpolini, 'Krauss-Maffei Wegmann: The Ever-lasting Leopard 2', *European Defence Review* (15 July 2021). https://www.edrmagazine.eu/krauss-maffei-wegmann-the-ever-lasting-leopard-2 accessed 6 January 2026.
9 Jen Judson, 'Dead on Arrival: Army Pulls Plug on M10 Booker Light Tank', *Defense News* (12 June 2025). https://www.defensenews.com/land/2025/06/12/dead-on-arrival-army-pulls-plug-on-m10-booker-light-tank/ accessed 6 January 2026.

CHAPTER 18

1 'German 120mm Tank Ammunition', German Armor (blog) (April 2020). https://germanarmor.blogspot.com/2020/04/german-120mm-tank-ammunition.html, accessed 4 January 2026.
2 Stijn Mitzer and Joost Oliemans, 'The Fight For Nagorno-Karabakh: Documenting Losses On The Sides Of Armenia And Azerbaijan', Oryxspioenkop. https://www.oryxspioenkop.com/2020/09/the-fight-for-nagorno-karabakh.html accessed 27 December 2025.
3 'Armenia's Investigative Committee Provides Updated Data on Casualties in 2020 War in Nagorno-Karabakh', Arka News Agency. https://arka.am/en/news/politics/armenia_s_investigative_committee_

provides_updated_data_on_casualties_in_2020_war_in_nagorno_karabak/ accessed 27 December 2025.

4 'List of the Servicemen Fallen (Shehids) in the Patriotic War', Ministry of Defense of the Republic of Azerbaijan. https://mod.gov.az/en/news/list-of-the-servicemen-fallen-shehids-in-the-patriotic-war-38076.html accessed 27 December 2025.

5 Mitzer and Oliemans, 'Fight For Nagorno-Karabakh'.

6 John Spencer and Liam Collins, 'Urban Warfare Project Case Study #13: Battle of Hadrut', Modern War Institute (25 April 2025). https://mwi.westpoint.edu/urban-warfare-project-case-study-13-battle-of-hadrut/ accessed 27 December 2025.

7 Liam Collins, Jayson Geroux, and John Spencer, 'Urban Warfare Project Case Study #15: Battle of Shusha', Modern War Institute (26 September 2025). https://mwi.westpoint.edu/urban-warfare-project-case-study-15-battle-of-shusha/ accessed 27 December 2025.

8 Dr Jack Watling and Sidharth Kaushal, 'The Democratisation of Precision Strike in the Nagorno-Karabakh Conflict', RUSI (22 October 2020). https://www.rusi.org/explore-our-research/publications/commentary/democratisation-precision-strike-nagorno-karabakh-conflict accessed 27 December 2025.

9 Kelly McCoy, 'The Road to Multi-Domain Battle: An Origin Story', Modern War Institute (27 October 2017). https://mwi.westpoint.edu/road-multi-domain-battle-origin-story/ accessed 4 January 2026.

10 Sam Cranny-Evans, 'IDF Orders Fire Weaver Network Fire Control System', Janes Information Group (4 February 2020). https://www.janes.com/osint-insights/defence-news/idf-orders-fire-weaver-network-fire-control-system accessed 4 January 2026.

11 Thomas Withington, 'Clouds on the Horizon', *European Security and Defence* (25 September 2023). https://euro-sd.com/2023/09/articles/33982/clouds-on-the-horizon/ accessed 5 January 2026.

12 Cranny-Evans and Hawkes, *Jane's Armoured Fighting Vehicles*, p.163.

13 Ibid, p.178.

14 Maj Robert Brown, 'The Armored Brigade Combat Team 2014–2024: Improving Abrams Lethality', *Armor* (January–February 2014), p.11.

15 'Infrared Sensors', Leonardo DRS. https://www.leonardodrs.com/what-we-do/our-solutions/advanced-sensing/infrared-sensors/ accessed 5 January 2026.

16 Hensoldt, *PERI RTWL Digital: Digital Commander's Periscope with Uncooled Thermal Imager* (Hensoldt, Taufkirchen, n.d.), https://dam.hensoldt.net/m/3b7fec3f1797a6e7/original/PERI-RTWL-Digital-Datasheet-English.pdf.

17 Sam Cranny-Evans, 'Challenger 3: Inside the TrueHunter Commander Sight with Thales', *Calibre Defence* (18 November 2025). https://www.calibredefence.co.uk/challenger-3-inside-the-truehunter-commander-sight-with-thales/ accessed 30 December 2025.

CHAPTER 19

1 Sam Cranny-Evans, 'Calibre Interview: Tristam Constant, Applied Intuition UK', *Calibre Defence* (11 August 2025). https://www.calibredefence.co.uk/calibre-interview-tristam-constant-applied-intuition-uk/ accessed 29 December 2025.

2 Sam Cranny-Evans, 'Oshkosh Receives $29.9 mn Contract for ROGUE Autonomy', *Calibre Defence* (14 January 2025). https://www.calibredefence.co.uk/oshkosh-receives-29-9-mn-contract-for-rogue-autonomy/ accessed 29 December 2025.

3 Sam Cranny-Evans, 'Helsing and General Dynamics Detail AI for Bowman Network to Help Double Lethality', *Shepherd* (6 November 2024). https://www.shephardmedia.com/news/landwarfareintl/helsing-and-general-dynamics-detail-ai-for-bowman-network-to-help-double-lethality/ accessed 30 December 2025.

4 Cranny-Evans, 'Inside the TrueHunter Commander Sight with Thales'.

5 Ogorkiewicz, *Tanks*, p.304.

6 Paolo Valpolini, 'Ascalon: Nexter's Solution for the MGCS Main Gun', *European Defence Review* (4 July 2022). https://www.edrmagazine.eu/ascalon-nexters-solution-for-the-mgcs-main-gun accessed 31 December 2025.

7 'Abrams Main Battle Tank', United States Army Acquisition Support Center. https://asc.army.mil/web/portfolio-item/abrams-main-battle-tank/ accessed 30 December 2025,

8 'Army Announces Plans for M1E3 Abrams Tank Modernization', Army.mil, 6 September 2023. https://www.army.mil/article/269706/army_announces_plans_for_m1e3_abrams_tank_modernization, accessed 30 December 2025.

9 'Army Announces Plans for M1E3 Abrams Tank Modernization'.

10 Jen Judson, 'US Army Plans to Dramatically Accelerate Abrams Tank Modernization', *Defense News* (14 April 2025). https://www.defensenews.com/land/2025/04/14/us-army-plans-to-dramatically-accelerate-abrams-tank-modernization/ accessed 30 December 2025.

11 Ibid.

12 Hope Hodge Seck, 'Next-gen Tank to Reach Soldiers for Testing by End of 2026', *Defense News* (15 October 2025). https://www.defensenews.com/land/2025/10/15/next-gen-tank-to-reach-soldiers-for-testing-by-end-of-2026/ accessed 30 December 2025.
13 Hunnicutt, *Abrams*, p.200.
14 JH, 'KF51 Panther Unveiled', *European Security and Defence* (14 June 2022). https://euro-sd.com/2022/06/articles/exclusive/26592/kf51-panther/ accessed 30 December 2025.
15 'LRMV Details the Italian Army MBT and AIFV programmes', *European Defence Review* (3 February 2025). https://www.edrmagazine.eu/lrmv-details-the-italian-army-mbt-and-aifv-programmes accessed 30 December 2025.
16 Paolo Valpolini, 'ADEX 2023 – Hyundai Rotem Exhibits its NG-MBT Concept While it Continues Delivering K2 tanks to ROKA', *European Defence Review* (26 October 2025). https://www.edrmagazine.eu/hyundai-rotem-exhibits-its-ng-mbt-concept-while-it-continues-delivering-k2-tanks-to-roka accessed 30 December 2025.
17 Alexey Ivanov, 'The Russian Armata Tank was Tested in Unmanned Mode', *Rossiyskaya Gazeta* (4 July 2020). https://rg.ru/2020/07/04/rossijskij-tank-armata-ispytali-v-bespilotnom-rezhime.html accessed 30 December 2025.
18 Gerhard Heiming, 'IAV 2025: Multi-platform MGCS Continues on its Path Undeterred', *European Security and Defence* (24 January 2025). https://euro-sd.com/2025/01/major-news/42246/mgcs-continues-on-its-path/ accessed 30 December 2025.
19 Sam Cranny-Evans, 'Arondite Raises $12 Million in Seed Funding', *Calibre Defence* (6 May 2025). https://www.calibredefence.co.uk/arondite-raises-12-million-in-seed-funding/ accessed 31 December 2025.

FINAL THOUGHTS

1 Sam Cranny-Evans, 'Israel to Increase Merkava, Namer and Eitan Production', *Calibre Defence* (20 August 2025). https://www.calibredefence.co.uk/israel-to-increase-merkava-namer-and-eitan-production/ accessed 29 December 2025.

Index

Page numbers in *italic* refer to tables